W9-APE-895

HADRIAN'S WALL:

The North-West Frontier of Rome

HADRIAN'S WALL:

The North-West Frontier of Rome

David Divine

This edition published by Barnes & Noble, Inc.,
by arrangement with Harold Ober Associates, Inc.

1995 Barnes & Noble Books

ISBN 1-56619-757-0

Printed and bound in the United States of America

M 9 8 7 6 5 4 3 2

Author's Note

Hadrian's Wall is the essential element in an elaborate military complex—a frontier developed to a higher level of defensive efficiency than any other in the history of Rome. In the two separate and distinct plans which brought it to completion, it incorporates two revolutionary concepts in military theory. Triumphantly successful for more than three and a half centuries of effective occupation, it was nevertheless overrun twice as a result of the disorder of the internal government of the Province of Britain, and once by the coincidence of provincial corruption and external alliance. This book is an analysis of its military effectiveness. It is not an archaeological study. For its necessary content of archaeological description I have borrowed from a list of predecessors which begins with Caesar and Tacitus and runs through Gildas and Bede and Camden to the great moderns, Simpson, Richmond and Birley, and my debt to the *Handbook of the Roman Wall* is unlimited as must be that of any writer who comes in from the outside. I have endeavoured at all times to acknowledge that indebtedness. For the book's military interpretations I acknowledge no debt. When, upon rare occasions, I agree with the scholars, it is by the necessity of the inescapable parallel. When I disagree it is because I believe that the military realities have been repetitively misappreciated.

To Janet Campbell

Contents

List of illustrations

1

Hadrian's Britain

The land has changed less here perhaps than anywhere in Britain since the last cohorts of the frontier guard went south with Maximus sixteen hundred years ago to challenge the Emperor of Rome.

It is a naked land. The grass on the long rigs is thin and sere. The sparse rushes are bent with the wind. The scattered farmsteads are hidden for the most part in the hollows and only the ancient field walls are new since Hadrian's day. From any point along the backbones of the rigs you can see the Wall he built as the men of the north saw it for close upon three centuries—a hard black rampart crowning the air ridge of the Great Whin Sill, uncompromising as the whinstone crags themselves, still striding implacably from height to height, still terrible as it must have seemed to them.

The crenellations and the towers are gone, the north gates of the milecastles are fallen in, Housesteads is a grey ruin and Greatchesters is an oblong of grass-covered mounds, but for eighty Roman miles from Solway to the Tyne you can trace the Wall of Britain, the Wall that is the classic triumph of frontier building, that stands today the greatest surviving monument to the military power of Rome.

It is, moreover, greatly more than a monument. It is in its existing structure a synthesis of all the factors which coalesced to maintain the Roman occupation of Britain. In a strong sense it was the core and kernel of that occupation—for the Roman conquest was a failure.

Because the conquest itself was a failure, the Roman occupation of Britain over the four hundred years of its existence was intrinsically a failure also. The historians, the classic historians at least, endlessly disagree upon this, but the evidence of failure is sharply apparent in four circumstances. The continuing necessity throughout the occupation to maintain an excessive garrison for the defence of Britain. The permanent military requirement of the Wall itself. The exorbitant cost of the military structure in relation to the resources of a relatively unproductive province. And, finally, the inability of Romanisation to establish—and ultimately to leave behind it—an enduring social structure for the island Province.

Because of these failures the land, when Rome left, dwined and dwindled to the shadow of a shadow. From the north, from across the Irish Sea, from over the German Ocean, Saxons and Angli, Norsemen and Danes and Scots began again the process of repetitive invasion that was to end only with the Normans.

The Roman invasion itself was a victory of sophistication. A powerful detachment of the Roman army, trained in a brilliant and ruthless tradition, admirably led, superbly equipped, overleapt the Channel and crushed the ineffective armies of the barbarians.

Attackers and attacked are so essentially different that to understand the processes of the invasion it is necessary to consider each separately.

Who were the barbarians?

In origin the word derives from the onomatopoeic representation of the gabble of non-Greek speakers speaking. It is the quintessence of Chauvinism, a portmanteau word for everything that was un-Greek. The Romans borrowed it and its attitudes, as they borrowed so much else, from the Greeks. The population of South-Eastern Britain at the moment of attack consisted primarily of an Iron Age people derived from the nearest tribes along the coast of the Continent and themselves recent invaders. They were, because of the necessity to cross the sea, of a relatively advanced culture. With them they brought the civilisation of Gaul. They had a strong artistic development. Their metallurgy within the limits of its materials was admirable. They had brought with them sound tribal organisations, oligarchic structures, in which strong individual leadership could at intervals establish effective control. Their sub-division and the characters of the differing tribes, however, were unfavourable towards the establishment of common defensive methods. Militarily they had great strength in conditions of inter-tribal war in which the tribal levy was adequate against the scale of opposition likely to arise. The same system was inadequate in relation to the possibilities of major invasion by trained armies.

Offensively they had developed the chariot to a remarkable degree. Where earlier civilisations had already abandoned it, they used it as their major instrument of attack. The chariots were large, carrying a crew often of four men and operating with runners. The fighting men in the chariot itself traditionally moved out on the shaft between the horses in close combat. Tactically they represented a mechanised infantry in a role strikingly similar to that of the armoured personnel carriers of the armies of today. With the chariot the tribes operated irregular cavalry mounted on wiry and manoeuvrable ponies and trained to utilise the heavily-grown terrain of the forests and the thorn scrub. The infantry also was irregular, not trained to the disciplined formations of Rome but capable of swift attack. It used a long sword, inadequate for the in-fighting which was a traditional Roman tactic, a relatively small shield, helmets varying from tribe to tribe and individual to individual, and armour, limited probably to the chiefs and senior officers.

Defensively the tribes relied on two clearly differentiated types of fortification. The first, used temporarily in mobile warfare, consisted of a system of stockades in woodland or thorn scrub rapidly constructed of felled tree trunks in dense areas, difficult to come at in strength, impossible to attack with cavalry, and hostile to regular formations.

For static defence they had a vast system of entrenched camps. Largely inherited from earlier waves of invasion, the system had been elaborately improved, in the main by refugees from the Continent at the time of Caesar's conquest of Gaul and in the years which followed it. It began, significantly perhaps, on the great headland of the East Cliff of Dover, with an enormous ditched camp extending for half a mile inland from the cliff edge above the mouth of the Dour.

Across the long downland areas that run parallel with the coast to the Solent, over the wide stretches of Salisbury Plain, clear across Hampshire and Wiltshire and Dorset and into Devon, there was an endless succession of hilltop forts. Dover itself was enormous, Cissbury Ring, Hambledon Hill in Dorset, Hod Hill, Warminster and a score of others were huge. Maiden Castle—Mai Dun, the great fort—the greatest of them all, was spread over a hundred and fifteen acres with, at points, eight lines of defence. Beyond the downland fortresses were the promontory forts of the coast stretching deep into Cornwall.

Basically the hilltop forts were cities of refuge. The permanent population even in this rich Southern country was relatively thin. Into the great earthworks, in time of war, the flocks and the cattle of the dispersed population of the country round them could be driven. The people formed their garrisons. They were not conceived in any sense as a national defence. Essentially they were local and independent, but in their numbers they offered an obstacle to the path of an invader and they were to play a role in the invasion.

The society of the tribes was fundamentally aristocratic, swinging from the pivot of chieftaincy. At its upper levels at least it clearly had artistic perception. Its housing followed relatively primitive forms, the large farm, for example, being basically a collection of huts rather than a planned building. Its dress was by Roman standards rugged—but so was the climate of Britain. It cannot have been as barbaric as the more fastidious and cynical Roman authors have suggested, for there is an index of fashionable commitment. That it is largely frivolous is unimportant. Socially, frivolity has its own place. It is established by the hand mirror. From the first century "Lady's Barrow" in Yorkshire, from Desborough in Northamptonshire, from St. Keverne in Cornwall and from half a hundred other places have been recovered hand mirrors which prove a high level of craftsmanship, high attainment in artistic design and, most important of all, a high degree of social ambition among the women who used them. A hand mirror is a competitive weapon. It is the instrument of self-assurance. Its perfected existence presupposes an organisation capable of supplying the requirements of fashionable adornment. It justifies by itself suppositions of attractiveness, at least in the womenfolk of the higher levels of the tribes, far beyond modern concepts of "barbarianism". It argues indeed a degree of "politeness" in society of a kind comparable at the very least to the deodorants of the twentieth century.

There was indeed a positive degree of Romanisation, in Southern Britain at least, before the Romans came. It moved in with the refugees from Caesar, with subsequent waves of exiles, and in the ordinary course of trade. The record of "finds" along the south coast areas in particular and up the eastern coasts as far as Yorkshire indicates an existing market for Roman artifacts from a relatively early date. A market implies a taste and a taste implies a readiness to accept Roman amenities and Roman standards, at least at the top levels of the Southern tribes, in the early years of the pacification.

Whatever the status of the society in relation to the assimilation of Roman cultures and perhaps manners, the system as a whole was probably inadequate in the face of threat and certainly so in the face of actual invasion. Basically this was the result of a failure of unity. The tribes existed normally in a mild antagonism, flaring apart under internal stresses, coalescing uncertainly under external threat. In the period immediately prior to the invasion and perhaps partially at least because of the earlier threats in Caligula's reign, Cunobelinus —Shakespeare's Cymbeline—king of the Catuvellauni, whose own tribal area covered what is now Hertfordshire north of London, accomplished a federation of the major tribes of the South-East. Cunobelinus established his federal capital at Camulodunum, which is today Colchester in Essex, fifty miles north-east of London. There he enclosed an area of about twelve square miles by dykes to cover the port of Colchester and a number of smaller villages.

It was the tragedy of Britain that Cunobelinus died less than two years before the invasion. It is possible indeed that his death was a factor in Claudius' decision to undertake it. With his death the nascent union of the tribes was at once affected by the division of the kingdom between his sons Togodumnus and Caratacus. There was thus at the vital moment a disruption of the slender tradition of central leadership. It was exaggerated by the normal fissiparous tendencies of the tribes. Of all the factors responsible for the failure of the resistance in the South it is this absence of central leadership, compounded as it was by the death of Togodumnus in the earlier stages of the fighting, that is the most significant. Despite the heroic efforts of Caratacus, the "barbarians" failed against the Romans—as other barbarians elsewhere—through lack of leadership in unity.

Who were the Romans?

It is a simple fact, much neglected in the consideration of the conquest and of its social consequences, that the majority of the Romans involved in the invasion were "barbarians".

Four legions were assigned to the invasion by the Emperor Claudius plus a force of auxiliaries, almost certainly stronger numerically than the legions, with an important element of cavalry. The four legions were beyond question Roman. Legionaries were still, at the time of the invasion, and for a quarter of a century afterwards, Roman citizens recruited in Italy if not in Rome itself. The auxiliaries, cavalry and infantry alike, on the other hand, were recruited in the provinces. Inscriptions in the camps and forts that were the staging posts of the conquest and subsequently in the permanent militarised area of the Wall make it clear that the army of Britain, apart from the legions, was built up of Tungrians and Asturians, Batavians and Sabines, Frisiavones and Thracians, Dalmatians and Gauls and Nervii and Moors and Spaniards.

The strength of the Roman army lay in two separate areas: the extreme professionalism of its main force, the legions; and its ability to use and control the widely differentiated provincials.

There was, remarkably, no General Staff. Cynics have suggested that its principal strength lay in that fact. The army was in the single control of the Emperor. The Emperor's position rested in part on his personal qualities, in part upon the Praetorian Guard. The Guard was an élite formation approximately nine thousand strong, quartered in or near Rome. As the single effective body of troops at the capital it exercised a strong degree of control over the city, over the

Senate, and not infrequently over the Emperor himself. On occasion it created him. Claudius, found hiding behind a curtain after the assassination of Caligula, was established as Emperor by the Guard against the attempt of the Senate to reconstitute the Republic.

The legions held the provinces. They were separated widely to prevent the establishment of private armies which might threaten Rome—and which, despite separation, sometimes did. Pannonia on the Upper Danube had the strongest garrison, four legions; Britain after the conquest, three; Asia Minor, two; Spain, one.

The legions themselves conformed to an unvarying pattern. Their strength lay in their tradition, their training and their discipline. Each had a complement of five thousand six hundred men, basically heavy infantry, but with a light infantry component and a small cavalry element. They wore heavy leather tunics variously reinforced with metal plates, they had metal helmets, and they used a tall, oblong shield designed to interlock with the shield of the next man in defence. They fought in three ranks, the first two ranks using the *pilum* (the short throwing spear), the rear rank using the long spear. At close quarters they fought with the short and deadly stabbing sword. Siege weapons were developed from the traditional *catapulta* and *ballista*. Primarily assault weapons, they were not of major importance in Britain where there were no walled cities to besiege. There is some evidence, however, that they were mounted defensively on the Antonine Wall and a tradition that they were used on Hadrian's.

The auxiliaries tended to use the weapons of their provinces: the curved sword of the Dacians, the Syrian bow of the Hamians, the sling of the Balearics. The cavalry was drawn primarily from the great horse tribes, but fought in formation and under discipline.

Regiments tended in differing degrees to use part at least of their traditional clothing. In the early years of their formation at any rate they used little Latin. They were not Roman citizens. Citizenship was the bait and the reward for twenty-five years of impeccable service. They were officered in the main by Romans.

The fleet divided into two classes: the heavy transports,

basically simple trading vessels built on the Brittany coast and in the Seine; and the light, oared warships with one square sail, which could be beached. Their crews were almost wholly provincials. Authorities differ as to the precise numbers involved in the landings. It seems improbable that there could have been fewer than fifty thousand men. The legions at full strength would have numbered roughly twenty-two thousand five hundred.

The theory that Romanisation was primarily a by-product of contact with the Roman army scarcely bears scrutiny. Even in the first two phases of the operation, when the main forces were still concentrated in the South, contact with the civil population must have been limited largely to the contacts of campaign. The conquest itself and the subsequent mopping-up measures can scarcely have been conducive to amity. With the second phase, however, the armies moved north of the frontier proclaimed by the Governor, Ostorius Scapula, in A.D. 47. Wroxeter first, and then Chester and York, and finally Caerleon, became legionary establishments, and the field army moved farther north still with the conquest of Brigantia.

Fifteen years from the landing the Roman army had virtually moved clear of the South, and except in the condign punitive campaign which followed Boudicca's revolt, the Southerners had little contact with the legions save on ceremonial occasions or with the auxiliaries except in the late established garrison of Londinium.

The evidence of effective Romanisation, however, is almost wholly confined to the South.

The most convenient yardstick for the assessment of Romanisation is the Villa.

It does not, of course, represent the first step in the process of pacification. This was taken with the beginning of the Roman road system. There was a road network before the Romans came. It was extensive, complex, and unsuitable to development. The authorities still quarrel over the degree to which it was adapted to Roman purposes. Certainly parts of the great stretches of tribal tracks were utilised in the line of the Roman surveys, but largely the tribal communications ran with the ridgeways along the crests of the downland or used the high ground above the swamps and the forest. The Roman requirement was in the first place strategic—the need to provide fast, direct movement for troops over the country as a whole. The great roads like the Fosse Way, running diagonally across Southern England from the Somerset coast to the River Humber in the north-east, Watling Street, the opposite diagonal, which connected the invasion ports with Chester by way of London, and Ermine Street, the great northern road, are masterpieces of military communication, designed to carry the heavy transport of armies and the swift movements of the Roman Post alike.

How soon the villa followed the roads is not certain. About the year 70 work began on the enormous "Palace of Cogidubnus" at Fishbourne on the outskirts of Chichester. The first stage of the excavation, recently completed, has revealed a structure, the largest single building in Britain, admirably proportioned, lavishly equipped with mosaic floors, having a vast colonnaded garden, a monumental arcaded entrance hall, and a great pedimented audience chamber.

Possibly it should not be classed as a villa. Yet it was a residence, incorporating all those adjuncts to the good life that are the primary characteristics of the villa. It was the largest exemplar, as it was demonstrably one of the earliest, of the new wave of building that surged up from the south like the slow green wave of the English spring.

Whether it was built by Cogidubnus—who was clearly a Quisling of the occupation—or by his successor, or even by some Roman official put in authority over Noviomagus, the capital of the Regnenses (which today is Chichester), is perhaps unimportant. Its significance lies in the fact that it was an exemplar, that it set a standard of possibility and a standard of excellence.

It lasted for two hundred years.

Generally the villa was an agricultural establishment. The great villas, like those at Woodchester or Bignor or Northleigh, were the focal points of a farm complex. They developed from relatively small, and sometimes disjointed, beginnings, often on or near traditional sites, into comfortable and finally luxurious establishments. As the Britons were made aware of the chill of their climate, they acquired hypocausts and central heating. As their artistic perception increased, they discovered the need for better and bigger mosaic designs, for more artistic façades, for better proportioned halls.

To meet the requirement for these things they created an industrial complex which could supply roofing tiles and flooring slabs, piping for water supply and drainage, metal work for fittings. Simultaneously they established an employment market for artisans skilled not only in mosaic laying but in the new and elaborate joinery demanded, in plastering, in tiling, in the stone cutting and mason work involved in columnar structures as much as in the simple ashlar of walls. And because of these requirements they made necessary, in conjunction with the similar requirements of the rising towns, another villa form—the industrial villa, the home and perhaps the offices of the master tiler, the kiln owner, the owner of tin and lead and copper mines, the importer and the exporter.

Simultaneously the urban centres of the Romanisation began to rise. The first capital, almost certainly, was the captured capital of Camulodunum—Colchester. It was rapidly superseded. Because the network of the Roman Road system centred on the bridge that was built early across the Thames at Londinium, the capital moved south to the river. It grew. Even by the time of Boudicca's revolt in 61, barely eighteen years from the landings, it was sufficiently important to be the main target of her campaign. Colchester, rapidly expanded as a *colonia* of time-expired soldiery, and enriched by the temple of the deified Claudius, was burned before Londinium; Verulamium—St. Albans to the north-east of London—was burned later, with immense slaughter.

The towns were rebuilt. Londinium, with a new basilica of enormous size and a range of temples from Diana to Mithras, became one of the five largest cities north of the Alps.

Complementing Londinium and the four *coloniae* set up at Colchester, Gloucester, Lincoln and York, were the cantonal towns. These were largely original tribal headquarters elaborated as the focal points of the *civitates*—which provided the administrative substitute for the independent kingdoms. There were fourteen of these. In addition, in the slow process of the occupation, there rose a score of lesser walled towns.

These with the villas are the visible manifestations of Romanisation. They were—except for the ex-soldiery of the *coloniae* and the garrison of London—a civilian manifestation. But beginning a little later there was another and a different growth dependent entirely upon the military. Outside the legionary establishments and at the gates of the main forts, and most particularly at the southern entrances of the forts of the Wall, the *vicus* became an important element in civilian life in the North.

It began probably as a collection of wattle and daub huts housing women—soldiers, for the use of—drinking shops gaming houses and cockpits. It grew both in variety and respectability. The small temples of the *vici* are a vital factor in the life of the Wall zone. The size and importance of the *vicus* is plainly apparent in the remarkable air-shot of Housesteads opposite page 33. The wine shops provided a necessary alternative to the watered vinegar of the marching troops or the thin drink of the garrisons. The food shops supplied a variant to the carbohydrates of the official ration. The brothels were never like those of Italy with their calculated phallic ornament, but clearly they sufficed. They provided a strip of vulgar and bustling Romanisation behind the barrier of the Wall, less spectacular than the culture of the villas but more elaborate and more varied than anything else in the northern half of Britain except perhaps the area around York itself. They provided for the Tired Military Man.

There are three other aspects of Romanisation: religion, entertainment, and the bath.

A resolute opposition to Druidism was either a part of the first intention of the invasion or an early addition to its objectives. Druidism was the principal alternative to the chieftaincies as a possible form of unification. It appears at this time to have covered most of Britain, and though it played no overt part in politics, it seems to have had a large command of the hearts and minds of the people. Little is recorded of its extirpation in the general body of the country, but the fury of its destruction in Anglesey is a sufficient indication of the position it occupied in the Roman assessment of Britain.

The remarkable thing is that the Romans appear to have provided no adequate substitute for it following the desecration of its sacred places and the massacre of its priesthood. Colchester had its temple to the Divine Claudius—a singular deity. Its massive podium survives today as a part of the foundations of its Norman keep, a mordant commentary on the transitory nature of fabricated gods. The towns, like Londinium, had their temples, and over the countryside and mainly in the south a score or so of temples apart from those of the Wall have been identified—all of them small, most of them insignificant.

Organised entertainment fared even less well. Only three theatres have been identified in Britain: the admirably excavated example at St. Albans (which was Verulamium), and that at Canterbury, and a third outside Colchester of considerable size in association with a small temple. There may have been others, now lost, in the towns. Amphitheatres were more frequent, for they were a normal feature of military areas and towns. They survive, as at Dorchester and Silchester, and are discernible on the outskirts of a number of others of the Roman towns.

There remain the baths. They were mandatory at all permanent military establishments. The best surviving military bath in Britain is that at Chesters on the bank of the North Tyne in the angle between the eastern wall of the fort and the wall that leads to the great bridge. It is brilliantly clear in the aerial picture of Chesters opposite page 81. The military bath with its large dressing room, its three separate chambers for different heat levels and its *unctorium*, where the bather's skin was rubbed with oil, was almost more a club than a bathhouse. On a lesser scale baths were essential with the villa culture. Some of them, as at Fishbourne, were elaborate; some, as at Brading in the Isle of Wight, simple.

In two instances, however, at Bath (its Roman name was Aquae Sulis) and at Buxton (Aquae Arnemetiae), spas were developed in the course of the occupation. The baths at Buxton have disappeared. At Bath they are magnificent. At the height of its fashion it had three great plunge baths. The largest of these, the Great Bath, fed by a natural spring at a temperature of a hundred and twenty degrees Fahrenheit, was originally open to the sky. Subsequently it was roofed by an enormous tunnel vault thirty-five feet across and supported by cross-ribbed arches. Bath was, in fact, a small town, walled, covering over twenty acres, and enclosing temples and inns and the dwelling places of the priests and servants of the hot springs and the baths. It was the greatest establishment of its kind in Western Europe. It is in its unquestioned opulence the effective monument of the Villa plutocracy, for it stands in the densest concentration of villas in the countryside, thirty-five miles from the nearest cantonal town—Cirencester—almost forty miles from Gloucester and almost the same distance from Ilchester. Its clientele, then, must have been drawn from the people of the villas in the main, and its genuine magnificence is an index of their status.

The towns, the villas and the spas are the measure of Romanisation, the evidence of its achievement. The most remarkable and possibly the most intriguing aspect of this evidence is that Romanisation was fundamentally confined to the South. The frontier of Ostorius Scapula—the line from the valley of the Severn to the River Trent at Winteringham—enclosed almost precisely half the area of the subsequent Province of Britain. Of just over two hundred villas positively identified a hundred and eighty-six are south of Ostorius's line. Of two hundred and fifty major buildings of different classes two hundred and thirty are south of the line. London and twenty-six of the walled towns are below it, only York and nine small towns above it.

The sharpness of the contrast between South and North has attracted surprisingly little attention from the historians. Yet the division is so abrupt as to place the North in an altogether different category.

It would be simple if one could ascribe it to some political aspect of the promulgation of the first frontier. But in fact the line was announced in A.D. 47, only four years after the landings and certainly before the villa building began. With the invasion of South Wales three years later, the defeat of Caratacus in the Wroxeter area in the following year, and the setting up of the temporary double legionary camp at Wroxeter, the frontier was effectively disestablished. It is impossible that anything in the nature of frontier regulations can have affected the general adaptation of the Northern area.

The conquest was, it is true, in these areas delayed mainly by the stubborn refusal of the tribes to accept defeat. These were tribes of an earlier series of waves of invasion than those of the South-East. They had had nothing to do with the Romanisation of Gaul and little, if anything, to do with the Romanisation of trade. Logically, they were less amenable towards the process, and it can have reached them effectively only after the final pacification of Northern Wales by Agricola in 78, thirty-five years after the conquest, and of Brigantia in the following year. But this delay considered in terms of the four hundred years of the occupation is negligible, perhaps even irrelevant. The failure of Romanisation in the North is due to other causes. In part it is, naturally, due to a different terrain. The mountainous character of Wales itself and, farther north, of the Lake District, the bleak high ground of the Pennines which comprised the bulk of the territory of the Brigantes, did not lend itself easily to modernisation. Despite this, however, there was still ample good agricultural land on either side of the central spine.

It is frequently claimed that the vital difference between the two areas was that the Northern tribes, with their high grazing grounds, were predominantly a cattle and sheep people while the South, following the advent of the deep plough with the invasion of the Belgae, had converted to a grain people. The argument is unconvincing. There was a Roman market for cattle products almost as considerable as the market for grain—the Roman soldier's tunic was of dressed leather, his breeches and boots of leather, his tents of leather, and the by-products of tallow and animal fats were an important item in both the Roman military and civil economies. In any event there were already by this time in the South corn villas and cattle villas.

In the North the villa system in reality never got under way at all. In all Wales there are only two authenticated villas, both are on the sea coast west of Cardiff. There are seven more in the general area of the Welsh Marshes. East of the central spine there are eleven, making a total of twenty altogether north of the Severn-Trent line.

It is difficult to avoid the conclusion that Romanisation as a policy ran out of steam relatively early in the occupation.

It had moved up from the South swiftly enough at the beginning of the second phase. The lead mines in Flintshire in the extreme north of Wales were producing dated pigs of metal as early as A.D. 74, the mines of Yorkshire by 81. Lead, copper, tin and the single gold mine at Dolaucouthi in South Wales were treated as first priorities. With these, real progress ceased. Roman administration appears about this time to have become, or was constrained to become, satisfied.

A number of explanations have been put forward for this. The first is that as an exporting country Britain lacked a realistic market. Strabo—who never visited Britain—writing twenty years before the landings, described the important British exports as corn, cattle, iron, silver and gold.

Corn certainly was being exported to the Rhineland as late as the fourth century, but the quantities do not appear to have been significant. Britain as an island was faced with an almost insuperable problem in the area of transportation. Grain, for example, had to be transported first to the south coast, loaded on ships, ferried across the Channel, and reloaded on land transport. The long haul over Gaul and reshipment to Ostia precluded direct export in quantity to Rome. The Continent was itself a grain producing area, and the market must have been limited and unprofitable. It seems quite possible that the Province, with its passion for Roman luxury goods, acquired quite early in the occupation a balance of payments problem. Certainly Strabo's gold helped little. The output of Dolaucouthi at its highest level cannot have been important. Cattle products came under the same damnation as grain, and the two items of export which paid their way in the simple economy of the Province must have been slaves and silver—silver derived as a by-product of the extensive lead mines.

The internal situation seems to have been even more difficult. The failure to consolidate the conquest of Scotland—discussed more fully in Chapter 4—is the single cause of the permanent retention of three legions and a proportionate strength of auxiliaries for the defence of the Province. The burden was beyond the powers of the Province to sustain in economic balance. The military demand for grain and hides itself diminished export potential. The tax requirement for the pay of the soldiery must at all times have strained the Provincial exchequer. The normal demand of Rome for revenue must have assured frequently a delicate imbalance. The availability of capital for development purposes, as vital in Roman times as it is in the present day, must have affected every major facet of Provincial life.

The problem is epitomised in the town of Silchester. Silchester lay fifty miles west and a little south of London. It was a cantonal capital—Calleva Atrebates. It became early a walled city. Its walls formed a great irregular octagonal, possibly because they followed original tribal boundaries. Its interior was laid out with an impeccable checkerboard of streets. It is today brooding and lonely; the only major Roman town that has escaped the modern builder. It could and it should one day be consolidated as the British Pompeii. But Silchester outlines the failure of Romanisation. It began in a high optimism. It achieved administrative buildings, public baths, pagan temples, and a major inn, in the first period of enthusiasm. Then enthusiasm faded, progress petered out. Unlike other cities in other Roman Provinces, unlike the medieval walled cities, it was never faced with the problem of overflowing its walls. The problem of Silchester was that it failed to fill its walls. It is the problem of the Province.

The virile era of Romanisation covered the first hundred and fifty years. For two generations of that period it operated secure behind the impregnable military barrier of the Wall. After that, security failed it—failed it not from without but from within.

The revolt of Clodius Albinus, Governor of Britain, in A.D. 196 is climactic. It is the pivot of the failure of the occupation, the demonstration of the failure of the system. Behind the security of the Wall the legions had been idle. Because the legions were idle, conspiracy was possible. Albinus took the army of Britain to Gaul to support his attempt on the throne of Rome. He was defeated and killed at Lyons, and behind him in Britain the barbarians flooded south as far as York, and perhaps as far as Chester.

The word security had never again the same meaning.

Rome, it is true, returned; ruins were made good, the line was manned again. But there must have been thereafter the knowledge that the legions would be idle once more and that conspiracy would return. It did. The North was never Romanised in a significant sense. The Province stagnated under the paradoxical protection of the Wall.

2

The Incomparable Memorial

It was never a simple wall.

Two plans were developed in swift succession. The first called for a standard fighting ditch 30 feet wide by 13 feet 6 inches deep, with a 60-foot glacis to the north made from its spoil. A level berm 20 feet wide separated the ditch from the face of the rampart. The Wall itself was planned of squared ashlar 21 feet 6 inches high to the capping stones of its crenellations, 10 feet thick. At every Roman mile was a fortlet with a turreted gate opening through the Wall to the north. Between each pair of these "milecastles" were two defensive turrets. It was designed to start at the bridge across the Tyne—built to serve it where Newcastle stands today—eight miles inland from the North Sea coast. It was laid boldly across the crags of the hill country of Northumberland and it reached the sea again at Bowness at the mouth of the Solway estuary on the Irish Channel, seventy-six Roman miles away. For reasons which are discussed in a later chapter the westernmost third of it, from the crossing of the River Irthing to Bowness, was to be built not of stone but of layered turf surmounted by wooden towers and pierced by wooden gateways.

Behind the Wall, for long distances close to it but in the hill country separated sometimes by as much as a quarter of a mile, was the Vallum, a 20-foot ditch of no apparent military purpose, 8 feet deep, with low continuous earthworks built from its spoil to north and south.

For most of its length either Ditch or Vallum or both can be discerned today, for more than twenty miles along the central sector enough of the main works stands to show what it was in the days of power. Long stretches of the Wall itself—some of it eight and ten feet high—turrets, milecastles, gate-

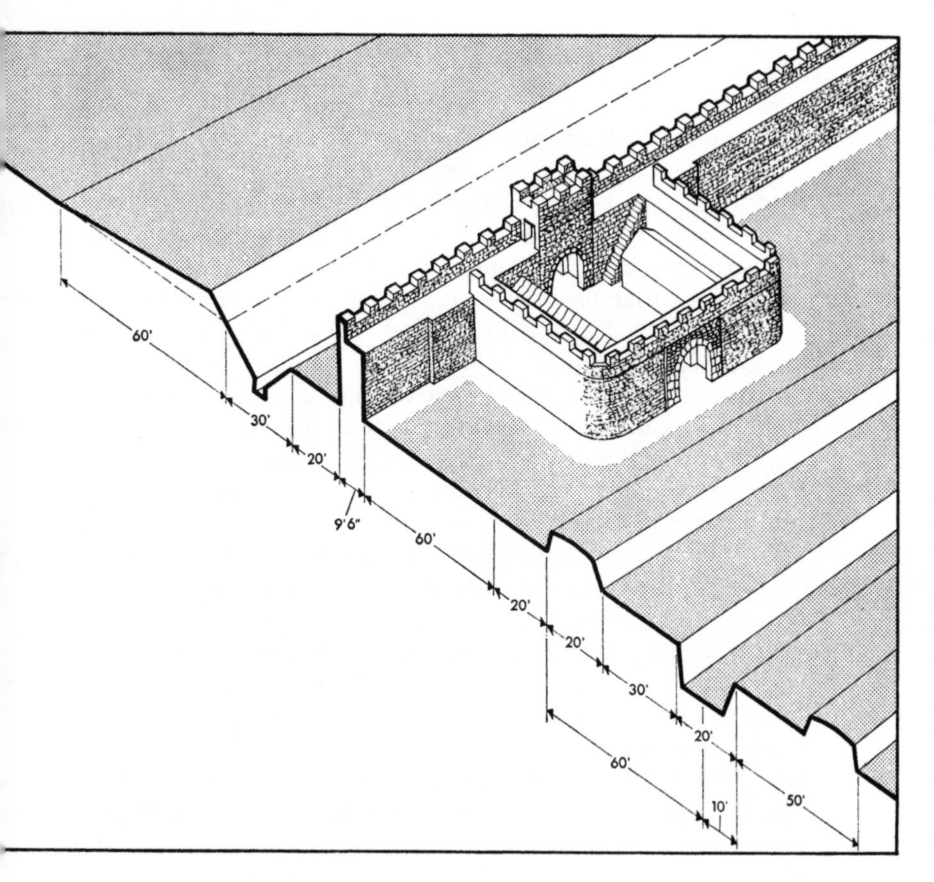

HADRIAN'S WALL : FIRST PLAN

The First Plan provided for a wall 10 ft. wide, 15 ft. 6 in. high and surmounted by a 6 ft. crenellation. To the north of this was a 20 ft. berm, a standard fighting ditch 30 ft. by 13 ft. 6 in. and a glacis composed of the spoil of the ditch, approximately 60 ft. in width. At each Roman mile was a milecastle with a north gate opening through the Wall, surmounted by a defensive turret and a south gate. In the original plan there were two barracks and the milecastle maintained a turret on either hand for the patrol garrison. South of the milecastle was the Vallum, a complex consisting of a 20 ft. ditch with a wide bottom section and mounds composed of the spoil to north and south. The Wall was built to the designed width only on the eastern slope. The milecastles built before the change of plan had 10 ft. wings on either side. The curtain wall as finally built was substantially narrower and the join is indicated in the diagram.

ways and bridge abutments have been expertly excavated. At Chesters, at Housesteads, at Birdoswald the great forts of the final development are largely cleared and consolidated. Almost everywhere it can be approached on foot. The great eighteenth century Military Road that runs on it or to its rear is the fast road from Newcastle to Carlisle. Farm roads cut across it. But in the centre along the high crags of the spine of Britain it still strides splendidly alone.

The First Plan for it was a masterpiece of military economy. It exploited the dramatic escarpment of the Great Whin Sill to the limit of its potential. It utilised the materials of the area to the maximum. It employed the existing fighting equipment——the Stanegate and the still serviceable forts of the Agricolan conquest—to the utmost extent of its effectiveness. It subscribed to the best precepts of the economics of war. But in its subtlety it went beyond all these things: it established a new technique in frontier defence, a technique that had not been developed anywhere along the line of the German *limes* or in the vast earthworks of the Dobruja—the technique of an established offensive-defensive. The Wall itself was to be defended basically only as a last resort. The milecastles were essentially fortified gateways opening towards the enemy. The concept relied upon sorties. The garrisons of single milecastles were adequate against small raiding parties and attempts at infiltration. Against heavy attacks garrisons could be concentrated in cover to strike at the optimum point of an enemy's weakness.

It represents a revolution in frontier tactics.

The Second Plan moved it a dimension higher in the philosophy of war. With a strange, still unexplained drama, work on the Wall was suspended—apparently over-night. At intervals of a rough average of five miles along its line the courses of the Wall that were already laid were torn down; at Chesters, at Housesteads, at Birdoswald and Burgh-by-Sands turrets that were all but built were demolished; at Greatchesters and at Bowness milecastles were levelled. Straddling the unfinished line of the Wall, great fortified cantonments covering five, six, even nine acres, equipped basically for cavalry—except in the central sector—were erected in the densest concentration of defensive strength in the history of the Roman frontier.

The Fighting Ditch that had been an essential element in the concept was sacrificed to the new design; the Vallum, however, was completed—with diversions to avoid the new forts. Bridges were built, the Turf Wall was replaced in stages by a stone wall. A lateral road to accelerate communication between the sections was in due course laid down. Link forts with the holding system of Eskdale and Annandale and Nithsdale were established, and for two hundred and sixty-one years sixty-three per cent of the garrison of the Province of Britain was deployed across this harsh upland or lay in support of it in the great legionary anchors to the line at York and Chester.

In time in the lee of the forts the *vici*—the civilian townlets—grew with their tally of wives and brothels, of drinking shops and baths and cockpits, of temples to the gods of Rome and to the gods of the Brigantes, until Kipling could describe the complex as "a vast town—long like a snake, and wicked like a snake. Yes, a snake basking beside a warm wall!"

Who planned the first Wall? Who countermanded that plan?

From Rome herself there is little help. No contemporary allusion to the Wall survives; there are no inscriptions, no dedications that establish its beginnings. If Dio Cassius, the first effective historian of the British conquest, dealt with it, the description is gone with the lost books of his history. Not until a century and a half after Hadrian's death does the definitive reference appear. Spartianus, writing the Emperor's biography for the *Augustan History,* says, with a qualified enthusiasm: "... he set out for Britain, and there he corrected many abuses and was the first to construct a wall, eighty miles in length, which was to separate the barbarians from the Romans."

... murumque per octoginta milia passuum primus duxit.... It is at least clear and unequivocal but it leaves endless questions unanswered.

From Britain the help is even less. The first fragmentary chronicles ignore it. Only Gildas, writing more than a century and a half after the disasters which followed the withdrawal of Maximus and the end of Roman rule, offers even a theory as to its origins.

Gildas outlines it in the famous passage on the Groans of

Britain. After Maximus, the barbarians of the North had broken across the abandoned defences. Penitently Britain appealed to Rome for help and Rome sent a legion. The barbarians were thrust back. Britain was told to build a wall to hold them for the future, and the legion returned across the Channel. It neglected, says Gildas, to provide information on construction methods—and the Britons built their wall of turf.

A second time the barbarians flooded across inadequate defences. The Britons appealed to Rome again. Once more a legion came; once more the barbarians were defeated; once more the Romans left, leaving instructions this time on how to build a wall of stone.

In its turn the wall of stone failed, and the Britons sent a third appeal addressed: "To Agitius, consul for the third time, the groans of the Britons . . ." This time no legion came.

It is a pretty story, told in admirable literary form. Gildas was not a military historian, he was a churchman devoted to the sulphurous castigation of the vices of his contemporaries, but the events that he described had ended barely seventy years before his birth; there should at least have been folk memories available of the centuries of history that already hung above the debatable frontier.

Gildas is the great inaugurator of error on the Wall. After him follows an unbroken and distinguished line. It is not yet complete.

Bede came next—Bede, the quiet, gentle monk of Jarrow, whose monastery was built probably in part of the robbing of the Roman base at Arbeia in South Shields. Looking across the Tyne, he could see from its fields the Wall where it came down to its end in the river and wrote of it as "eight feet wide and twelve high, in a straight line from east to west as is clear to beholders to this day".

Though his figures have been questioned, there is not the slightest doubt that they were reasonably accurate. Bede's contribution to error was to christen the earthwork that runs for most of the length of the Wall the "Vallum". A Roman general would surely have called it the Fosse.

After Bede there is Nennius, who is unimportant, and then a long period of silence with only casual allusion and incidental reference. John Leland, King's Antiquary under the Great Seal to Henry VIII, takes up the story again. In the course of his great tour he was at Bowness where "ys part of the *Pict* Wal evidently remayning". Leland got most of his information from Robert Davell, a parson of Newcastle, whose knowledge of the Wall was detailed. He records that it was built of squared stones, that it had been robbed heavily where "the Grownd ys best enhabited", that "on the farther side toward the *Pictes*" the Wall was strongly ditched and that "an Arow Shot a this side the Stone Wal" there were traces of a turf wall.

Leland's contribution to error was that he wrote positively of the Vallum as another wall. His actual words are "*vestigia muri cespititii*". For good measure he adds "that it was thoroughly made as the Stone wal was yt doth not wel appere there".

Leland died and in due course Camden succeeded him and lifted much of his information from Leland's copious papers. Towards the end of Elizabeth's reign, however, Camden went to Cumberland and began an examination of the Wall complex as far south as the coastal fort at Moresby. At Bowness he wrote: "...here that Vallum and the Wall, the most famous works of the Romans, begin." At Carlisle, he writes, "the Picts wall, which was later superimposed on the vallum of Severus, is to be seen at the village of Stanwix, not far beyond the *Ituna* or Eden...."

The carefree way in which the early historians varied the names of the Wall is unimportant. Archdeacon Threlkeld, who seems to have been one of Camden's earlier sources, begins a note: "As towching Hadrian's wall, begyning abowt a town called Bonus standing vppon the river Sulway..." They knew, despite the inconsistencies, that it *was* Roman, they knew that part of it at least had been built by Hadrian, they knew that in its later years it had served against the Picts. Archaeology was not yet an exact science. It may not be today.

Camden, though he explored assiduously, did not see all the Wall. He had a very proper concern for his person as newly-made Clarenceux King-of-Arms. He left out the sector "near to Busy Gap—a place infamous for thieving and robbing; where stood some castles (chesters they called them), as I heard, but I could not with safety take the full survey of it, for the rank robbers thereabouts". And Camden, where he did not see, sometimes invented. He seems, amongst other things, to have fudged his figures as to the width of the Wall near Carvoran.

The eighteenth century saw the first great flowering of a more precise enthusiasm. Horsley's *Britannia Romana* is one of the remarkable works that appeared in Britain in that remarkable era. Horsley was a Presbyterian minister and the proprietor of a private school at Morpeth. From these improbable beginnings he became the primary expert on Roman Britain. With the publication of the *Britannia* he established his place as the first of the scholars of the Wall. Through the rest of the century he had his imitators and successors, but he was the first to see the Wall not merely as a whole but in its relationship to the wider problem of the Province of Britain. Two centuries and a half later he remains the standard by which other men's work is judged.

Ironically the eighteenth century was also the age of the great iconoclasts. From as far back as the year of the Groans of Britain the Wall had been robbed. Sheep folds and cattle pens, farm houses, churches, inns and border keeps had been built of its stone. But destruction reached its climax with Marshal Wade. In 1745 Wade misappreciated the line of Prince Charles' advance. While he still lay at Newcastle, Charles with his army came down the western roads, crossed the Eden and besieged Carlisle. The carter's track across the high ground was too light to take Wade's artillery, the river road was inadequate; Wade had to go south to find a crossing. With the end of the '45 he proposed a military road to link Tyne and Solway against the possibility of future trouble. In 1751, though Wade himself was dead, Parliament authorised it.

For twenty-seven miles its route ran along the complex of Ditch and Wall and Vallum. Still-standing stonework was

---

The north-west corner of the Roman Empire—Limestone Corner ▶ on the Newcastle-Carlisle road. The picture shows the Fighting Ditch at the point where construction was finally abandoned; the broken stone in the foreground indicates the area. The line of the ditch to east and west of it is clearly visible. Immediately south of the road the Vallum ditch with its mounds and the crossing points where it was slighted stand out in detail.
Photograph: Aerofilms Ltd.

thrown down to make the road bed; at points ditch and Vallum were overlaid, but for more than a century a stubborn skeleton lifted through the road metal in time of drought. It was the greatest single act of vandalism in the history of Britain.

In the nineteenth century industrialisation went farther. It obliterated the Wall in the east as Newcastle and Wallsend grew. In the west there was destruction at Carlisle and over the marshlands of the Solway. But in the centre, by paradox, it was also the age of the first great conservators.

In 1801 William Hutton of Birmingham, walking the length of the Wall at the age of seventy-eight, came to a point where he should have seen a perfect sector two hundred and twenty-four yards long—"a sight not to be found in the whole line. But the proprietor, Henry Tulip, Esq., is now taking it down, to erect a farmhouse with the materials."

William Hutton wept.

What remained of the sector was saved. It still stands, cleared and cared for, and the long process of rescue that was not to end until World War II was begun.

John Clayton of Chesters, Town Clerk of Newcastle, was the giant of them all. Influenced largely by the work of Hodgson of Jarrow, another of the remarkable clergymen who loved the Wall, Clayton purchased in turn the forts of Carrawburgh, Housesteads, Chesterholm and Carvoran; Chesters he had already. To them he added miles of the course of the Wall and on his lands he began an enormously ambitious programme of excavation and restoration.

Some of Clayton's work was over-eager, some of it was clumsy—the age of scientific excavation had not yet begun—but even with his mistakes he illuminated the history of Britain.

◀ Housesteads from the air. The clarity of Dr. St. Joseph's remarkable photograph makes it possible for it to be used as a diagram for an infantry fort. The *praetorium,* the granaries, the four main gateways and the turrets are wholly clear. The original line of the Wall with the turret that was demolished at the change of plan is apparent just inside the north wall. The clumsy junction between Wall and fort at the western end and again at the eastern corner is plainly illustrated. Outside the walls the shapes of the houses and shops of the *vicus* show with the quality of an X-ray plate, as does the western line of the Military Way.
Photograph: Dr. St. Joseph

The Museum at Chesters, the fort itself and the abutment of the great bridge across the river are his just memorial.

Bruce—John Collingwood Bruce—was another schoolmaster. In 1849, with a few friends, he organised the first Pilgrimage of the Wall. A hundred and ten years later his memory was strong still along that debatable line, and the eighth Pilgrimage was not so much a tribute of piety as an act of scholarship.

Bruce's first essay was the "forming of a pilgrimage like that described by Chaucer, consisting of both ladies and gentlemen" —but not, presumably, a wife of Bath. The pilgrims travelled on foot along the Wall, their baggage went with them on a "commodious brake" (its horses were called Romulus and Remus), and they dug a little, talked a lot and were disarmingly early Victorian. Bruce himself was the "Chief Expositor".

Out of the work that he had done along the Wall before the Pilgrimage and out of that engaging experience he began the monograph on the Wall which he published in 1851. It made him the leading authority on Hadrian's defensive system for his lifetime. In 1863, with the study for a much larger book all but complete, he published *The Handbook to the Roman Wall*. Twelve editions have appeared, revised in their generation by almost every one of the great scholars of the Wall. It remains the indispensable compendium for all who hope to understand it.

Scholarship flourished through the end of the nineteenth century and to its aid the early twentieth brought science and method. The springing point of the new era begins with the excavation of the fort at the Haltwhistle Burn by Simpson and Gibson in 1908. At Haltwhistle for the first time along the complex of the Wall the new techniques were fully exploited, the new disciplines observed. Out of that tentative beginning came guide lines for all subsequent excavation in the area. The antiquarian had become the archaeologist and archaeology itself was reaching towards science.

The fifty years after the Haltwhistle Burn excavations are the age of scientific scholarship. Simpson and Gibson themselves, Haverfield in his last years, Collingwood and Bosanquet, particular specialists like Salway, Mrs. Heywood, C. E. Stevens and Dr. J. K. St. Joseph, and finally the great figures of Birley and Richmond, had at their disposal tools that their predecessors had lacked, techniques that had not been available, knowledge that had been impossible.

In the traditional irony of scholarship it became the age of heightened controversy. Science, as in other fields, did not always clarify. New theories multiplied, contra-theories established themselves overnight; heresies manifested themselves. From the hot and sweating war of the trenches of the excavations to the leisurely flight of arrows from ivory towers the Wall became again a battlefield.

Two hundred years after Horsley, sixty years after the excavations at the Haltwhistle Burn, there are major problems still unsolved, basic questions unanswered:

Who drafted the First Plan for the Wall? And when?

Who countermanded it? And why?

Who conceived the new and sophisticated theory by which cavalry was employed to defend a rampart?

Who drafted the Second Plan so that its six main elements differ fundamentally one from another?

Why was the great Fighting Ditch abandoned?

Were the fortified cantonments designed initially to stand by themselves?

What was the relationship between the line west of the Irthing river and the tightly garrisoned area of Cumberland and Dumfriesshire beyond?

How was it that the Durham coast was left undefended and the Cumberland coast fortified to St. Bees Head?

The list can be prolonged. The answers to the questions will still in every instance be wholly military. With all appropriate humility, it must seem to the layman that scientific scholarship has tended increasingly to lose sight of the fundamental fact that Hadrian's Wall was a military exercise. Its problems were those of soldiers. Its solutions are those of the sword. Its origins are rooted in the greatest military misjudgement of British history—the failure to complete the conquest of the Caledones.

On that misjudgement all British history hangs and something at least of the history of Northern Europe with it. Domitian's decision after the victory at Mons Graupius can be explained. It cannot be condoned. The failure to complete the Agricolan design by the pacification of the Highland area with the system of roads and forts that had succeeded brilliantly in Brigantia set in motion a succession of cause and effect that has much of the inevitabilities of classic tragedy.

The apparent destruction of the Caledones inspired an over-confidence which led to the withdrawal of II Adiutrix from Britain.

The withdrawal of the Second Legion destroyed the balance of forces available for Northern Scotland.

Within four years the resultant inadequacy compelled the evacuation of the legionary fortress at Inchtuthil.

The evacuation of Inchtuthil led within five years to the abandonment of the remainder of the forts of Scotland.

The inroads into the Border country that followed that abandonment forced the establishment of a new frontier.

The need for a defended frontier made the Wall essential.

The demands of the Wall in turn made necessary a Provincial garrison of three legions, an abnormal strength in auxiliary troops and a wholly disproportionate share of the scarce and costly cavalry of the Roman army for the duration of the occupation.

All Spain, it may be remembered, was for long held by a single legion.

Inevitably the cost of this garrison dominated the finances of the Province for three hundred years. It is doubtful if in terms of economics Britain ever justified its conquest.

Last of all, the very excellences of the Wall system led to recurrent disaster. In the long decades of peace that it secured an idle and over-concentrated army turned from time to time furiously to politics. Six conspiracies, secessions, revolutionary attempts upon the throne of Rome itself had their origins in the Province of Britain.

The history of the frontier legions through the rise and fall of Rome is a history of turbulence. They were commanded by men of senatorial rank, young men, vigorous, ambitious—professional soldiers who, like English admirals in the eighteenth and nineteenth centuries, were also active professional politicians. Their connections in Rome and their communications with Rome by the fast and admirable Roman post were adequate for conspiracy. Vespasian, for example, was proclaimed Emperor by the troops in Egypt. Severus marched on Rome from the Danube. From Britain Clodius Albinus challenged him for the throne, crossed the Channel and was narrowly defeated at Lyons. Carausius, Admiral of the Roman Fleet, forced his own inclusion in a Triumvirate of Emperors. Magnus Maximus seized Gaul and Spain. Constantine III led the army of Britain to set up a capital of the west at Arles. There were other conspiracies.

Their consequences brought catastrophe to the Province and at intervals disruption to Northern Europe.

3

Resolutely Opposed to Rome

In one of his most masterful compressions of insolence and information Edward Gibbon wrote of the conquest of Britain:

> After a war of about forty years, undertaken by the most stupid, maintained by the most dissolute, and terminated by the most timid of all the emperors, the far greater part of the island submitted to the Roman yoke.

Accepting the exquisite appropriateness of his summing-up of Claudius, Nero and Domitian, it is, none the less, important to establish the fact that the matter might have been differently expressed. Gibbon could with equal scholarship have said: "A vital sector of the island remained resolutely opposed to Roman rule."

To understand the requirements of Hadrian's Wall it is necessary to understand at least the fundamentals of the Roman conquest.

In a sense it began earlier even than Gibbon's most stupid Emperor. Julius Caesar's campaign in 55 B.C. is, it is true, customarily accepted to have been no more than a reconnaissance in force. Acknowledging this, it was still in fact an ill-judged venture, inadequately prepared and incompetently executed, and all the nineteenth century adulation of Caesar cannot hide this fact.

His preliminary intelligence efforts were deplorable. Neither the interrogation of the men who ran the existing highly organised cross-Channel trade nor the five-day exploration of the Kentish coast by Gaius Volusenus succeeded in discovering a sheltered harbour for an amphibious force—though one existed.

Next, the fleet was sailed in two divisions, with the cavalry ordered to button up off Ambleteuse on passage—and the cavalry missed the tide. Then the infantry was landed hastily on an open beach, probably where Walmer is today, certainly exposed to every wind from north-north-east to south—though the sheltered channel between Thanet and the mainland lay a bare seven miles beyond.

The attempt failed not in battle but because the fleet, incautiously beached, was all but destroyed by a conjunction of the high water of the spring tide and an onshore breeze—it cannot have been the "violent storm" that Caesar subsequently claimed, for the heavily-laden horse transports weathered it at sea without loss. Afterwards he explained everything away by a declaration that Romans did not understand the conjunction of spring tide and full moon. The explanation is inadequate. His ships were requisitioned from Gaulish traders who knew every nuance of the Channel waters. His own sea captains had for the best part of a year campaigned against and defeated the Veneti along the coast of the Bay of Biscay and in the Gulf of Morbihan. They too must have known the rhythm of the tides.

The size of his army—he took two legions only with him—and the fact that the attack was made late in the season go far, however, to justify the reconnaissance theory. When he invaded Britain the following year he took five legions and two thousand cavalry with him—and compounded his error.

Once more he landed on the same beach. His ships were left on the same lee shore—this time at anchor. Once more spring tide and wind battered his rear. He was forced at the very outset to abandon the pursuit of the beaten enemy of the first battle and to fall back to the coast to haul the undamaged galleys clear of the water and to begin the giant task of cannibalising the damaged ships and enclosing his base in a vast fortification.

Thereafter his campaign was brief and triumphant. New tactics defeated the British chariot arm, a series of victories broke the tenuous confederacy of the tribes, the legions crossed the Thames in a swift and ruthless advance, and Cassivelaunus asked for terms. Caesar granted them and accepted an offer of tribute, not because the military problem was beyond his means but because he was aware now that his rear was insecure. Behind him the Gaulish harvest had failed and the tribes of the North were smouldering in revolt.

The tribute, of course, was not paid.

The problem was too much for his successors. Dio says that Augustus flirted with it twenty years later. Caligula certainly moved an army to the coast of Gaul in A.D. 40 and built a pharos at Boulogne to light the galleys. But at the last moment, at the very point of embarkation, he lost his nerve; again, so far as one can judge, not because he feared the military problem but because he feared his rear—in Rome this time.

His apprehensions were justified—early in the new year he was suitably murdered.

Claudius, his successor, achieved the laurels—not without dust and heat and some respectful manipulation of campaign history. Early in 43 he ordered the concentration of four legions at Boulogne: II Augusta from Strasbourg, XIV Gemina from Mainz, XX Valeria Victrix from Cologne and IX Hispana from Pannonia. With them he authorised a powerful force of auxiliaries and an exceptional element of cavalry. The force as a whole was approximately forty thousand strong.

Whether some lingering memory of Caesar's amphibious failures still lived in the Roman army we cannot know. Dio, the best authority for the campaign, says that the legions refused to sail "outside the world". On the beaches of Boulogne they staged a singularly good-tempered mutiny. From Rome Claudius sent his chief secretary, the freedman Narcissus, to reason with them. They jeered at him with catch phrases but Narcissus ignored the jeers and talked them over. The mutiny faded, and with three great fleets Claudius' general Aulus Plautius invaded Britain.

With this landing the necessary harbour was known—the great Claudian encampment at Richborough on the channel between Thanet and the mainland marks Plautius' base. Swiftly, efficiently, he cleared the country in its vicinity. The tribes, led by Caratacus, one of the sons of Cunobelinus, stood against him at a point between Richborough and the Medway. Plautius dislodged him from a strong defensive position and harried him up the line of what in due course came to be called Watling Street. Britain, misled by the reports of the mutiny, had been caught unprepared but the holding actions in eastern Kent gave time for the levies of the tribes to concentrate on the Medway. In a bitterly fought battle on the river they lasted two days against the full weight of Plautius' attack. Then, cut up by cavalry that had swum the Medway, taken in flank by the Second Legion, which had found a ford, they broke and fled; Togodumnus was dead, Caratacus fled with them. The battle of the Medway was the crucial point in the first stage of the conquest of Britain. It was also a crucial point in Plautius' career, for the plan of campaign as laid down by the Emperor had provided that Claudius himself should take command at the decisive moment—and win the victory. Personally!

Plautius could not break off a hot pursuit. While his army drove the Britons north across an all but undefended Thames to the Lea marshes, he sent urgently for Claudius. Claudius, according to Dio Cassius, had made the necessary preparations "including elephants". Possibly he was already at Boulogne, though Dio says that the message reached him at Rome. Classical military historians are notoriously partisan where the Emperors are concerned. Dio claims that Claudius fought the decisive battle, other authors suggest that the whole affair was stage-managed to ensure the Emperor's popularity.

It is unnecessary—it is perhaps, in the light of the existing evidence, impossible—to examine in detail the early years of the occupation. Using first the prehistoric roads that ran from Colchester and from the Great Ford across the Thames above London, subsequently constructing the magnificent Roman network, the legions fanned out to consolidate the conquest. The tribes in Britain at the moment of the invasion existed in loose and temporary alliances. Richborough, the landing point, was in Kent, the territory of the Cantiaci, who had clearly at least a defensive agreement with the federation established by Cunobelinus. This consisted of the Atrebates and the Trinovantes, who held the Thames valley, and the Catuvellauni, who reached up into Hertfordshire, north of Londinium. With the second phase of the occupation new tribes were involved. The Ninth Legion struck north to build a base at Lincoln, and in the process subdued the Trinovantes and the Iceni. The Fourteenth and the Twentieth moved

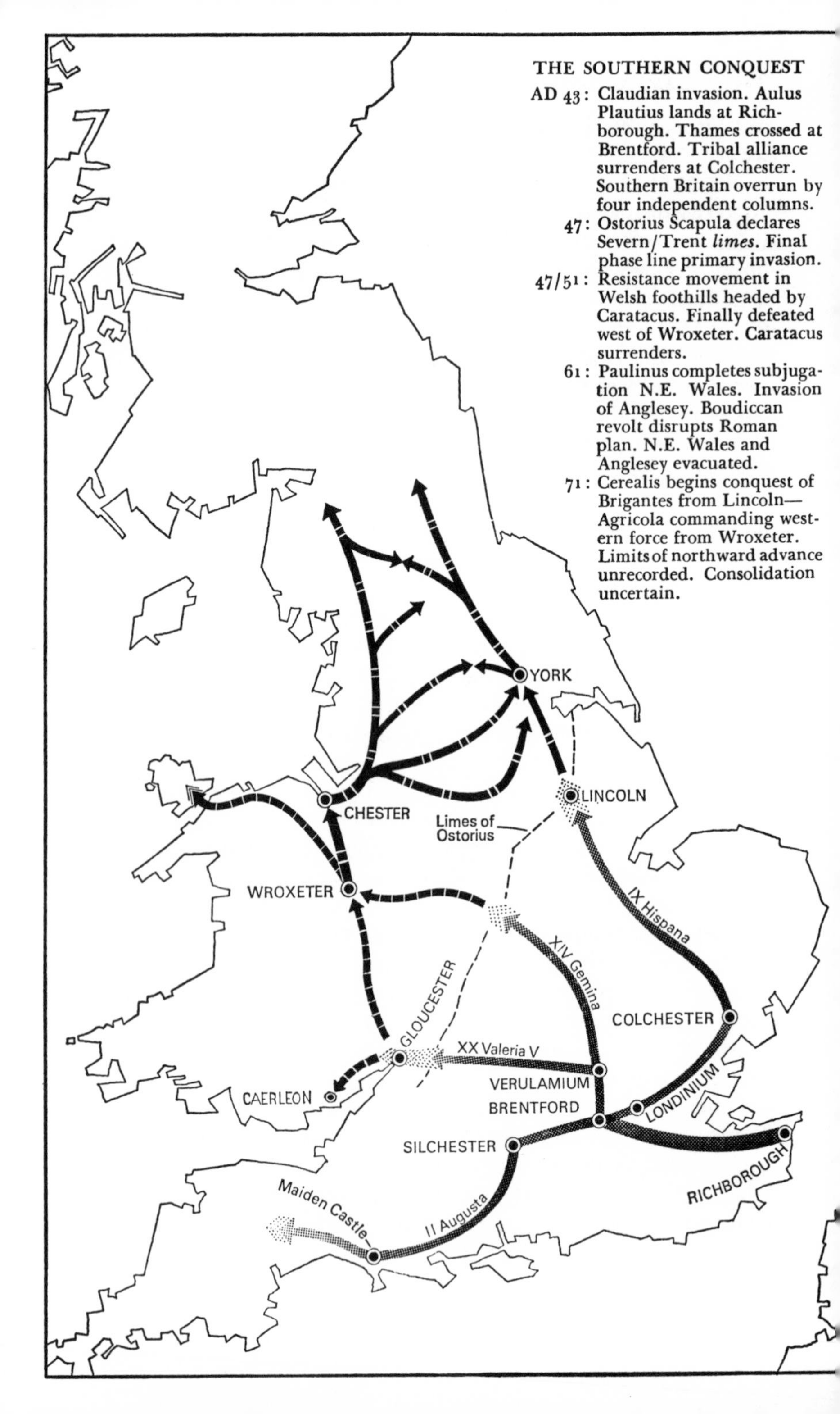
THE SOUTHERN CONQUEST
AD 43: Claudian invasion. Aulus Plautius lands at Richborough. Thames crossed at Brentford. Tribal alliance surrenders at Colchester. Southern Britain overrun by four independent columns.
47: Ostorius Scapula declares Severn/Trent *limes*. Final phase line primary invasion.
47/51: Resistance movement in Welsh foothills headed by Caratacus. Finally defeated west of Wroxeter. Caratacus surrenders.
61: Paulinus completes subjugation N.E. Wales. Invasion of Anglesey. Boudiccan revolt disrupts Roman plan. N.E. Wales and Anglesey evacuated.
71: Cerealis begins conquest of Brigantes from Lincoln—Agricola commanding western force from Wroxeter. Limits of northward advance unrecorded. Consolidation uncertain.
YORK
LINCOLN
CHESTER
Limes of Ostorius
WROXETER
IX Hispana
XIV Gemina
GLOUCESTER
XX Valeria V
COLCHESTER
VERULAMIUM
CAERLEON
BRENTFORD
LONDINIUM
SILCHESTER
RICHBOROUGH
Maiden Castle
II Augusta

north-west into the Midlands and the country of the Dobunni. The Second Legion cut south-west to Silchester, accepted the submission of the Regni of the south coast as it moved, and struck into the fortress country of the Belgae and the Durotriges in Hampshire and Dorset.

Four years after the landing Ostorius Scapula, who had succeeded Plautius as Governor, decided, as earlier indicated, that he had consolidated Southern Britain sufficiently to declare a frontier. On the line of the Fosse Way between the valley of the Severn and the Trent he established a *limes.*

Essentially a *limes* was a demarcated frontier. In its primary stages it frequently consisted of a path or unmade road marking a boundary or even a line of advance. Whether it was defended or not depended basically on the likelihood of attack. Ostorius' *limes* was anchored militarily on the fortress of the Second Legion at Gloucester in the south—though archaeological evidence is meagre—and on the fortress of the Ninth Legion at Lincoln in the north-east. There is no evidence of temporary forts along it.

Little remains of it except the road. It is probable, despite the orthodox historians, that Ostorius never considered it as more than a temporary expedient, for already the relatively simple process of the Southern conquest was complicated by the factor of Welsh intransigence.

The third phase of the conquest brought Rome into sharp conflict with Wales. Three main tribes were involved—the Silures in the south, the Ordovices in the centre, and the Deceangli in the north. Their precise relationship to the eastern tribes is obscure. Basically they were of different stock, yet they accepted Caratacus in flight and permitted him to establish himself as a leader. Legend and to some extent history has perhaps made too much of this, for the Welsh tribes inhabited a mountain country, difficult of access and therefore defensible, and were in consequence a naturally resistant people. Even without his leadership they would have presented a difficult military proposition to the legions.

Caratacus, when he made up his mind instantly after the battle of the Medway as to the impossibility of challenging the Roman military power in the lowland country, had three possible choices. He might have made his way west in the hope that the great fortresses like Maiden Castle would stand against a Roman siege. He might have made his way north-west to the Brigantes to stir them to an attempt to hold the central massif of Britain. He chose instead to head for Wales in consideration, quite certainly, of the known stubbornness of the mountain tribes—though he might possibly have been additionally influenced by the political jealousies both of the Belgae and the Brigantes.

By the time Ostorius' *limes* was completed the valley of the Severn above Gloucester was already suffering from raids. Before he could deal with these Ostorius had to settle a rising of the Iceni, the first of the rebellions of the Province of Britain. The Iceni, with the other tribes below the line, had been ordered to surrender their arms. Their refusal brought a condign punishment. Thereafter, with his rear area quiet, Ostorius began the subjection of Wales.

Again it is unnecessary to attempt to trace the complex campaigns involved, but the Silures were reduced to a temporary impotence. Caratacus moved northwards, stirring up the Ordovices and the Deceangli. Ostorius countered the move—probably (though the archaeological evidence is still indefinite) by establishing a temporary double legionary post at Wroxeter. In a last heroic stand on one of the great spurs of the Welsh uplands that thrust across the Shropshire border Caratacus and the Ordovices were defeated. Leaving his wife and daughter behind him, Caratacus fled to Cartimandua, Queen of the Brigantes.

The Brigantes were the largest tribe in Britain. Their southern limit is ill-defined but was probably a little north of the modern line Lincoln-Leeds-Chester. From there, except for the Parisi in the area about the River Humber, they held the country to the Lowlands of Scotland around the Solway Firth and probably down the valley of the Tyne to the North Sea. Their subjugation marks the next phase of the conquest.

Cartimandua ruled a turbulent tribe. Once already she had called in Roman aid to survive an insurrection. Effectively she had accepted client status. She was not now prepared to abandon the advantages that this had brought. She surrendered Caratacus to the Romans. In the interim the Silures had got their second wind; extensive raids were launched into the

Roman area and Ostorius' attempt at the consolidation of the new territory by a system of fortlets was disrupted by fierce attacks. In the middle of the turmoil he died.

Didius Gallus, who succeeded him, inherited the local problem and almost at once, in addition, a fresh Brigantian civil war. For the second time Cartimandua was supported by a force of auxiliaries and again her authority was re-established with Roman aid. It was already obvious that Rome would require some time to settle the Brigantian problem, but for five years there was relative quiet while first the elderly Didius Gallus and then for a brief period Veranius Nepos contented themselves with holding down the Silures.

Nepos died suddenly and was succeeded by Suetonius Paulinus. One of the tough soldiers of the epoch, Paulinus decided to move forward again. From the Wroxeter position he marched north, heading for the Welsh coast to break the Druid hierarchy, to deny the granary of Anglesey to the mountain tribes, and with the eventual intention of outflanking Snowdonia. On his staff was a young tribune, Gnaeus Julius Agricola, in process of being blooded to war.

The battle of the Menai Straits is one of the bizarre episodes of British history. Against an enemy of priests of the Druid faith, women of the religion and warriors, Paulinus forced the crossing, his infantry in shallow-draught boats, his cavalry swimming. Brief opposition ended in massacre.

Before he could complete the conquest of the island, Britain flared into flames behind him. Boudicca—Boadicea, there is no absolute canon for either spelling—was the widow of Prasutagus, King of the Iceni. Nero was Emperor in Rome. Prasutagus, following the established practice under tyranny, made the Emperor co-heir to his estates, trusting that—for half his property—Nero would do justice to his family. When he died, Decianus Cato, the Procurator, may have communicated with Nero; more probably he acted on his own authority. Whatever the event, the succession was broken, the estates confiscated and Boudicca, protesting at the invasions of her palace and her inheritance, was flogged, her daughters raped.

The neglect of Boudicca among British historians is a by-product of that uncritical adulation of Roman arms and of

Roman achievement which began with the English acceptance of the Renaissance and reached its peak in the romantic Latinity of Victorianism. The brief and tragic story of the revolt of the Iceni is also in fact the story of one of the major breakdowns of the Roman military machine.

The Iceni themselves had been rigorously disarmed at the conclusion of the revolt against Ostorius twelve years before. Caister, the headquarters of the tribe, was barely ninety miles from the fortress of the Ninth Legion at Lincoln. Despite police espionage and the civilian control inevitable to the reign of Nero, Boudicca raised the tribe with astonishing speed, supplied it in secret with minimal arms, secured the support of the Trinovantes, and led a devastating attack against the Roman *colonia* at Colchester (Camulodonum), fifty miles to the south.

Before Cerealis, Legate of the Ninth—the nearest major force—could move to the defence of the *colonia*, Boudicca had carried it in a brutal two-day assault. At the end of the second day she burned the great temple of Claudius, the sacred place of the Conquest, with its defenders, and thrust west to challenge Cerealis. Somewhere north of Braughing on the road from Lincoln to London she met him. Cerealis had started south with a vexillation of barely two thousand men plus the cavalry of the Legion. The depth of his error of judgment was at once apparent. In a swift and brilliant action the Ninth was totally defeated. His infantry annihilated, Cerealis fled with the remnants of the cavalry, harried to the gates of Lincoln. There, with a masterful judgment, Boudicca resisted the temptation to besiege the battered Legion and turned south for London.

The strategic reaction of the Roman army command is at this point of the utmost interest. Suetonius Paulinus was still embroiled in Anglesey, but his immediate decisions were immaculately professional. Detaching half the infantry of the Twentieth Legion to Wroxeter to cover the Welsh frontier, he ordered the Fourteenth and the remainder of the Twentieth down Watling Street—the great diagonal road towards Verulamium and London and the coast. Simultaneously, he sent urgent dispatches to the Second Legion at Gloucester to move west immediately to cover the cities. He himself rode with the cavalry in a desperate attempt to reach London first.

He accomplished his objective. At London, however, he learned that Boudicca was already thrusting south from Lincoln. Presumably he learned also that Cerealis had not moved again from the safety of his camp. Certainly he learned that the Second Legion had not moved at all. In the absence of its Legate, Poenius Postumus, the *praefectus castrorum,* in command, had ignored the Governor's orders. It is accepted that this was due to the threat of the Silures—always present—to the west. Whether this was so is immaterial; what was material was that Paulinus' plan of campaign had already collapsed; it was no longer possible to cover London.

The city was still unwalled, a straggling entrepot without garrison, with scarcely more than guards for the military stores area and the civic headquarters. Paulinus abandoned it at once and rode back to St. Albans (Verulamium). The reports that he received there of the progress of his main force must have made it clear that there was small hope even of saving Verulamium. Again he abandoned a city to its fate and rode grimly up the road past Towcester to regain his legions.

Behind him, as he rode, Boudicca fell upon London. In a day and a night of slaughter the Iceni overwhelmed an exiguous resistance. In the morning the city was burned and dead. With that iron control over the tribesmen that she had exercised even in the drunkenness of loot and victory after Camulodunum, Boudicca broke away from London and struck with lightning brilliance to the north-west.

Verulamium, third of the three great cities of Romanised Britain, was destroyed in a fury of revenge. The Roman figure for the dead at this point was seventy thousand. Statistics of casualties in early history are open to question. The slaughter in the three cities was, however, beyond question shattering. That the Ninth Legion subsequently required replacements totalling two thousand men is an inescapable index of the scale of disaster. As the fires died, Boudicca marched north to challenge the strength of Paulinus.

It has been described as suicide—the march of a death wish. It was in reality a warrior's choice. She could have gone south again, endlessly devastating the countryside as the tribes rose to join her, but logically, inevitably, the legions would recover and concentrate, and after that the end was certain. It must have seemed to her that if she struck in time, fate would strike with her. And time was short.

How good her intelligence was we cannot tell. Certainly she must have known that the battered Ninth was still at Lincoln. Probably the friendly tribes would have told her that the second had not moved from Gloucester. She had outfaced the Ninth, now she was prepared to face the main body.

Somewhere on the edge of the great Midland forest Paulinus waited for her. He chose his position with the cold, dispassionate skill of a Roman general. Dense woodland backed the line of the Fourteenth and the five cohorts of the Twentieth. His weary cavalry was disposed on either side, backed also by the forest. Tactically it may be that Boudicca's judgement was inadequate, despite the thrashing of the Ninth. Encumbered by a vast waggon train with the loot of the three cities, her dispositions were clearly faulty. The waggon train was allowed to block the ground which she required for radical manoeuvre when the legions pressed. Beyond that single fact we have no account of the action, only the knowledge that Roman training and Roman arms overweighted the fanatic courage of the tribes. Harassed by the cavalry, thrown back against their waggons, the Iceni died. Afterwards the Romans claimed eighty thousand dead. Again the figure may be challenged. But the tribes had gathered to Boudicca's banner by this time, their women and children moved with them, and battle ended in holocaust.

It was the Götterdämmerung of the South Britons.

The story of Boudicca has all the attributes of valour. Ill-armed, unorganised, inexperienced, she threw the great professional military machine of Rome off balance, the civil machine was for a time wrecked, the cost to Rome of the burning of the cities and the breakdown of the administration has never been assessed. In the end she died by her own hand. She stands high in the line of warrior women.

Sixty miles away in the fortress at Gloucester Poenius Postumus fell upon his sword. By his failure to obey an impera-

---

The West Gate at Housesteads. The quality of the masonry of the gateway proper is admirably clear. The picture shows the guard turrets on either side which formed the base of the western tower. *Photograph: Ministry of Public Building and Works* ▶

tive order he had failed the army of Rome in crisis. Death was necessary as it was inevitable.

The decade that follows is obscure and untidy. The revolt had curbed the thirst for conquest. Paulinus was recalled to Rome for—according to Tacitus—the brutality of his revenge upon revenge, and in the enclave of Roman control the legions sat idle in the camps and, following the custom of idle legions, intrigued. In due time the reign of Nero came to its bloodied end and over the Empire the cloud of civil war spread like a dust storm. Galba, Otho and Vitellius—the first the meanest of Emperors, the second the cuckolded husband of Poppaea, the third the greatest glutton of Rome—appeared and disappeared with the flamboyance of a Hollywood spectacular in a welter of murder, suicide and violent battle. The legions in Britain, separated by the Channel from the main focus of disruption, backed different claimants to the Roman throne until finally they chased a Governor, Trebellius Maximus, across the Channel.

Of this Maximus, Tacitus says bitingly in Mattingley's translation: "He was deficient in energy and without military experience, but he governed his province like a gentleman."

For a time Britain was ruled by a triumvirate of the legates of the three legions. Then Vettius Bolanus was sent to replace Trebellius. The rule of Bolanus is even more indistinct than that of some of his immediate predecessors, but he clung to his governorate, watching inactively the growth of the threat of the Brigantes. Cartimandua had failed at last. She had divorced her husband, married his standard bearer and scandalised the elaborate relationships by which the Brigantian throne was supported. Now her ex-husband came back with allies from the north, and though a distracted Province sent units of auxiliaries to rescue her, they saved only her life. Her kingdom broke with Rome.

In the final months of the governorate of Bolanus Agricola

◀ A conjectural reconstruction of Housesteads by Alan Sorrell showing the line of the Wall, the buildings of the interior of the fort, its four great gateways and the crowded buildings of the *vicus* below and to the east.
Photograph: Ministry of Public Building and Works

returned to Britain as Legate of the Twentieth, charged by the new Emperor, Vespasian, with bringing it back from mutiny to discipline.

The second phase of the conquest of Britain was moving to its end. By the time Agricola had completed his task Vespasian, the civil war ended, had sent Cerealis as Governor to settle the problem of the Brigantes. This was the Cerealis who ten years before had been hounded by Boudicca to the walls of Lincoln. The campaign that follows marks the beginning of the third phase.

It is a masterly and methodical exercise of absolute military power. The Brigantes were the most numerous tribe in Britain. The limits of the kingdom were never positive, but for military purposes the Brigantes occupied the central massif of the Pennines from Derbyshire to the frontiers of the Selgovae above the Solway Firth and, with the exception of the country of the Parisi, the coastal plains as well. It was a strong tribe, but it was separated by the natural divisions of the terrain.

In this first campaigning season Cerealis advanced the main eastern legionary base from his old camp at Lincoln to York—Eburacum—strategically placed on the land ridge between the dales and the wolds. On the western side Agricola, striking north from Wroxeter, matched his movement. The results are apparent on the map of Roman Britain today. As they moved north, the two forces cut the Brigantes into segments. Roads, or tracks which subsequently became roads, were driven across the spine of the Pennines, forts were planted on the roads, and what were effectively temporary *limes* were established up the backbone of Britain.

The accounts of the campaign are exiguous except for Tacitus, and Tacitus' own version is brief; it suggests a testing period under a tough senior general in which Agricola developed the power of command. There is no formal end to the advance, but in 74 Cerealis was recalled to Rome and by that time the Brigantes were peaceful, held down by the forts of the consolidation. Agricola himself was already gone, in the year of Cerealis' recall he was appointed Praetorian Legate in Aquitania, three years later he was Consul in Rome. He had climbed swiftly the other ladder of power.

Behind him in Britain Frontinus was Governor, and the

Brigantes were smouldering but quiet. Frontinus, a sound soldier, decided that the immediate task was to take out the Welsh threat. In a brisk and harsh campaign he broke the Silures, thrust into the mountains and, following the pattern of the Brigantian conquest, built roads and studded them with fortresses.

In 78 Agricola replaced him. He arrived after midsummer; theoretically the campaigning season was over, but the fourth phase of the conquest of Britain dates from that moment. Frontinus in the course of his Welsh campaign had advanced the western legion to Chester. Now somewhere in the hills to the west of Chester the Ordovices wiped out a Roman cavalry force. In the fag end of the summer, when the legions normally gave themselves over to ceremonial duties and preparations for the long hibernation of the winter, Agricola assembled a disenchanted punitive force, thrust ruthlessly into the Welsh mountains, broke the Ordovician resistance, took a swift chance and crossed the Menai Straits and completed, at last, the conquest of Anglesey. At the very beginning of his governorate his reputation was dramatically established and through the winter he readied the army for his main purpose.

The fatal disunity of Britain had once again played its part. As has been said, the Welsh tribes were of different stock from that of the Brythonic and Belgic peoples who had overrun south-eastern Britain. It was perhaps inevitable that, secure within their mountain fastnesses, they had rejected alliance with the rest of the tribes. Agricola thus was able to deal with the constituent parts of the island piecemeal. Methodically with the spring he began the final conquest of the Brigantes.

The precise nature of the early part of the campaign is not recorded. How much of Brigantia was hostile is unclear. What is clear is that Agricola moved north on either side of the Pennines. Tacitus says: "Himself he chose the sites for camps . . . he gave the enemy no rest . . . when he had done enough to inspire fear . . . they accepted the curb of garrisons and forts."

The forts derived directly from the traditional camp of the Roman army. The camp consisted of a ditch dug at the end of the march in the form of a rectangle with rounded corners.

The rampart was built of its spoil and strengthened with stakes carried in the transport. "Army" camps, as at Keithock, on the line of the advance through Eastern Scotland, might cover as much as 63 acres or even, as at Kair House, 120, but the temporary fort derived essentially from the cohort camp, which had an area of approximately three acres and held a quingenary cohort of five hundred men. When forts were made permanent they were given high layered turf walls and complex ditch systems; gateways, corner turrets and parapets were built of heavy timber, headquarters buildings, barracks and storehouses were of wood, and all were laid down to a standard pattern. Not until after A.D. 100 was masoned stone employed, first in Wales, then spreading rapidly from there to the north.

Simultaneously the road system was completed. It stands today like a ladder to the north. Its uprights are the great main roads to east and west of the Pennines, the rungs of the ladder are the passes across the hills. Each of them was controlled by a road, each road studded with forts and fortlets and signal stations. Tacitus is not explicit, but almost certainly by the end of the second summer Agricola was already consolidating the isthmus of the Solway-Tyne and the lowland of Dumfriesshire beyond it.

The third summer he thrust north by two roads—contrary to the accepted canon—to the Tweed. The line Newstead-Lyne-Castledykes-Loudoun Hill probably marks the limit of that year's advance. By 81 he was established on the high ground of the isthmus between Firth of Forth and Clyde and the Lowlands of Scotland were entire in his hands. He spent the summer consolidating what he had gained, using his fleet to explore the western coasts. Clearly he was already searching for a means to outflank the Highland massif, but the sea lochs failed him. Always there is a meticulous, intricate attention to detail.

In 83 he crossed the Highland line.

His route lay through Strath Allan to the Tay crossings and from there through Strath Mor. As he advanced he planted a fort at the mouth of each of the glens that came down from the Highland massif—Bochastle, Dalginross, Fendoch, Inchtuthil, Gourdie, Cardean—like an earth stopper blocking the mouths of the earths on the line of a hunt.

On his right flank the fleet kept pace with him, meeting him

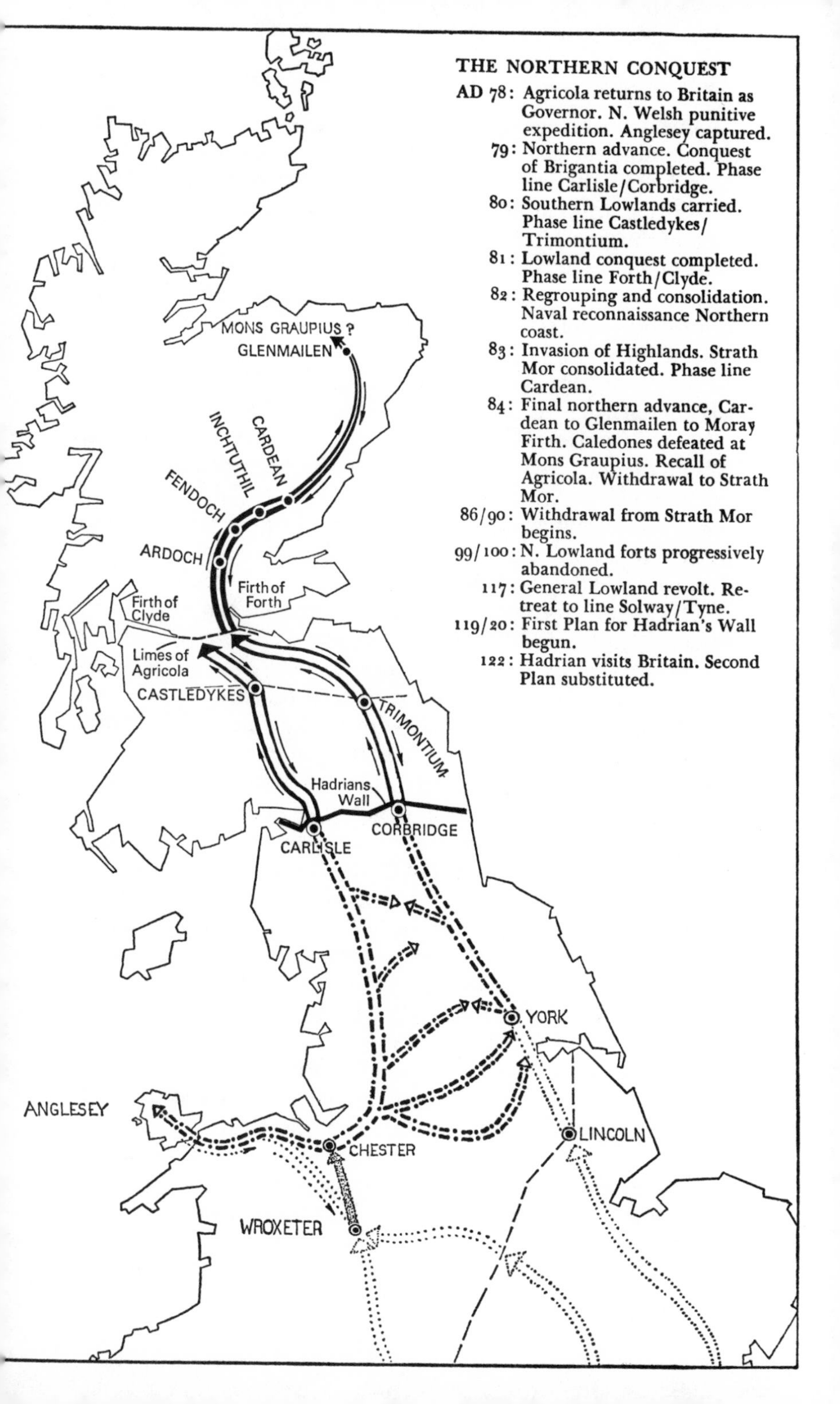
THE NORTHERN CONQUEST
AD 78: Agricola returns to Britain as Governor. N. Welsh punitive expedition. Anglesey captured.
79: Northern advance. Conquest of Brigantia completed. Phase line Carlisle/Corbridge.
80: Southern Lowlands carried. Phase line Castledykes/Trimontium.
81: Lowland conquest completed. Phase line Forth/Clyde.
82: Regrouping and consolidation. Naval reconnaissance Northern coast.
83: Invasion of Highlands. Strath Mor consolidated. Phase line Cardean.
84: Final northern advance, Cardean to Glenmailen to Moray Firth. Caledones defeated at Mons Graupius. Recall of Agricola. Withdrawal to Strath Mor.
86/90: Withdrawal from Strath Mor begins.
99/100: N. Lowland forts progressively abandoned.
117: General Lowland revolt. Retreat to line Solway/Tyne.
119/20: First Plan for Hadrian's Wall begun.
122: Hadrian visits Britain. Second Plan substituted.
MONS GRAUPIUS ?
GLENMAILEN
CARDEAN
INCHTUTHIL
FENDOCH
ARDOCH
Firth of Forth
Firth of Clyde
Limes of Agricola
CASTLEDYKES
TRIMONTIUM
Hadrians Wall
CARLISLE
CORBRIDGE
YORK
LINCOLN
ANGLESEY
CHESTER
WROXETER

at the Tay, bringing up supplies, carrying reinforcements, threatening the coastal settlements. He was halfway up Strath Mor before the tribes gathered to challenge him. The first major operation of the resistance was an attack on one of the forts of the glens; it was beaten off, but the incident was held by the opponents of Agricola's strategy to be a warning. His lines of communication were dangerously stretched and the possibilities of reinforcement remote. Officers in council pleaded for a strategic withdrawal.

Before the pleas could gather weight the Caledones attacked again. Agricola's intelligence had warned him of the probability. His force was moving in three divisions. The unlucky Ninth Legion, reduced in strength by the detachment of a vexillation for the army of the Rhine, was rushed in camp at night. Agricola, marching instantly on receipt of news, arrived in time to save it. The Caledonian offensive broke in its opening phase and the tribes dispersed again.

The attack on the Ninth Legion marks the end of the slow consolidating period of Agricola's advance. Through the winter he appears to have developed a newer, more fluid strategy. As the campaigning season opened he sent the fleet up the east coast to raid and harass. Now "with an army marching light", according to Tacitus, he moved straight up the edge of the Highland massif towards the Moray Firth. Though much remains to be done by way of archaeological investigation, the patient interpretation of one of archaeology's newest techniques, aerial photography, has made clear his line of advance. A chain of marching camps of exceptional size runs from the consolidated area close to Inchtuthil by Oathlaw, Keithock and Kair House to Raedykes above Stonehaven. At Raedykes it trends north and a little east to Normandykes and Kintore, more easterly still to Glenmailen at the Wells of Ythan, and reaches to within sight of the Moray Firth at Auchinhove, two miles from Keith. At Fochabers on Speyside there are traces of what may be the final camp in the line. It has still to be positively identified, but it is not important, for even at Auchinhove Agricola had effectively turned the flank of the Highland massif. He was on the coastal strip, less than fifty miles of easy country lay between him and the mouth of the Great Glen.

As Gibbon scathingly points out, the conquest now swiftly approaching the climax of the battle of Mons Graupius had taken "about forty years". Many, perhaps indeed most of those years, had however been spent in a dubious peace, and it is Agricola's campaign which provides the standards for the potential of the Roman army of Britain.

Disregarding the lightning thrust to Anglesey, Agricola's northern campaign was launched against the Brigantes in the early summer of A.D. 79. He established his winter quarters on the line Solway-Tyne, having conquered the whole of what is now the North of England—a rough parallelogram 120 miles from south to north with an average width of 110 miles and an area of rather more than 13,000 square miles—in a single season.

The campaigns of subsequent seasons covered less ground. There is no "average" capability in conquest. Terrain, the numbers and valour of the enemy, and above all his leadership are determining factors, but Agricola's seasonal results are the index of the Roman army's potential. He had under command four legions in Britain, but one and possibly the larger part of two must have been retained in the south to hold Wales and to cover the garrisons of the newly conquered areas. Unquestionably he had more auxiliaries in the field than legionaries.

His plan of campaign is clear and bold. Its strategy was the strategy that had broken the Brigantes—a simultaneous operation on either side of the enemy heartland, dual thrusts from east and west to cut off segment by segment of the tribes in turn. The routes of today's roads demonstrate how it could have been carried out in the Highlands: the rungs of the northern ladder would have rested on Carrbridge and Grantown, on Dalwhinnie and Blair Atholl, on Crianlarich and Lochearnhead.

Years of embittered archaeological argument have not yet solved the mystery of the site of the battle of Mons Graupius. Certainly it was in the far north. Tacitus says after the battle "summer was almost over", and the line of the marching camps suggests that that calculated, deliberate advance must have taken the whole of the campaigning season. In logic Agricola's force should have been at its weakest at the summer's end; his lines of communication were stretched to the utmost, he could scarcely yet have established full contact with his ships, his troops must have been close to exhaustion.

To Calgacus, heading the new confederacy of the northern tribes, it was essential to halt the advance before Agricola reached the mouth of the Great Glen and perhaps went into winter quarters.

Calgacus chose his battle ground facing one of the marching camps, for Tacitus says that the legions were drawn up "outside the wall". Estimates of enemy strengths in early history are invariably unreliable; the strength of the Caledones before the battle is estimated as thirty thousand, with more men flocking in.

The account of the battle itself is, as always, superbly confusing. The brunt of the Caledones' attack was borne by the auxiliaries. The legions, above the battle, watched. Agricola himself fought on foot in front of the colours. In the opening stages of the battle the Caledones attacked furiously, but their chariots were routed by the Roman cavalry. The cohorts of the Batavi and the Tungri were sent in to close up the fighting and use the short sword, and Calgacus attempted to counter the move by sending forward his reserves from the high ground. Agricola had kept back the main strength of his cavalry for this moment. Now they went in in strength, and the Caledones broke. In the late afternoon the challenge had become a slaughter, with the Romans combing the thin woodlands for survivors and the cavalry mopping up the open areas. Agricola had won his last battle. The Caledones were crushingly defeated.

It should have been the Götterdämmerung of the North Britons.

4

Consequences of Agricola's Recall

Before the opening of the campaigning season of 84 Agricola was recalled to Rome.

The decision to abandon the completion of the conquest of Northern Scotland is, as has already been claimed, the greatest single strategic blunder in the history of Roman Britain. Its consequences are apparent in every aspect of the story of the Province for more than three centuries.

Tacitus wrote the first anguished comment: "*perdomita Britannia et statim omissa.*" The scholars have quarrelled over the precise implications of the phrase, but it is sufficiently clear to the layman: 'Britain was subjugated—and immediately thrown away.' The failure to consolidate the conquest of the Caledones after the established pattern of Wales, Brigantia and the Lowlands was to shape the military requirement of an indefinite future.

In Britain the period immediately after Agricola's return to Rome and the emblems of a triumph is obscure, it lacks both a Tacitus *and* an Agricola. For the first two seasons, however, it is sufficiently evident that the Caledones and their immediate allies lay quiet in the hills, catching their breath. In 86 Domitian, deceived by the apparent acceptance of defeat and harassed by the rising tide of trouble on the German frontiers, withdrew the Second Legion, II Adiutrix (which had been brought to Britain by Cerialis for the Brigantian campaign), and posted it to Pannonia. Britain was left with three legions. With these, three main areas were covered: at Isca (Caerleon on Usk), II Augusta held down the southern end of Wales; at Deva (Chester) XX Valeria Victrix dominated North Wales and the Brigantes; and at Eburacum (York) IX Hispana was based, with the far-ranging task of covering the eastern side of Britain from Inchtuthil to the south.

The task was manifestly beyond the capacity of a single legion. It is desirable at this point to stress the importance of the legions. They embodied the vital qualities of the Roman army. Approximately 5,600 strong, they were formed of heavy and brilliantly trained infantry with a small component of cavalry for reconnaissance purposes. In addition, however, they provided the expertise of the Roman army in its widest sense. They surveyed its roads and built its bridges, they erected its forts and constructed its buildings. In Britain they were to build the Wall itself.

Inchtuthil—set up originally as a camp to command the valley of the Tay where it issues from the Highlands to the west of what is now Dundee—had been expanded as a legionary fortress. Its decline began with the decision to withdraw II Adiutrix, but the great camp itself was not at once abandoned: a garrison of auxiliaries held it for at least four more years. The legionaries, however, pulled back by stages to Newstead, the huge fortress that the Romans called Trimontium on the southern slope of the Tweed valley. Archaeological evidence indicates a period of confused fighting in which the Strath Mor forts were repeatedly attacked and finally deserted and the Agricolan chain across the Forth-Clyde isthmus was found indefensible and in due course abandoned.

The time scale of the retreat from Scotland is closely bound up with the growth levels of the new generation after Mons Graupius. Agricola's crushing defeat of the Caledones and their allies in his last battle had wrecked the fighting strength of the tribes. But the boys who had been eleven and too young to fight at that disaster were men of eighteen when Inchtuthil was evacuated. At the close of the century, the accepted date for the abandonment of Scotland north of the Cheviot, they were mature men and the three-year-olds of the time of Mons Graupius were in the fighting line, reared in the tradition of revenge.

The set battles occupy the front of the stage of history, but it was the failure to permit Agricola to complete the consolidation by roads and fortlets through the Highland massif that, after less than a generation, unleashed again the fury of the North.

Domitian and his policies were dead by now. Nerva, whose brief reign leaves no trace in Britain, was dead also. Trajan, one of the great fighting Emperors of Rome, had begun his tragic search for the glory of victory. But for the hard-pressed force on the British frontier there was small comfort, for Trajan's first concern was the subjugation of Dacia—today's Rumania—with its rich prize of gold and silver mines. After Dacia, urgent and enormous dreams of conquest drew him across the Mediterranean to the East. Britain has no place in Rome's consideration in this period.

Trajan in the fullness of time died, sighing with all old generals: "Ah, had I Alexander's years!", and Hadrian succeeded him.

The conjunction of Hadrian's succession and the slow retreat from Scotland engendered the Wall.

Publius Aelius Hadrianus subscribed to none of his adoptive father's dreams of military splendour. He was a consolidator. He saw the purpose of his reign as the rationalisation of the frontiers of Europe. Trajan's acquisitions in Armenia, in Mesopotamia and in Parthia were restored to their original status. To the north he drew new frontiers and behind them he accelerated the enormous task of the Romanisation of the conquered nations. Despite the degree to which history has associated his name with Britain, his interest in Rome's farthest Province was limited to a single journey and not, it would appear from the lack of historical references, afterwards resumed. It was, despite this, highly significant.

His movements in the first year of his reign are the subject of one of the more spectacular brawls of the historians, but by the summer of 118 he was at least installed in Rome and intensely preoccupied by the aftermath of the "affair of the murder of the four consulars". Two, or possibly three years later, he began the first of his tremendous journeys. In the year of his arrival at Rome he sent a new Governor to Britain from Lower Moesia—Pompeius Falco.

The appointment of Falco marks the end of the second period of strategic policy in the Province of Britain. For the first forty-two years it had been a strategy of advance, conditioned by resistance, complicated by revolt, but always thrusting doggedly to the north, until Agricola built the last of his marching camps on the high latitude of the Moray Firth. Following this, it became—for thirty-five years—effectively a strategy of withdrawal, harshly contested. The years witnessed a slow forcing back of the armies of Rome over a distance of two hundred miles, a slow compression of Roman power in the southern half of the island. It was accompanied not by set campaigns but by raids, by ambushes, by local and *ad hoc* alliances for local and immediate strategems. It brought an accelerating accretion of strength to Rome's most determined enemies in the north—the Caledones—by the addition of the Taezali, the Venicones, the Damnonii, and possibly already the Selgovae and the Novantae to the list of the potential enemies in what is now Scotland.

Hadrian's new Governor *must* have been sent to Britain with a charge to define, to declare and to defend a frontier. Nothing less would have matched the purpose and the policy of the Emperor.

It has in the past been accepted for writ that Hadrian planned the Wall and that Aulus Platorius Nepos, second Governor of Britain in his reign, built it. There are a score of inscriptions to prove the fact. Yet the chronology of building nowhere fits, for the existence of two distinct plans—and it is no longer possible to reject their existence—demands an interval between them. The stage which work on the First Plan had reached at the time of its supersession demonstrably required at least a season's labour, preceded by a necessary planning period. The Second Plan most clearly demands, because of its cost, its scope, and its effect for the foreseeable future on the numbers and dispositions of Roman troops, an Imperial intervention.

Accepted chronology claims, with one school, that Nepos brought the Sixth Legion to Britain. A second school claims that the Emperor brought it. A third that Hadrian and Nepos, and possibly the Legion, arrived simultaneously. There is, in fact, no conclusive proof whatever. Nepos alone, on the evidence of a discharge certificate, was certainly in Britain before 17 July, 122. Hadrian, by the datal evidence for his presence previously on the German frontier and subsequently in Provence, must also have been in Britain in 122. If they coincided in a single building season, the accepted chronology of the Wall is out of the question.

What time-table fits the wall?

The changes enforced by the Second Plan are changes in principle not in detail. Because they exist, they have been accepted by too many of the scholars of the Wall as mere modifications. The point will be examined in Chapter 5. But, if, as has been claimed earlier, their size and their consequences demanded the direct fiat of the Emperor, it follows in logic that since they were imposed upon what was clearly at least a season's, and quite possibly two seasons', building work, the First Plan must have been drafted no later than the winter of 120/121 and consequently in the governorate of Pompeius Falco. The point is made briefly by C. E. Stevens in the second version of his paper on *The Building of Hadrian's Wall*, but it has been apparent for a long time in the endless archaeological controversies that have wrapped themselves about the time-table.

If Falco made the First Plan, what was the nature of the directive given to him on his appointment?

It has been assumed that because Hadrian established his early reputation as a maker of frontiers, he gave whoever was appointed to the task something of the character of a blue print. But Hadrian himself cannot have reached the Hoch Taunus, the sector of the German *limes* where he established this reputation, before 121. That detailed instructions for a wholly different type of *limes*—a difference so great as to amount to a revolution in Roman military practice—could have been written by him at the time of Falco's appointment or would even have suggested themselves to him before he had had practical experience on the German frontier, appears to be in the highest degree improbable.

It seems, in view of the fluidity of the situation in Northern Britain, Hadrian's lack of knowledge of the terrain, and Falco's own ignorance of the area (he was not, like Agricola, a British "expert"), most probable that he was given his instructions in general terms, something blunt and simple—"Set up a *limes* and stop the rot."

What were his options? In its most urgent aspect his task was to concentrate sufficient force in the north of the Province to block the remorseless southward pressure of the tribes. To accomplish this while leaving sufficient troops permanently in the west to dominate the Welsh, he had to select the shortest possible line and thereby produce the maximum possible concentration.

The Forth-Clyde line on which Agricola had set up his temporary *limes*—and which later was to be used for the wall of Antoninus—had long passed from Roman hands. He had to find his short line south of the debated territory.

It is one of the shibboleths of the faith that the shortest possible line was the isthmus of the Solway-Tyne. In point of fact a line between the Solway at the mouth of the Esk and the Firth of Forth at Inveresk is marginally shorter. The line between the head of Morecambe Bay and the Tees is approximately the same, and the line between the Mersey and the Humber not seriously longer. But Falco, whether he made the First Plan or not, must have realised with the troubles of the first year of his governorate that his most urgent strategic responsibility was to prevent permanently at any possible cost a conjunction between the northern tribes and the largest, the most cohesive and probably the most war-like tribe in the south—the Brigantes.

An alliance between the northern tribes and the Brigantes would have presented Rome with an all but insuperable task in the existing temper of the northern warriors, fed, as they must have been, on the long process of victorious recovery. The first line was already clearly out of Falco's reach. It was in any sense militarily unrealistic and it would have required a major campaign to establish its possibility. Under Hadrian major aggressive campaigns were out of the question. The Morecambe Bay–Tees route would have released a substantial part of the Brigantes to co-operation with the North and could scarcely be contemplated. The Mersey–Humber line was a stark impossibility; it would have surrendered all that was significant in Brigantia to the enemy. Falco *had* no options. The Solway–Tyne position forced itself upon him.

He still had, however, local alternatives. The south bank of the Tyne valley offered advantageous ground, except when the tributary streams cut through it, all the way from the lowest ford of the Tyne at Newburn to Broomhouse, south-west of Haltwhistle. High ground, well adapted to defence, ran above the valley of the Tipalt Burn all the five miles to the Willowford crossing. The south bank of the Irthing river offered sound defensive positions as far as Brampton and from there the Irthing–Eden Valley provided at that time the substantial protection of marshes almost all the way to Luguvalium (which is Carlisle). The rivers were not, it is true, insuperable but long stretches of them could be crossed only at fords even in summer. The slopes of the valleys, cleared of trees, would have provided difficult ground for the attacker at most points.

A defensive wall from the Ryton area to Carlisle would have been less costly than the Wall of the First Plan and—save for the twelve-mile sector of the Great Whin Sill—would have offered substantially greater problems to the attack. Nowhere along its entire length would it have had the deplorable defensive situation of the sector from Stanwix to the Willowford crossing, as it was finally built, or the hardly less unsatisfactory sector from Sewingshields to the bridge at Pons Aelius (which is Newcastle).

The northern line was adopted, according to the experts of the Wall, for three principal reasons. First, it followed in general terms the line of the existing road—Agricola's road—the Stanegate. Second, along that line were the surviving forts of Agricola's chain. Third, above it stretched the all but unscaleable barrier of the Great Whin Sill. By Falco's time some at least of the Agricolan forts had been refurbished, others had been in continuous occupation as part of the consolidation network of Brigantia. The Stanegate was in daily use and, as the northern pressure grew, it is reasonable in the knowledge of Roman military practice to assume that the high ground of the Great Whin Sill was an established patrol line. It remains, none the less, doubtful that any or all of these factors determined the First Plan.

The analysts of the Wall have for some reason largely ignored the fact that the Agricolan system offered no advantage at all for the first quarter of the Wall's length except the presence of the Dere Street crossing. East of milecastle 22, at the time the plan was drafted, there was neither fort nor road nor, so far as has been ascertained, even a single signal station between Dere Street and the sea. The Agricolan consolidation disregarded the wide band of low country bordering the sea—except at the fort of Alauna and one or two minor posts—from the Firth of Forth to the Yorkshire wolds. From this, two assumptions may be drawn: the first, that the area was sparsely populated; the second, and more probable, that it was inhabited by a peace-loving people closely tied to Rome. With the oncoming pressure from the north, however, it was clear that it could no longer be regarded as immune from danger.

In the next quarter of the line of the Wall as built there were three Agricolan establishments only, intermittently occupied: the fort of the bridgehead at Corbridge (Corstopitum), the starting point of the Stanegate; the fortlet at Newborough; and the strongly sited encampment at Chesterholm (Vindolanda).

The third twenty miles, however, was firmly covered either by Agricolan, Trajanic or very early Hadrianic forts. Banna, Throp, Nether Denton, Castlehill, Castlesteads, Old Church, High Crosby and Carlisle stood in varying degrees of serviceability behind it.

The last quarter along the estuary of the Solway need not be considered at this point.

The greater part of the existing military facilities, therefore, were concentrated in the area of the third sector. In a remarkable degree the Wall, as finally erected, disregarded them. Instead of using the capacity of the existing Agricolan forts and the road of the Stanegate for rapid support and reinforcement (as many commentators on the Wall have stated), the decision-maker chose the northern ridge of the Irthing valley for the line of the new works and accepted a slow rate of communication and reinforcement across the Irthing valley even in summer when the river was at all times fordable.

Thus, of the three existing advantages which the historians have claimed as dictating the choice of the northern rim of the Tyne and Irthing valleys, only the twelve miles of the Great Whin Sill supplied, in fact, an integral part of the First Plan.

Why then did Falco select the northern line?

In the simplest terms he chose it because he had evolved a concept wholly new in the history of the Roman army—the concept of the offensive-defensive operating from a static defended position. The Wall was the start line for counter-force movements calculated according to estimates of enemy strength made either by forward patrols or assessed from the patrol line of the Wall, and designed to take the enemy in flank or to utilise the tactical advantages of a known terrain by the selection of the most advantageous line of attack. To this end the Wall was planned with a strongly defended sally port at every Roman mile—1620 yards.

It was not intended to fight major actions on the Wall itself—though it is wrong to assume, as a growing number of commentators appear to be assuming, that the Wall itself could not be defended. The intention was clearly to utilise the superior tactical abilities, the marked advantages of Roman equipment, and in an important degree the greater discipline in mobility of the Roman auxiliaries, to operate in the open country beyond the Wall with all the contingent advantages of surprise, speed and security.

The concept has no precursors. Defensive walls existed of course in relation to encampments, to fortresses and to protected cities in varying degree in all provinces. The sally port existed in a number of types of construction. The combination of the two in a fixed-base offensive-defensive theory extending for scores of miles along a frontier, however, had been attempted nowhere else.

Were there any contemporary military engineering works in Britain which might have provided an inspirational point for the concept?

One development that must have helped Falco originated at Caerleon, where the fortress of the Second Legion was rebuilt in stone in the year 99. Following this, at Caerhun, Caernarvon and others of the Welsh forts, the replacement of turf walls began. Four years later the reconstruction of Chester started and by 108, ten years before the arrival of Falco, the northernmost remaining legionary fort at York was converting to stone. Falco, therefore, could fall back for constructional expertise on legions equipped for quarrying, skilled in mason's work and trained by recent experience in wall construction in stone.

These things were fundamental to the execution of the scheme, for the First Plan called for a wall forty-four miles long, twenty-one feet six inches high to the top of the crenellations, and ten feet wide. It was to be built of solid stone, with the defended sally ports—the so-called milecastles—at every Roman mile, equipped with two massive gateways north and south, two turrets of substantial proportions between each two milecastles, three major bridges—over the Tyne, the North Tyne and the Irthing, with possibly a fourth over the Eden—signal towers, stores and barrack accommodation. The whole was to be fronted by a fighting ditch thirty feet across and thirteen feet six inches deep. To the west it was to be complemented by a defensive line at least as far as the Eden at Carlisle. One new main road from Dere Street at a point near Binchester to the site of the Tyne bridge at Pons Aelius was called for and an extension of the eastern road from York through Chester-le-Street.

No contemporary account of either of the two Plans exists, but their details are explicit in the archaeological record. Where the Second Plan is superimposed upon the First the alterations in construction can be read like a palimpsest.

No date exists for the beginning of construction.

Falco was posted to Britain in 118. It seems improbable that he reached it until late in the year. He was, as has already been said, embroiled immediately upon arrival in frontier trouble. Though exact evidence of the nature of the trouble does not exist, a victory coinage was unquestionably minted in 119, and it is necessary to build backwards from that point. The historians have adopted a singularly varied and speculative approach to the matter. Henderson, in *The Life and Principate of the Emperor Hadrian,* asserts that "the Brigantes of Yorkshire and Northumberland were in wild insurrection" and derives from this the remarkable conclusion that the Wall "looked southwards as a means of pacification as well as northwards". Stewart Perowne says that the climax of British non-co-operation "came in the year of Hadrian's accession when once again the northern Britons rose against their invaders". Haverfield says: "The north rose and not in vain." Collingwood quotes an "ancient writer" to the effect that "the Britons were in successful rebellion against Roman rule."

The sole literary evidence, in reality, appears to be that of the *Augustan History.* Spartianus states with simplicity, in a list of Hadrian's early troubles, "the Britons could not be kept under Roman sway." There is no indication anywhere that the trouble was, in fact, more than a powerful flare-up of the process that had continued intermittently since the withdrawal of Agricola. But the primary effect of it must have been to establish absolutely the need for a defended frontier.

Until the defensive campaign involved was brought to a successful end it is obvious that Falco would have had no time to initiate the vast effort that the plan required, but in 119 it may be assumed that the survey at least could have been begun. The spring of the following year seems, then, the most probable moment for the actual start of operations for, between the survey and the start, time was needed for the very considerable administrative programme necessary to concentrate a minimum of two legions—later three—plus auxiliaries and a substantial amount of local labour in the area, to begin the building of the internal roads demanded by the system, to open the quarries and dig the wells and build the lime kilns, and arrange for stores, supply and the feeding of a force of men that can never have been less than fifteen to twenty thousand and may well have reached thirty thousand at maximum strength.

The plan of operations is itself elaborate. Three distinct types of working party began simultaneously along the main line of the Wall: the first digging the great Fighting Ditch; the second laying what has come to be known as the Broad Foundation; the third beginning the construction of the milecastles with their gateways through the main wall and the turrets that were recessed into the solid bulk of the structure. Milecastles and turrets alike were created with wings on the Broad Foundation, ready to bond into the running wall when it came to be built.

The evidence for the time-table and for the methods of construction has been made singularly clear by excavation, by aerial photography and by the precise analysis of existing structures. The time-table is apparent in such things as the superimposition of the Narrow Wall on the Broad Foundation or the adjustment of the broad wings of turret and milecastle to accept the narrow gauge. The quarries that the work gangs drew upon still remain, the lime pits are visible, the abandonment of work—at Limestone Corner or Allolee Farm, for example—is plain, while beneath the cavalry forts of the Second Plan, foundation, ditch, turrets, even milecastles exist to prove the change.

The bald description of the component parts of the plan is wholly inadequate. To visualise the gigantic nature of the enterprise it is necessary to attempt to see it in its entirety. For twenty-seven miles from the North Tyne eastwards over the high shoulder of the Cumberland plain there were at the very outset of the scheme working parties engaged on the Fighting Ditch—it can still be seen for miles along the Military Road that Parliament imposed upon the Wall. Over wide sectors at intervals of a third of a mile there were groups working on the basic structure of milecastles and of turrets. South of them there were quarry details cutting rock—first, for the flagstones of the Broad Foundation; then, wedge-shaped, beautifully fashioned to an average size of seven inches by ten, with a depth of twenty inches, the ashlar for the faces of the Wall. Somewhere in the same area the smoke of the lime burning rose high. Between the Broad Foundation, the quarries and the kilns was a perpetual traffic of mules and sledges and men carrying loads. Far out in front of it all a covering force waited in the forward hills, patrolling the valleys, making certain that the workers and the work was at all times wholly protected.

For twenty-two miles westward from the North Tyne there were the same working parties, the same mule trains, the same quarries, the same smoke rising from kilns, but along the twelve miles of the crags of the Great Whin Sill the whole pattern rose breathlessly, magnificently, to the heights of the spine of England, climbing the last slopes, leaping from crest to crest, superbly challenging under the protests of the raven and the crow and the querulous complaining of the plover.

In the bed of the Irthing at the entrance to the gorge of the river the twenty miles of the lowland sector began. The first parties there must have been stretched out to clear a way for the Wall, to cut timber and to slash out the scrub to open a fighting space before the great Ditch so that the sentries who watched while the men of the legions worked beside their arms could see the approach routes of an enemy.

5

Hadrian the Decision-Maker

At Winshields Crag the Wall stands one thousand two hundred and thirty feet above the sea.

On a clear day, under the great and brilliant shapes of the clouds that lift above the high ground, the Wall patrols could see far into Dumfriesshire and the western Lowlands. To the north-east the hills rise in ridge on ridge to the Cheviots, to the south the turning sentinel could look deep into the country of the Brigantes above the lakes or over the wide central barrier of the Pennines to the vales of Durham. You can see today almost unmarred the view the Romans saw. Only one achievement of the technological age lifts out of it. West-north-west of Winshields, where once the sentries watched for the beacon fires on Gillalees, rise the missile-testing towers of Spadeadam Waste.

There is an odd significance in this, for between the Blue Streak missile, Britain's single venture into the technologies of a new era in war, and the Wall itself there is a strange affinity.

Blue Streak was designed to meet the threat of the Soviet Intermediate Range Ballistic Missile. It was abandoned primarily because, as a liquid-fuelled missile of the generation before storable liquid fuels were developed, it took so long to be filled on the launching pad and to be readied for firing that it was finally recognised that it could be destroyed before it could be launched.

In the jargon of missilry, its reaction time was unacceptably slow.

The First Plan for the Wall was abandoned because, precisely as with Blue Streak, it was recognised in the course of development that with the distance of the Agricolan forts from the gates of the milecastles its reaction time was entirely inadequate to the enemy threat.

The debatable point in relation to the Wall is the identity of the decision-maker.

Hadrian, as was outlined earlier, moved out of Rome on the first of his great journeys probably early in the summer of 121. By way of Gaul he proceeded to the frontier are beyond what is now Frankfurt. The progenitor of the long German *limes* had been established by Vespasian half a century earlier. It was a road studded with small forts. Twenty years after Vespasian, Domitian set up a system of wooden watch-towers and strengthened the fortlets. Hadrian readjusted the line both there and possibly to the south in Raetia and initiated a series of improvements. The process can most conveniently be examined in the developments at the Saalburg. At this point in the Hoch Taunus the *limes* utilised the crest of the hills that run transversely north-east and south-west of Bad Homburg. At the Saalburg there was a small Domitian fortlet with a weak earth wall. It lay back from the actual line of the *limes* by almost two hundred yards and it formed a rallying point for a system of wooden Domitian watch-towers, a duty it shared with its nearest neighbour at Heidenstock, four and a half kilometres to the south-west, and Lochmuhle, two kilometres to the north-east. It was markedly weaker than the milecastles planned for the Wall in Britain. Once again, the evidence is that of patient excavation and the analysis of surviving structures, but both Aelius Spartianus and Dio Cassius pay tribute to the new emperor's energy.

Hadrian's inspection of the area resulted first in the deepening of the ditch which marked the *limes*, and which probably already existed, and the construction of a wooden palisade of split tree trunks in front of it. The Saalburg earthwork he replaced with a cohort fort. Earth-walled and defended with a single ditch, the fort was approximately seven hundred and twenty-five feet by four hundred and eighty. It was designed to hold five hundred men. The present and remarkably interesting reconstruction on the Saalburg is not of this Hadrianic fort but of the stone version that in due course replaced it under Caracalla. In Britain as early as Trajan's time the legionary forts at Caerleon, Chester and eventually York had similarly been rebuilt in stone.

Hadrian's frontier in the Taunus was, at the time of his departure, at a relatively low level of development, and the principal interest of the area rests unquestionably in his decision to establish the Second Cohort of Raetians on the site. Prior to this the area had been covered by the main military base at Trajectum ad Moenum (which is Frankfurt), the delay consequent on the distance between the *limes* and the legionary base, about eleven miles, the equivalent of more than a third of a day's march, being accepted. The decision was obviously made in the interest of the speed of reaction to any threat to the frontier.

The fort lies at the junction of two roads—one, and possibly both, of which existed in Roman times—and it connotes a forward strategy such as that which formed the basis of the thinking of the British First Plan. With, however, only a single relatively narrow gate in its northern wall and its main exits in the southern half of the enclosure, it lacked the urgency of the British design. Broadly speaking, it followed the traditional pattern of major Roman encampments. It was oblong, its corners were rounded in the customary style of earthworks, and its internal dispositions were probably identical in principle with its British counterparts. It would be wrong to assume that it represents a major increase in the general strength of the frontier forces, for through the main Taunus area, for ten miles to the south-west, no other fort of similar size was set up either in Hadrian's time or subsequently.

Armed with experience acquired in these adjustments, Hadrian moved to Britain. His route is uncertain, but since in the course of it he established the new town of Forum Hadriani (which today is Voorburg) in Holland, it seems reasonable that he went down the Rhine. From the Rhine mouths he crossed to Britain, probably coasting to the narrows and crossing to Rutupiae on the Thanet channel. No absolute dates exist for the journey but the summer of 122 is generally accepted as the time of his arrival on the Tyne-Solway isthmus.

The duration of his stay is equally uncertain; through an odd little scrap of verse, however, it is apparent that it was discussed widely, and possibly even cynically, in court circles in Rome itself. The well-known doggerel by Florus

Ego nolo Caesar esse,
Ambulare per Britannos . . .

does *not* mean, as at least two of the pundits have humourlessly interpreted it, that Hadrian walked the line of the Wall but that Florus did not envy him his job if it entailed uncomfortable wanderings in primitive parts.

Hadrian's journeys in later years were elaborate—at times baroque—and copiously annotated. His Egyptian journey, with the death of his youthful favourite Antinous and the extravagant creation of a city for his tomb, is remarkable even in terms of present-day moralities. But in Britain, as on the German frontier, he was a soldier carrying out a stringent professional inspection. Certainly he did not walk. The time-table suggests that he rode swiftly with a small staff and a compact escort. Certainly he moved rapidly to the north, carried out his inspection, and moved rapidly south again heading, as others after him, for Provence, still riding hard.

Borysthenes, his favourite hunter, died at Apt. It is at least possible that his death was the result of the journeying. To him Hadrian built a memorial. And at Nimes he erected a temple to Plotina, widow of Trajan and his wise and courageous supporter in the first days of his accession. It was the beginning of an endless largesse of architecture.

Apart from Florus, the documentary evidence, as has already been indicated, is the single sentence from Spartianus—". . . he was the first to construct a wall, eighty miles in length, which was to separate the barbarians from the Romans."

The statement is direct and, on the surface, simple. None the less, it requires attention. Hadrian was Emperor. Any major work of his reign, therefore, was by custom and tradition attributable to him. The fact that the First Plan must have been started earlier than his visit does not in any way militate against this. That the Wall is specifically and correctly described as eighty miles long has generally been accepted by the experts as conclusive proof that he was the planner of the entire scheme. In fact, however, the Wall, when Hadrian left the area, was certainly not more than seventy-six Roman miles in length—the Wallsend extension is definitely a later addition. Even more importantly, the Wall may not have extended, or been designed to extend at that date, beyond the Eden at Carlisle. The possibility that the fourteen Roman miles from the Eden crossing to Bowness are an addition at least as late as the Wallsend sector will be examined subsequently. Hadrian's personal "share" of the Wall, then, may be in fact only sixty-two miles. Spartianus, as has been stated, wrote a century and a half after his death.

In the infuriating capriciousness of the survival of documents and inscriptions there is nothing whatever that proves conclusively that Hadrian fathered one single section of the Wall, and it is necessary in consequence to argue inferentially.

The fundamentals of the argument are that there was a plan —the First Plan—and that it was overruled. It was the plan of the "man on the spot". Whether it was that of Falco or, as the traditionalists believe, of Nepos is relatively unimportant. It was in any case the plan of a Provincial Governor responsible for the finances of his Province, as well as for the safety of his Province, acting, as has been assumed, on the original directive of his Emperor and seeking an economic solution of an unavoidably expensive requirement.

The First Plan, then, represents a practicable solution both in military and in financial terms. An adjustment of such a plan by a succeeding Governor—Nepos, if the First Plan was devised by Falco—is conceivable, but it is conceivable only within reasonable limits. The Second Plan, by the demands it made in terms of construction, but very much more largely by the permanent demands it made in terms of manpower, represents a quantum leap forward. Brusquely and ruthlessly overriding a scheme itself of great sophistication and designed, as has been claimed, to the limits of the capacities of the Province, it appears to be far beyond the limits permissible or probable to a new Governor still unacquainted with the conditions and demands of his governorate.

The time factor is explicitly important. Nepos, if he did not indeed accompany his Emperor, must have known that Hadrian would follow him within a matter of months. It seems irrational to suppose that he would have overruled the First Plan and substituted for it a second and infinitely more expensive scheme of his own without waiting for the Emperor's word.

That Nepos might have begun the *drafting* of a second plan is, of course, within the bounds of probability, but once again the time factor is relevant. The necessities of the normal ceremonial of the take-over of the governorate and of the investigation into the civil and financial side, which must have been an indispensable preliminary to any new term of office, would almost certainly have precluded the possibility.

The factor that dominates the whole of the Second Plan, however, is that it represents a precise and inevitable move forward from the point in defensive thought which the Emperor had already reached at the Saalburg. It is the logical projection of Hadrian's personal determination to reduce the reaction time of defence to an absolute minimum.

Was this an inevitable consequence of events?

The historians have in succession repeated the assumption that the changes in the design of the Wall are contingent on the indignant reaction of the local population to the "iron control" imposed by the new frontier.

The local population over most of the zone of the Wall was, in fact, exiguous—the density of earthworks and enclosures in the strip five miles wide on either side of the line of the Wall is, except only in the valley of the North Tyne, singularly below that of, for example, the valleys of Dumfriesshire or the dales of Northumberland. This is not of course an absolute criterion, but it is a strong pointer to the "settled" areas. It appears, in fact, in the highest degree improbable that the planners of the Wall took or needed to take the slightest notice of "popular" reaction, local or distant, except in relation to the main threat from the north. The construction work on the Wall settled that problem by itself, for it brought to the area a concentration of fighting men all but unprecedented in British history—two legions on the construction line of the First Plan alone plus the auxiliary forces covering them—and it would have required an astonishing temerity to interfere directly with it. In addition, in the older and at least partially Romanised areas of the forty-year-old Agricolan pacification it is probable that the local inhabitants were grateful for the assurance of permanent protection against the active and "barbarian" Northerners.

That there *was* opposition to the construction of the Wall is of course certain, but it is surely more appropriate to assume that it was the transmitted opposition of the Northern pressure

—of the process of de-Romanisation of the conquered territories against which the Wall was specifically designed.

It is in this aspect of the threat to the Province that the reason for the sharp and sudden upgrading of the potential of the Wall must be sought. And it is in this connection that the fate of the Ninth Legion is important.

No one has yet attempted an historical whodunit with the title *The Mystery of the Ninth Legion*. Possibly this is due to the paucity of evidence—the mystery itself is incontrovertible.

IX Hispana was one of the legions of the conquest—the founding fathers, as it were, of Roman Britain. It was allotted the eastern coastal area in the original pacification; consolidated the control of the kingdoms of the Iceni and of the Trinovantes; moved north to Lincoln, dominated the Parisi, and established the beginning of the remote control of the Brigantes.

Boudicca, as has been related, dealt it a humiliating blow. It is possible perhaps to argue that it was a mortal blow. Certainly the Ninth recovered temporarily, its strength was made up by drafts from Europe—two thousand men were sent across—and certainly it was employed with effect by Cerialis in the Brigantian conquest; but it is questionable that it ever recovered its panache. In Agricola's campaign in Strath Mor it was humiliated for a second time—overrun in camp. This was a marching camp, but it will be remembered that Tacitus wrote positively of Agricola's fortifications: "None was ever stormed, ever capitulated, or was ever abandoned." The Ninth was, in fact, rescued at the last lamentable moment by Agricola himself and must have survived to be reminded of the matter often and acidly. In 108 it was at York—an inscription proves it. Somewhere before this time it may also have been at Carlisle—a tile with the Legion's mark survives, but is undatable. There is nothing else. The Ninth disappeared.

Every historian puts forward a different theory and a different date. Haverfield says that the Legion "then [in 117] stationed at York, was annihilated", but offers no evidence. Richmond says: "It was cashiered, there is no doubt," and Hadrian cashiered it—but also offers no evidence. C. E. Stevens differs from all others by postulating a rising as late as 124/5, which "led to a defeat in which legion IX disappeared from the

Army List". Ritterling, with a masterly ingenuity, produces evidence of two tribunes of the Legion who not only survived but achieved subsequent promotion in their senatorial careers at a time which argued the end of the Legion somewhere about the middle of the building of the Wall.

The one hard conclusive piece of evidence is that it was replaced by VI Victrix from Vetera on the Lower Rhine in 121 or 122.

Again the matter is one which can be dealt with only by inference and logical assumption. It is, to start with, improbable that the Ninth was totally destroyed in the first nine years of the decade immediately after 108. Despite Trajan's preoccupation with the settlement of Dacia in this period and his preparations for the Persian expedition, it is inconceivable that a major disaster involving the destruction of a third of the legionary strength of the Province of Britain would have had no reaction in Rome, that no replacement, no reinforcement would have been sent.

It is even less conceivable that it would have happened without reaction within the Province. The archaeological evidence suggests that in the first part of this period work on the rebuilding of York went on steadily. Nothing in the record of the other legionary fortresses suggests any large-scale movement to the north. Since neither the Second nor the Twentieth appear to have been engaged on major punitive expeditions outside their own general territory, the occasion for a major disaster seems to be narrowed into the period of the "rising" of 117/8, which Fronto said was accompanied by "heavy" Roman casualties.

Though Ritterling suggests that even this is too early for the chronology of the promotion of the tribunes, it is at least not too early for the decision taken by Hadrian to transfer the Sixth to Britain. It will be remembered that the victory coinage was struck in 119. If it is assumed that punitive action sufficiently drastic to justify the minting of victory coins was carried out late in 118 or in the opening of the campaign season of 119, its results would have kept the border area sufficiently pacified to permit the deliberate transfer of a replacement legion in accordance with Hadrian's plans and movements in 121 or 122.

The Legion, it is obvious, was not "annihilated"; the survival of the tribunes alone is proof of this. What is clear is that it was broken beyond hope of rebuilding by drafts from other legions. It seems logical to assume, then, that Hadrian, on his arrival at York, held a stringent enquiry with the survivors and examined the record both of the disaster—or the succession of disasters—and of the precedent campaigns of the northern recession.

On the evidence of these enquiries and, presumably, on the advice of the senior officers directly concerned, Hadrian must have formulated estimates as to the weight of the future threat from the north, the nature of the strategy likely to be employed, and the levels of the Roman forces necessary to hold it in permanent check. With these estimates prepared, he quite certainly went up Dere Street to the frontier area to examine the work in progress and to survey the terrain in order to make his own tactical appreciations.

This is implicit in the structure of the Second Plan. It is in no sense a general "strengthening" of the First, as has too frequently been suggested. It is in substance the exposition of a wholly new solution for the frontier problem, utilising new values in time and space, and devising new methods of accomplishing purpose. It adapts itself to the wide differences in the possible lines of enemy approach so fundamentally that there are three distinct strategical and tactical responses made possible by it for the three main sectors of the Wall—the sector covering the Northumberland lowlands from Pons Aelius to the North Tyne valley, the high central sector along the Great Whin Sill, and the strangely anomalous area between the Irthing and Carlisle.

For the sector from Pons Aelius to Chesters on the west bank of the North Tyne the archaeological evidence of the forts erected across the partly built Wall proves conclusively that a purely cavalry solution was selected. Construction, accommodation and equipment, plus a series of inscriptions naming the units of the garrisons, supply the necessary confirmation. The approach to the Wall from the north in this area is over the Cumberland plain except in the high ground along the line of Dere Street. Even on the high ground the slopes tend to be easy and though on the plain itself there was probably a considerable area of forest in Roman times, there were also long stretches of open moorland and grass country. It was, in fact, excellent cavalry terrain, and the four forts of the Second Plan—Benwell (approximately two and a half miles from the bridge, at Newcastle, that was in process of building), Rudchester (six and a half miles to the west), Haltonchesters (seven miles to the west again) and finally Chesters (five and a half miles away on the North Tyne)—are placed approximately half an hour's riding distance apart.

The system permits, then, of the concentration of a thousand horsemen at a depth of almost ten miles at any point along this portion of the line within the hour, a riposte capable of dealing with anything except major attack. Cavalry patrols from these secure bases could cover a belt fifteen to twenty miles deep to the north of the Wall in the normal working day and fighting patrols could investigate the whole of the plains area to the foothills of the Cheviots.

The one region not adequately covered was the seaward reach beyond Pons Aelius itself. The Wallsend extension was not necessarily an afterthought, though it is improbable that it was completed until the end of the Wall construction, after 128. It provided in the final result the necessary protection. It was planned beyond question, with its three gates to the north, as a cavalry post capable of operating five hundred horse, and it seems at one time to have held a mixed force of cavalry and infantry.

From Chesters to the Irthing crossing, on the other hand, the evidence is equally clear that an infantry system was decided upon. The great five-acre cantonment of Housesteads is an infantry fort, its buildings follow the standard infantry pattern as do those of Greatchesters. Though the addition of Carrawburgh at a later date—it is built over the Vallum—and the precise employment of Carvoran and the fort at the Haltwhistle Burn complicate the original picture, they are all three infantry forts. Even without them Housesteads and Greatchesters dominated the escarpment of the Great Whin Sill.

It is generally assumed that the natural difficulties of the escarpment zone entirely precluded the use of cavalry. This is of course not necessarily the case. At the Knag Burn, immediately below Housesteads, at Milking Gap, at the Peel Gap and at Greatchesters itself, perfectly good cavalry access to the area under the escarpment existed, and it is probably safer to assume that the condition of the soil—the bogs, undrained then, and the loughs, more numerous possibly than today—precluded or at least diminished the effective tactical use of horses. The natural barrier of the Sill, on the other hand, reduced stringently the number of points at which heavy attacks on the Wall itself could be launched, and the general difficulties of the approach over the high ground of the Kielder area probably convinced Hadrian that infantry defence was adequate—provided, that is, that numbers in the immediate front line were substantially increased.

The third sector, from the Irthing crossing to the Carlisle bridge, is, once again, a cavalry area. Birdoswald was built athwart the line of the Turf Wall with the statutory three gates to the north, but after Birdoswald there is for more than sixteen Roman miles no fort on the Wall at all. Only Castlesteads, an Agricolan fort rebuilt in stone a quarter of a mile to the south of the Wall, offers any effective reserve strength—and that in terms of infantry—until the great base at Stanwix, across the river north of Carlisle, is reached. Stanwix, the Petriana of all the early references, was the base of the *ala Petriana,* one of the rare milliary regiments of cavalry in the Roman army. Stanwix and the Carlisle crossing formed the vital strategic nexus of the western road system.

The distance between Birdoswald and Stanwix is well over twice the permitted distance between the eastern cavalry forts. The Wall over that distance was Turf Wall, markedly weaker than the broad stone wall of the eastern side. The milecastles themselves were built of turf. The defences of the seventeen Roman miles between milecastle 49 above the Willowford bridge and milecastle 66 above the Eden bridge are so disproportionately inferior to those of the central and eastern sectors that the question requires to be examined subsequently in detail. With due acknowledgment to this fact, the solution of the Second Plan none the less strengthened the area substantially in terms of man-power and very substantially in terms of speed of reaction.

The execution of the Second Plan was not achieved without the sacrifice of certain essential elements of the First. Of these the most significant is the effective abandonment of the Fighting Ditch which was designed to front the Wall from the Tyne crossing to the Eden save where the crags of the Whin Sill made it unnecessary.

The superb Ordnance Survey map of Hadrian's Wall marks at milecastle 30—Limestone Corner—the well-known and incomplete rock cutting with the words hallowed by generations of antiquarians: "Ditch unfinished owing to hardness of rock." Uncounted generations of Roman engineers must have turned in their graves over that unconscionable insult to their capabilities. The Ditch at Limestone Corner was unfinished because orders were issued that it was not to be completed. It is probable that the hardness of the rock had delayed the digging, but it was the decision that a ditch was no longer essential that stopped the work. Eighteen months, perhaps two years later, the engineers of the Vallum cut a ditch through the same stretch of rock a few score feet to the south, completed it, and passed on to the next task.

By itself the Limestone Corner episode would not justify an assumption that the Ditch as a whole was abandoned, but in addition to it there is clear evidence at a number of points along the line that work on the Ditch stopped in, as it were, the middle of a shift. At Appletree and at Wall Fell, for example, the glacis which was constructed to the north of the Ditch from the material dug out of it is still unsmoothed, the spoil lies in small mounds and rough heaps precisely as it was thrown up, indicating that nobody ever bothered to finish it off. At Cockmount Hill, half a mile from Greatchesters, the Ditch was dug to a bare half the normal depth. Near Allolee Farm it was not even begun, though the nature of the approach to the Wall required it. It is reasonable to assume that these areas had not reached completion—as with the area at Limestone Corner—when the Ditch was declared redundant.

A precise date for this is not, in the nature of things, possible

Monolithic Roman columns from the headquarters building at Chesters support the south aisle of Chollerton Church. A Roman altar, hollowed to hold water, formed at one time the font. *Photograph: Ian Yeomans* ▶

but the logic of it suggests that it coincides with the decision to put the cavalry forts athwart the Wall. That decision involved the filling in of the Ditch where it had been fully dug at at least four important points in the eastern sector, one more in the western area, and the provision of exit points for the eastern and western gates at all the cavalry forts except Stanwix, which involved further obliteration of the Ditch.

The real issue is not one of timing but of the acceptance of the new strategic principle. It is desirable to re-state this in simple terms. By superimposing cavalry forts on the line of the Wall it was possible to fight the battle for the Wall far to the north of it. The desirability of this appears to have been established by the fighting of the early period of Hadrian's reign and underscored probably by the loss of the Ninth Legion. It is not the result of the development of new weapons or of major changes in the balance of forces available but of the inspirational development of a new concept.

Clearly the status of the Ditch was drastically affected by the development of the Second Plan. What was the position in relation to the Wall itself?

In the final upshot one part only of the Wall was completed according to the specifications of the First Plan—the Broad Wall sector from the abutment of the bridge across the North Tyne to the bridgehead fort at Newcastle. Twenty-one foot six high, ten Roman feet wide, it was, despite all the theorists, an effective defensive wall. Its fighting platform was eight foot six

---

◀ Chesters from the air. The picture shows in the foreground the steep bank of the North Tyne and the ruins of the great bath house (probably the best of its type in existence) with to the right of it a short sector of the Wall exposed. It demonstrates exactly the character of the cavalry forts, built with rather more than one-third projecting to the north of the Wall line. The east gate is clearly visible above the exposed portion of the Wall, with, to the left, the Commander's residence and to the right barrack blocks. The headquarters building occupies the central area. Further to the left the rounded corners, the intermediate turrets and the south gate itself are admirably excavated. The house at the top of the picture belonged to the Clayton family and in it the preservation of the Wall was planned and carried out.
Photograph: Aerofilms Ltd.

across, perfectly adequate for the purposes of repelling an attack that must necessarily have begun at the bottom of a ditch roughly thirty feet below. That the eight foot six wall erected across the central sector provided less space for the defenders is, of course, obvious, but even from its narrower fighting platform a strong resistance was entirely possible against the reduced scale of direct attack anticipated in the theory that the Second Plan would provide for the interception of the enemy well to the north of the Wall line.

The original design provided for a sally port/milecastle with a garrison of thirty-two men at each Roman mile, two turrets between each pair of milecastles at intervals of a third of a mile, held—the estimates vary—by from six to ten men—a total of approximately fifty men to each milecastle unit. The weakest point in any sector was the central point between the turrets. An attack there could, however, have been met, if the turrets themselves were left unmanned, by twenty men within a minute and a half provided that the garrison was on the alert. It could have been supported by a further sixty men—less the gate guards left at the sally ports at either end of the sector—within approximately six minutes. A concentration of a hundred and eighty men was theoretically possible within a maximum of fifteen minutes of an alarm. The Wall was clearly defensible, given an effective fighting ditch in front of it, against anything except a major attack. Allowing the classic advantage to the defensive, a major attack would constitute an assault by more than five hundred men.

The tactical diagrams drawn by the late Professor Richmond and widely reproduced have certain obvious weaknesses. The idea that forces operating through the sally ports could "roll up the attackers against the barrier which they were attempting to cross" is basically unsound. It might perhaps have succeeded once, but the time factors involved give the advantage of withdrawal at all times to the attack except where cavalry could be brought to bear against an infantry assault.

But neither with the First nor with the Second Plan was the capacity of the Wall to defend itself against attack the primary qualification. The First Plan provided for an effective conventional defence of the Wall line, together with an effective capacity for offensive-defensive operations to the north of it. Its

ETHAN ALLEN INN®

THE BANQUET AND
CONFERENCE CENTER DON'T LEAVE HOME WHEN YOU TRAVEL

(203) 744-1776 FAX (203) 791-9673

defect was that as it was conceived in terms of infantry, and as the reserve forts in the valley were distant, it was inevitably slow. The Second Plan placed the main force on the Wall itself, substituted a cavalry for an infantry time scale, and accepted with equanimity the sacrifice of some of the conventional defensive capacity of the Wall itself.

The requirement for a fast counter-attack capability was, in fact, so urgent that it led clearly to important postponements in the completion of the Wall itself.

Though, as has been indicated, the eastern sector went ahead as planned, work on the central sector was patently suspended in favour of the construction of the fortified cantonments. The evidence for this lies in the anomalies apparent at the junction points of the curtain wall as it was eventually built and the actual structure of the forts.

The first visible example of this occurs at Chesters. Chesters has already been discussed as a cavalry fort of the eastern sector. Though in relation to its purpose it should properly be considered as a part of the eastern cavalry plan, it is physically in the central narrow wall sector. Built like its fellows athwart the line of the Broad Foundation and the Ditch, and incorporating turret 27a, it follows the normal pattern of the Roman camp with rounded corners and the specific pattern for the area of three exit gateways to the north of the line of the Wall. Following this same pattern, it had its own defensive ditch system.

What is remarkable about it is that the ends of the ditches against the south side of the Wall actually underlie the Broad Foundation and were packed with a blue-coloured clay according to Richmond's interpretation of the report of F. G. Simpson, who excavated the area in 1921. Collingwood, examining the same material in 1933, declares bluntly that the Wall "at these two points had been built across the ditches of the fort, which were filled in to support it".

At Housesteads a similar anomaly exists. Though again a turret—36b—is incorporated inside the fort, Housesteads was not built athwart the Wall as is the case with the cavalry forts. It could not have been, for the line is almost on the edge of the precipice. Its north wall was, however, built slightly in advance of the Broad Foundation (for reasons now obscure) and its western ditch undercut the Broad Foundation largely after the manner of the Chesters ditches.

The third example is at Greatchesters. Greatchesters was built, again for reasons best known to its engineers, not on the Broad Foundation but immediately south of it this time. The structure incorporates milecastle 43. The ditch plan here is more elaborate than at any other point. On the western face there are four, the first three of which were dug almost to the Broad Foundation. The innermost followed the outline of the fort to the Broad Foundation and curved through it, matching the curve of the north-west corner, into the original Fighting Ditch. All four ditches had to be filled when and where the Narrow Wall was built on the same alignment as the north wall of the fort.

It is possible to derive a number of conclusions from these facts, and the experts of the Wall have duly done so—most of them differ. Only one conclusion seems to fit all these oddities, that is that the forts were built substantially before the curtain wall was brought to them—built and occupied. If final proof is wanted it exists in the fact that at Housesteads the north-east corner turret was built on the curve of the fort wall in the traditional position and was demolished and a new turret built at the point of junction only when the running wall finally reached the area.

6

The Eastern Sector

How far is it possible for the ordinary man to see and judge for himself the evidence of alteration and change of plan which over the first decade of the Wall's history produced its effective shape?

The simple answer is that Hadrian's Wall is for the layman more accessible, better excavated and easier to see and understand than any other major monument of Roman military history. It has the additional quality that it runs over some of the finest country in the entire Province of Britain.

The excellences of its planning and of its construction ensured its survival.

It is true that in Newcastle and along the Wallsend extension the overlay of industrialisation masks its course, that the bleak ruin of the quarries in the central sector has destroyed altogether perhaps three-quarters of a Roman mile and that at Burgh Marsh on the Solway almost three miles of its line has been eroded by the sea. For the rest, however, something is visible always—the ditch, the enduring earthworks of the Vallum, the Wall itself magnificent along the high ground. Even the Military Road, damnable in its archaeological effects, should not be wholly condemned, for, considered militarily, it is in the direct line of succession from Hadrian's plan. It duplicates, in eighteenth-century aspect, the purpose of the Roman Military Way, providing, as it did, lateral communication for armies from east to west. In absolute terms, it is the last military work in the long history of the defence of the English frontier against the North and—provided always that Scottish Nationalism does not rise once more against an effete and exhausted Province—almost certainly the final one.

But the Military Road serves another and a present purpose.

Principally because of it the Wall, for the eighty Roman miles of its length, is nowhere as much as a mile from a motor road. From any point on the road the line can be reached by a twenty-minute walk.

Newcastle at the eastern end commands one half of it, Carlisle at the west the other. Hexham on the south bank of the Tyne, third of the three towns of the Wall, gives access with its own road network to all the wild centre from the Irthing crossing to Heddon-on-the-Wall.

From the valley of the river the small towns and villages provide alternatives as bases: Corbridge and Newborough, Haydon Bridge and Bardon Mill, Haltwhistle and Greenhead and—beyond the divide—Brampton.

On its course Wall and Chollerford and Gilsland lie almost astride it; and from end to end there are the pubs of the road. Only to the north there is nothing except in the North Tyne valley. It is as if here the no-man's-land that Rome created in front of the Wall—the depopulated zone—has after fifteen hundred years not yet recovered. Beyond the Wall it is still lonely, still bare, and sometimes subjectively hostile.

Everywhere along its length from Wallsend to Bowness the meticulous and brilliant work of the archaeologists has now fixed its line. Except only in the puzzling zig-zag immediately above Hadrian's bridge its structure and its course are known and the layman can wholly accept the results of that patient detective work and trust the guidance of the magnificent Ordnance Survey map that has been based upon it.

This map is essential to any exploration of the Wall. In Wallsend and central Newcastle, where the line can be followed at best only by the cracks in house walls that mark the points where the filling of ditch and Vallum has subsided under the weight of the nineteenth century, it would be impossible without it to form even the barest picture of the plan. Beyond the built-up areas it is essential for other reasons. It indicates not simply the course of the Wall but makes clear in detail the stretches where ditch and Wall, Military Way and Vallum are visible even to the uninstructed eye.

Traditionally exploration starts at Newcastle. The reason probably is that for long it was believed that the builders began there and that the great curtain of the Wall flowed west with a sense of inexorable purpose.

It didn't. It was as ordered and counter-ordered and as disordered as a modern Air Force contract. It was begun simultaneously at a score of points at least and it was certainly torn down again at nine more. None the less, it is still easier to start from the east not only because forty years ago Collingwood laid down the numbering of the milecastles, beginning at the north-east corner of Wallsend fort, but also because the road pattern starts from here, and because if you lack a car, buses and trains begin at Newcastle.

The east, however, should mean the sea. The Wall runs in military reality from the North Sea to the Irish Sea, shortened a little only by the convenience of the estuaries of the rivers. The remarkable point about the North Sea start point is—that there isn't one. South from the mouth of the Tyne there are no coast defences, nothing to compare with the forty-mile long chain of forts and fortlets that runs from the Bowness terminal of the rampart of the Wall to St. Bees Head. It is abundantly plain that the planners both of the First and of the Second Plan had no reason to fear seaborne attack down the coast from Northumberland or across the North Sea from the Saxons and the Northmen.

There was, however, a river defence. At South Shields—Arbeia of the Romans—a major establishment existed. Probably for its foundation it is necessary to go back as far as Agricola, who must have used the river for his fleet and would almost certainly have set up a protected base to cover seaborne supply for his advance. Certainly there are indications of an occupation in the Flavian period. References to the remains of the Hadrianic fort itself begin early; but knowledge was vague until in 1875 South Shields began a remarkable excavation of its own beginnings. The ramparts of the fort were found then to be six hundred and twenty feet in length by three hundred and sixty feet in width. It covered five acres. It faced north-west towards the river originally, and on its seaward side there was a notable bath house and the remains of a series of other buildings. In the second century it was manned by a cavalry cohort, the *ala Sabiniana*, a fact which appears to place doubts on the suggestions that South Shields was an islet at that date cut off from the mainland by a narrow creek. A cavalry regiment at that point—and it was built for cavalry—would have been expected to cover the whole of the coastal area as far south at least as the mouth of the Wear.

A fork of the road from Chester-le-Street to the new bridge at Pons Aelius led to Arbeia; it still leads to it, the modern A1005. The last two miles are lost in the tangle of small roads which covers the Tyne bank, but at its end Arbeia still stands. The excavation was one of the best of the nineteenth century, and South Shields Museum, with Richmond's careful consolidation of the walls and buildings that were excavated a hundred years ago, is an essential beginning to any understanding of the frontier system.

A hundred and eighty years after Hadrian it was a flourishing entrepot, manned by a cohort of lightermen from the Tigris, equipped with great granaries and storehouses for seaborne goods, and below it in the shelter of the river and the Milldam stream was built, according to Christopher Hunter of Durham, an "elevated pavement in the river Tine ... proper for their safe landing at different times of the flowing and ebbing tyde".

There was another Roman site south of the Tyne. The Ordnance Survey map marks it with reserve as an "unspecified building"—than which it can hardly be more cautious. John Hodgson, one of the great "antiquaries", was parson at Jarrow for many years and to him there was nothing unspecified about it. He described it positively as "an oblong square of about three acres, with its corners rounded off, overlooking the estuary of Jarrow Slake and Tinmouth harbour". Walls of strong masonry, whose foundations he said still existed, enclosed his own churchyard and "some ragged remains of the antient monastery of Jarrow". The *Notitia Dignitatum* lists a fort named, slightly doubtfully, Danum between Arbeia and Pons Aelius.

Roman masonry unquestionably exists in the Jarrow ruins and two inscribed fragments were found in the walls of Jarrow church in the eighteenth century. One of them was identified as "an altar erected in honour of all the adopted sons of the Emperor Hadrian". But no definite evidence of a fort has been discovered. Questions remain to be answered: did the industrious monks of Jarrow loot Arbeia to build their monastery, or was Hodgson right and did they carry out their looting nearer home? Jarrow needs something of the spirit that moved South Shields a hundred years ago. The area cries for investigation.

Even if the Jarrow "fort" is rediscovered, there was no Wall south of the river. The line ended at the head of the Long Reach where the great shipyard of Swan Hunter & Wigham Richardson lies today. What must have been almost the last few feet of it was discovered in 1933, when extensions to the slipways were cut deep into the river bank. Six feet six inches across, standing on a flagstone foundation approximately seven feet wide, its cut ashlar followed the sloping surface of the bank. It could not, unhappily, be left *in situ*. The site was marked by a tablet, and foundation and masonry were transferred to Wallsend Park.

It came from the last quarter of a mile of the curtain. How the Wall itself ended in the river no one knows, but the last quarter sprang from the south-east turret of Wallsend fort and it was traced there in the course of one of F. G. Simpson's most remarkable excavations. Unintimidated by the problems of a built-up area, tunnelling even below the surface of a major street, Simpson located the four gates of Segedunum, as the Romans called it. Three of them opened to the north for cavalry, only one communicated to the south and the area inside the Wall. The fort itself, it was determined, covered four acres, a ditch surrounded it, and from the south tower of the west gate the main Wall ran straight for three miles, swung slightly to the right to negotiate the steep valley of the Ouse Burn, crossed the stream presumably by a small bridge—now lost—and climbed to the heights of Newcastle.

The earliest known garrison of Segedunum was the Second Cohort of Nervians, but the fort was constructed, despite the angled ending of the Wall, precisely on the lines of the cavalry forts to the west of it. Its gates were cavalry gates, and clearly its task was to cover the wide area of the coastal plain. Five miles from Benwell fort, it was carefully positioned for the swiftest possible reaction to any threat in that area. At later periods it was garrisoned by mounted detachments brigaded with infantry, but at the start its efficient operation demanded cavalry.

The Wall to Newcastle was wider than the downhill section

to the river, but the archaeological evidence is that the whole of the scheme east of Newcastle was an afterthought, a wall decided upon subsequent to the inception of the Second Plan. With its eight-foot foundation—against ten feet six for the Broad Wall, and its width of seven feet six—against ten feet—it is patently the work of a different hand.

There has been a wide variety of explanations for this decision. The favourite is that the extension was built to prevent smuggling. No one so far has suggested what was smuggled or who smuggled it, or, for that matter, how they got the contraband across the swift-flowing tides of the river. Nobody, for that matter, has suggested why they should not have gone on smuggling below the Wallsend fort after it was built if they were, in fact, so enthusiastic about it. All the available evidence suggests that the population of the Cumberland plain—the Votadini—was docile, well-disposed towards the Romans and easy to handle. The Wall was not extended against them. It was built to provide a patrol outpost that could command the seaward plain against invaders from the distant north, and it achieved precisely that capability. Whether in addition it covered a small boat harbour at the mouth of the Lort Burn is probably irrelevant. The Wallsend extension is, simply and logically, an extension of the new defensive philosophy of the Second Plan and constitutes a valuable index of the extent of new estimates of the danger of attack from the north, both in space and in time of reaction.

The Broad Wall began at Newcastle. The line in the centre of the city is still obscure, but a prolongation of the presumed course along the eastern part of Westgate Street would bring it to the river close to the modern Tyne Bridge. The accepted point is the site of the existing Moot Hall. It seems improbable that it would have been carried over the Lort Burn by a bridge merely to protect a small craft harbour, as has been suggested. Militarily the proper course would have been to use the Lort Burn in the place of the Fighting Ditch. The matter is academic, however—no evidence exists. The course of the Wall and its eventual junction with the narrow extension of the Wallsend sector is speculative in this densely built over city centre, and in any event there is from the point of view of the layman nothing to see. Even the site of the fort of Pons Aelius is matter for scholarly dissension. Fragments of buildings, coins, and a variety of inscribed stones have been found over much of the city's heart, but the problem of attempting a methodical examination of the possibilities remained until 1929 daunting in the face of the accumulations of Saxon, Norman and industrial Newcastle.

In that year the North of England Excavation Committee, with exemplary courage, essayed the formidable task. The eleventh edition of the *Handbook*, discussing the Roman construction work that was found in the course of the attempt south and west of the keep of the Norman castle, declared, in a mildly despairing manner: "This, together with other positive and negative evidence, suggests a small fort, occupying a level spur some two acres in extent, with a steep fall to south, east and north." This is scarcely enough. Professor Birley in his classic compilation of evidence and informed opinion, *Research on Hadrian's Wall*, says drily: "A review of the evidence suggests the need for a reconsideration of the case." The case itself is simple. There *must* have been a fort. It is militarily inconceivable that a vital river crossing should have been established without a garrison to cover it. Pons Aelius was one of the major hinges of the First Plan. All that is necessary is to find the evidence—under the maze of foundations and basements, cellars and sewers, cable conduits, water mains, gas mains and drains that is the subsoil of a modern city. Birley makes that point also drily clear.

Research on Hadrian's Wall is, beyond all question, the essential volume for anyone who may wish to enquire into matters beyond the *Handbook*. Its detail as to the accounts of discovery and excavation, its crisp summing up of identifiable and identified remains is complete. Under the heading "Anatomy" it lists what is concretely known everywhere along the Wall. Of Newcastle fort it says sorrowfully: "Anatomy: nothing certain."

The one thing that *is* certain about Newcastle is Pons Aelius. The bridge across the Tyne was the most important single engineering accomplishment in the construction of the Wall. That the work was well executed is proven; in one shape or another it lasted for eleven hundred years. Begun certainly as one of the earliest structures of the First Plan—probably, as has been suggested, as early as the year 120—repaired and adapted when essential from century to century, it was the basis of the Saxon bridge which followed it and in turn of the Norman bridge which followed that. It survived at least until 1248. In that year construction of a medieval bridge to replace it began. This second bridge lasted for roughly five hundred years, and again the piers of the Roman work were partly used in its design.

A hundred years ago the eighteenth-century bridge which replaced it after a disastrous flood was itself replaced by the Swing Bridge. For the last time Pons Aelius thrusts into history. The Roman piles and the stone-work located then could not be incorporated in the new structure and were removed, but in the dredging that was inevitable a splendid altar to Oceanus was recovered, dedicated—with a twin altar to Neptunus—by the Sixth Legion, probably to celebrate its first arrival by sea from the Rhine after a notable voyage in ocean.

In Newcastle then, Wall, fort and bridge are all alike invisible. The altars remain.

They have a place of honour in the Museum of Antiquities. Admirably housed now in the quadrangle of the University, this is one of the key collections of the Roman period in Britain, the necessary starting point for any pilgrimage of the Wall; and the altars of the Sixth serve well to mark it. It holds the larger part of the important material of the western sectors, the best of the Northumbrian material, the great inscribed stones of the Dere Street forts and a treasure of lesser things. William Bulmer's model of the Wall from sea to sea is alone worth chapters of a book, and the Museum's astonishingly effective reconstruction of the Mithraeum at Carrawburgh is an essay in total recall.

The position of the fort at Newcastle, then, must be left to the accident of the future. There remains the western line of the Wall itself. From the medieval fortifications it is in contrast to its springing point splendidly clear. The west gate straddled it. The Westgate Road today, as straight and at sunset as dramatic an exit as that from any city in Britain, marks its course. Lifting from the complexity that once lay within the medieval ramparts with an assurance that is difficult to match anywhere, it runs for almost the whole of its length just clear of the Fighting Ditch, its southern pavement overlies it and, like the Wall before it, it strikes with the utmost boldness for the high ground of Benwell Hill.

At Benwell, four hundred feet above the tide-mark, it sweeps across the first of the great cavalry cantonments. The Romans called it Condercum. Like its fellows of the eastern watershed, it lay athwart the Wall, a third of it projecting to the north with its three wide cavalry gates.

The nineteenth century built a reservoir across that third, the twentieth century built a housing estate over the rest; but before it was swallowed up for all time the North of England and the Durham University Excavation Committees carried out a series of admirable rescue operations. The southern angle towers were located and measured. Most of the *principia,* the *praetorium,* parts of the granaries, the barracks, the stabling, and much of the hospital were examined and planned, and the main south gate, with the small west gate, was plotted. Downhill from the south gate itself the location of the Vallum diversion was finally determined and the Vallum crossing, revetted at the sides with Roman ashlar and still carrying the foundations of the arched gateway that led across the Vallum into the military area, was consolidated as an ancient monument. With the delightful little temple of Antenociticus a hundred yards to the east between the tidy houses of Broomridge Avenue—the suburban juxtaposition is irresistible—the Vallum crossing is all that is left visible to mark the first of the major defence works of the Second Plan.

To these fortunately can, however, be added an inscription of remarkable importance. At the south end of the granaries a stone was recovered which read: "For the Emperor Caesar Trajan Hadrian Augustus, under Aulus Platorius Nepos, Emperor's propraetorian legate, a detachment of the British Fleet...." The missing words must have read "erected this building" after the convention of such inscriptions. Its importance lies in the fact that it ascribes the fort, and by analogy the remainder of the cavalry forts, to the Emperor positively, that it dates it in the governate of Nepos, and that it indicates an urgency in the matter of skilled manpower which led to the builders' making demands on the Roman navy.

From the summit of Benwell Hill the road plunges straight for the valley of the Denton Burn. Just beyond the wide crossing at the burn bottom the map marks triumphantly: "The first extant fragment from the East." It lies in the grounds of the Public Library, tended now, standard Broad Wall, a little over nine feet wide, laid on a foundation of flagstones originally set in clay. Old drawings of it exist and, judging from them, it has not altered in more than a hundred years. How it escaped the last of the stone robbing no man knows, but it has an odd, indomitable air.

Uphill from it, still to the south of the road, are the first visible remains of a turret. Turrets, by Collingwood's notation, take their numbers from the nearest milecastle to the east; milecastles themselves are numbered by the Roman miles from Wallsend—this is turret 7b, the second turret to the west of milecastle 7.

A little down the slope on Denton Bank the Vallum is clear for the first time—with two crossings strongly marked in the fields.

Past Chapel House is what remains of the first positively identified milecastle—MC 9, excavated by Birley in 1929.

A quarter of a mile beyond this the ditch becomes visible, a deep, significant hollow to the north of the road.

So the component parts of the plan of Hadrian's frontier are made apparent, one upon the other, until the pattern of the Wall becomes a whole and, at Walbottle Dene, Vallum, milecastle and Fighting Ditch fuse into a single complex and only the Wall itself, lost now under the tarmac of the road, is absent.

At Throckley, just beyond, there was a treasure—five thousand silvered coins of the third century close to where milecastle 11 once stood.

This Newburn area has a particular importance, for at Newburn itself was the first ford at which men could cross the Tyne—a man-made ford in heavy stone.

At Newburn in 1346 David of Scotland crossed the river and marched to his defeat at Neville's Cross.

At Newburn three hundred years later Leslie defeated the army of Charles I, and Newcastle was left naked to the Scots.

Through Newburn in 1751 Parliament built the Military Road.

Over all this area, thirteen hundred years after the last appeal to the Consul Agitius—the appeal that expressed "the Groans of the Britons"—was left unanswered, the north slopes of the Tyne and the Eden valleys were still the fighting frontier of England.

At the entrance to Heddon-on-the-Wall, Vallum, Wall and ditch at last run visible together. A stretch of three hundred yards of well-preserved mason work survives, in places more than five feet high, where the road sheers away a little to the north. To the south the Vallum runs clearly for three-quarters of a mile, and on a high knoll the Saxon church of St. Andrew, its walls part built of Roman ashlar, a centurial stone on a window-sill, marks with its splendid Norman chancel other and later conquests.

Beyond Heddon the road divides.

The south fork is the medieval road that runs over the descending country to Corbridge and then by the Tyne banks to the divide at Gilsland. It was this road that failed Wade's artillery. The new road that he asked for runs straight with the Wall from the fork to the fort which is now called Rudchester but which Rome called Vindovala. At Rudchester cross-roads it cuts ruthlessly across the site.

The character of the road has changed here. This is open country. The housing estates, the schools, the ribbon villages have been left behind. Rudchester stands perhaps a bare fifty feet higher than Benwell seven miles back along the Wall, but it is set at the head of a great slope to the south. Except for the Rudchester farm buildings—constructed largely of Roman stone—it is curiously and peacefully alone. The cross-road skirts its eastern wall and tall trees mark its outline. It was recognised as early as Camden's day. Holland's translation says: "we beheld very plainly the expresse footings, in form four square, of a garison Castle, that joined hard to the wall."

In due course, towers, the ruins of buildings inside the walls, and gateways were identified. Horsley, as always, was singularly precise. Most of the antiquaries viewed it and described it, and Haverfield began the excavation. At the beginning of this century it was methodically examined. Measurements gave it an area of a little over four and a half acres, with a north-south length of five hundred and fifteen feet. Camden had recognised only the southern two-thirds of it. Like the rest of the eastern cavalry forts, it was built across the Wall with its three gates to the north of the line, the masonry of the rampart that had already been erected was demolished to make way for it, and the ditch that had been dug filled in. To the south-west of it was a Mithraeum, built in the third century and abandoned, presumably with the onset of Christianity, in the fourth.

The Wall runs direct for a quarter of a mile beyond Rudchester, alters course a little to the south for another quarter of a mile, and then aims straight for Harlow Hill. The road curves from it almost at the summit of the hill, slips round the summit itself, and comes back to it to plunge downhill across the Whittle Dean reservoirs and hurtle three miles dead straight to Carr Hill. It is here the prisoner of the frontier system. The ditch is deep on its northern side. To the south for two miles the Vallum seems almost to hem it in, running parallel a handful of yards down the valley slope, its mounds clear and well defined, its fosse strongly apparent, and the road held beyond the possibility of deviation between the two.

Over the seven hundred foot summit of Carr Hill the Wall turns southerly again for a little, strides over Down Hill while the road loops to the north of it and the Vallum zigzags to the south, and reaches Haltonchesters, Onnum of the Romans—Kipling's Hunnum. Halton is the fourth of the cavalry forts. As with Benwell and Rudchester, the part-built wall was pulled down to make place for it and the Fighting Ditch filled in. It had the customary three cavalry gates to the north and at some later date, needing more space, it was extended south of the Wall towards the west to make an L-shaped whole. Much has been made of the anomalies of its site. Its outlook to the north is hardly more than adequate, its outlook to the east was blocked by the spurs of Carr Hill, its outlook to the west was indifferent

---

The eastern sector of the Great Whin Sill. The Wall runs clear from Cuddy's Crag to the skyline above Milecastle 37. Beyond it Housesteads Wood stands above the lip of its crag and masks Housesteads fort. The line of the Wall follows the air-ridge of the Sill to Sewingshields Crag, the highest point against the sky, with Broomlee Lough below it. ▶
Photograph: Ian Yeomans

from a military point of view. But the problem that has bothered successions of experts is the evidence that it was built in total disregard of the fact that Dere Street crosses the planned line little more than half a mile to the west of its walls. Generations of opinion have felt uneasily that it should have been built to defend the crossing.

The position seems simple enough to the layman. Surely for the begetters of the First Plan at least, the crossing had little importance. After the completion of their Wall the country to the north would be a no-man's-land. Dere Street had served its purpose and in their view would have to be abandoned with its forts. They made no attempt even to alter the position of Milecastle 22—two hundred and sixty yards or so to the eastward—from its measured but arbitrary position to cover the road.

Horsley, it is true, recorded a *castellum* at the intersection. It projected, he said, for half its depth—he calculated it as sixty feet square—to the north of the Wall and he described it as, except for the projection, like the milecastles and claimed that the ditch "manifestly goes about" it.

It is possible that this gateway was in fact of later date than the Wall and that it belongs to the period of the advance to the Forth-Clyde line when Dere Street came back to its ancient importance. No proof exists either way. It might be found perhaps if Birley's splendidly practical suggestion could be adopted: "If ever a roundabout is made at the cross-roads it should be possible to uncover and preserve the remains of this structure."

Once again from the Dere Street crossing the road runs, hemmed by ditch and Vallum, up the fell to high ground, alters course to head due west, and comes boldly to Heaven Field.

Beside the road there is a simple wayside cross.

Almost two centuries after the frontier guard went south down Dere Street an earlier cross was planted there. Bede says that it was the first cross planted in all Northumbria. According

---

◀ The western sector of the Great Whin Sill. From the Hotbank Crags the Wall drops steeply to Milking Gap and the brilliance of the Crag Lough in the sun. Beyond the lough it climbs again to Winshields Crag, the highest point of the Wall, 1,200 feet above the sea.
Photograph: Ian Yeomans

to tradition, it was socketed in a Roman altar. Long ago that cross crumbled. The altar, like the altars of Pons Aelius, remains. It stands inside against the north wall of the little church across the Heaven Field, the church that the monks of Hexham built of the stones of the Wall to mark the place where Oswald, saint and king, advanced to the defeat of Caedwalla "with an army, small in number but strengthened with the faith of Christ...." The altar, with the rough hole cut in its upper surface, bridges the transition from pagan Rome to the Rome of Christ. Heofenfeld—Heaven Field—it is one of the moving places of the faith in Britain.

From the north-west corner of the churchyard the view swoops like a swallow to the valley of the North Tyne. Along the bottom the river runs blue past Cocklaw and Chollerton and Haughton Castle. Beyond the castle the recessional of the hills leads in fold after fold for ten miles to Bellingham and the ultimate implacable hollows of the dales.

The North Tyne valley is one of the beautiful valleys of England. It holds, as well, the richest concentration of Roman material between Tyne and Solway. Seven major sites lie within a circle of less than a mile of Chollerford bridge.

Appropriately the first of these, half a mile from the gate of Heaven Field, is that fine length of Wall that old William Hutton saved with his tears. You reach it by a stile across the field wall and it stands, upright still and almost arrogant, above the meadow grass. It has a special importance, for its eastern half is Broad Wall at the full gauge of nine foot six but it narrows abruptly to a width of six feet. The second of the sites reverses the pattern. A quarter of a mile down the Hexham road from the wide crossing at the valley bottom a path leads to Brunton Turret—26b. The turret, admirably preserved, is built in the Broad Wall, still seven feet high at this point with nine courses of its facing stones perfect and the ditch in front of it deep and splendidly sloped. Just east of the turret, however, the Broad Wall gives way abruptly again to a six-foot gauge. Argument about the significance of this began early and continues. One theory is that sectors here were unfinished at the change of plan and were filled by narrow gauge work; one that it was pulled down by the Roman army itself, for unexplained reasons, and rebuilt hastily to meet a new threat. Neither theory carries conviction. The older tradition that here the barbarians tore down the Wall with their bare hands in a fury of revenge after the great assault of the year 367 has much to commend it dramatically—and perhaps archaeologically also.

Chollerton Church lies a mile and a quarter to the north of Brunton cross-roads on A6079. Archaeologically speaking it is not a "site". It is instead the depository of the proceeds of one of the earliest and one of the greatest of the robbings of the Wall. About 1150 its Norman builders raised an arcade of four bays on the south side of the nave and used for the purpose five astonishingly perfect Roman columns, looted, beyond all question, from the *principia* of Chesters fort. The feather tooling is still clear on the easternmost of these, the simple moulding of the capitals is all but perfect, and at the western end of the arcade there is to match them an altar to Jupiter Optimus Maximus, hollowed to serve as a Christian font.

For two miles or so to the north of the line and five miles to the south no ancient building stands that has not borrowed from the Wall. Chollerton's builders were only the arch thieves of them all.

The North Tyne bridge, the fourth of the seven sites, is by contrast the most brilliant and the most honest piece of engineering between Tyne and Solway. The path to it starts at a gate on the south side of the approach to Chollerford bridge and follows the line of the abandoned railway. It reaches the Wall just below MC 27. The platform of the milecastle can be distinguished in the meadow to the east; the Wall itself emerges below the stiles—Narrow Wall, six foot four inches wide, rebuilt on the Broad Foundation and almost nine feet high in places. It ends at a tower, square and still upstanding, based on the superb eastern abutment of the third-century bridge that served the Wall.

The abutment itself is built of giant blocks of stone from the Black Pasture quarries on Brunton Bank. Beautifully tooled, perfectly finished, they stand immaculately preserved by the mud of some final winter flood that overwhelmed them after Maximus went south. In their own time the barbarians tore down the timbers of the bridge and wrecked its towers. The aggressive phallus on the upstream water face—that had brought good luck to generations of soldiery who passed that way—failed at last of its duty.

The great footing was constructed to take the second and larger of the two bridges built at Chesters. The First Plan provided for a narrow structure just large enough to carry the Wall across on low round arches. The voussoirs of some of those arches are incorporated in the later work. The first pier of this bridge can be seen embedded in the platform of the abutment and part of the third in a pier of the later bridge in mid-stream in dry summers, when the western abutment is also visible. They show conclusively that there was no roadway across the river in this period but only the patrol way of the Wall.

The second bridge is late, built probably in the time of Severus and offering perhaps a hint at the date of the construction of the Military Way. The main water face of the footing is twenty-two feet in length. As at Pons Aelius, it carried its roadway on a timber superstructure and it may have been defended by timber crenellations with a complex grating below to prevent infiltration. The width of its roadway must have been governed by the width of the tower through which it passed. Richmond says categorically that the abutment accommodated a roadway of about twenty feet in width. The tower in fact was twenty-two feet square, but almost a third of its eastern side was taken up by the thickness of the Wall's end, and the problem of the manner in which the road reached the decking of the bridge has scarcely been satisfactorily explained.

The tower served also a second purpose: it was a mill, one of the three known water-mills of the Wall—at Chesters, at the Haltwhistle Burn and at the Willowford bridge. A four-foot millrace covered with heavy slabs, now mostly broken, runs the whole length of the abutment and of the thirty-foot downstream extension which may have been made necessary by the scour of its fall. The hub of the wheel, of stone, slotted for eight spokes, is in Chesters Museum.

Properly speaking the North Tyne forms the topographical boundary between the eastern and the central sectors of the Wall even as the Irthing provides the boundary between the centre and the west. The cavalry cantonment at Chesters, however, was an integral part of the eastern system, a vital element of the cavalry aspect of the Second Plan, designed not simply to protect the bridge crossing, as has been too easily assumed, but to provide patrols and a striking force for the western slopes of the North Tyne valley and the relatively easy country between the river and the beginning of the Great Whin Sill. The eastern slopes of the valley were covered by the cavalry detachment at Haltonchesters, less than four and a half miles from the nearest point of the stream. Chesters fort therefore is properly included in the eastern march.

It must have been the most delectable of all the stations of the Wall. Classically sited on level ground above the river, it stands today in parkland. What trees there were in Roman times we cannot tell, but it would be difficult to impair the fundamental beauty of the valley. Below it the ground opens out towards the Tyne itself. Warden Hill, the tall hill a little south of west, frames one end of its vistas. To the north it opens past Humshaugh to the upper valley. The river runs below it, full and brawling for most of the year, and the sound of the fall across the weir at Chollerford makes counterpoint to the wind in the trees.

The museum, the fort, the bath house and the bridge are John Clayton's memorial. Chesters came into the possession of his family in 1796. In that year Nathaniel Clayton, having bought the estate, levelled the obtrusive portions of the ruins of the fort to improve the view from the simple Georgian house of the day. John Clayton was his second son. Whether his enthusiasm for the Wall was founded in a spirit of atonement is unclear, but in 1843 he began, with the careful examination of the house of the commander of the garrison, the long series of excavations which was to continue for almost half a century. Clayton's work was imperfect, for he employed necessarily the limited techniques of the period. Much that he cleared could have been saved in the light of present-day knowledge, but the immense enthusiasm of the man, the devotion and the strong protective spirit that he engendered did more to save what was left to be saved than any other single effort.

The museum underscores his achievement. Most of its specimens were recovered in the course of his digs or under his aegis or in areas that he purchased and protected for all time. The display is not adequate to its importance. This is one of the most significant assemblies of the Roman period in Britain, significant not only for its wealth of inscribed stones and altars but even more for the minutiae of everyday life on the frontiers of Rome: the toilet articles of the women of the *vicus*, the arrows and the armour of the soldiery, the altars and the offerings of the temples, the dedicatory stones that give us the names of emperors and governors, the centurial stones—"Sixth Cohort, Century of Lousius Suavis"—that form the record and give in an astonishing number of cases the names of the men who built the Wall.

Chesters supplied the greater part of these things. As a cavalry cantonment it had both military importance and a reasonable degree of wealth—for the cavalrymen were better paid than the infantry. The variety of the material from the site is elaborate, ranging from the well-known "diploma"—the *tabula honestae missionis* which was found in the eastern guard chamber of the south gate—to pins and shoe nails. The diploma is the copy in bronze of the decree conferring Roman citizenship issued to a time-expired man of the auxiliaries in the year 146. It lists the group of auxiliary regiments discharging men at that time and with six other known diplomas (the earliest of which dates from the year 98) supplies a valuable record of the regiments serving in Britain over half a century. The original is now in the British Museum, the Chesters exhibit is an electrotype.

There is one other exhibit that has an ironic interest—the splendid *modius*, a bronze corn measure found fifty years ago outside Carvoran fort. The inscription, partly erased, indicates that it was issued in the reign of Domitian, and it records that the measure was attested at seventeen and a half *sextarii*—roughly seventeen pints. In point of fact the measure holds twenty, and generations of cynical students have contemplated the iniquity of the quartermasters of the day swindling the innocent Briton to the tune of fifteen per cent in the corn levy. Anything, after all, was possible under Domitian.

More sober judges in recent years have pointed out that two small holes drilled in the side of the vessel might possibly have provided for the rivets of an indicator at the seventeen-pint level. It seems improbable, however, that they will overtake the sceptics.

The path to the fort lies across an easy meadow. Almost certainly there is little still to be found below the meadow save perhaps the course of the aqueduct that enters under the northern gate; this in its day was no-man's-land. But the archaeologists have located all the six gateways of the fort. The towers of the southern face have been cleared. Enough of the defensive wall—five feet thick, backed by a heavy earth bank and protected by a ditch—survives to prove its precise dimensions, and within its five and three-quarter acres the elaborate remains of the *praetorium* with its well, its courts, its regimental offices, its "Chapel of the Standards" and its underground treasury have been brilliantly excavated. The house and the baths of the commandant, built and rebuilt after the three disasters of the Wall, have been investigated. Barrack blocks and stables have been laid bare, and Chesters offers today, with Housesteads, the most perfect evidence of a major military establishment in Britain.

The course of the Vallum below the fort is still uncertain. Following the known line to east and west, it has been assumed that no deviation was necessary and that the ditch of the Vallum may possibly have provided the southern ditch of the fort. Tentative excavation and aerial photography suggest, however, the probability of a planned deviation to the south after the established precedents of Benwell and Haltonchesters, with a crossing below the southern gateway of the fort. The solution remains to be proved.

The seventh and the last of the valley sites is the great bath house. Admirably excavated by Sir George Macdonald, it stands on the bank of the river safely above flood level between the east wall of the fort and the water. One of the most impressive Roman buildings in Britain, its complex of warm and cold rooms, its furnaces, its provision for dry heat and wet heat, its arcade of niches is astonishingly complete. Even the wear of generations of naked feet across its flagstones is visible, and the tiny and human graffiti of its masons.

Much still requires to be done at Chesters. Its *vicus,* whether it straddles a deviation of the Vallum or whether it lies to the south of it, is still all but unexplored. It offers an exciting opportunity to determine further the status and the conditions of the Romanised British civilians in the north. Birley, making a plea for further investigation, suggests the possibility of a pre-Hadrianic fort on this portion of the site, perhaps to guard the river crossing. He calls for further work, too, to resolve problems in the cavalry stables. More excavation is necessary to determine once and for all the hotly disputed problem already referred to of the fort ditch and the Broad Foundation.

7

The Splendour of the High Sill

From Chesters the Wall runs west-north-west under the Victorian embellishments of John Clayton's original Georgian house. In a dry summer it appears as a low, straight lifting of the ground. Beyond the house it stands four courses high for a short stretch and subsides again to a flat mound that marks the Broad Foundation. As it leaves the edge of the plantation beyond the house, the road, arrow-straight from Chollerford bridge, turns sharply on to it and masks it to Walwick hamlet. At Walwick the road turns south and runs with the Vallum, and the Vallum runs straight for Teppermoor Hill. Once again the works are strongly marked. The Vallum ditch is deep, the mounds clearly defined, the Fighting Ditch clean and formidable to the north; and at turret 29a the Wall itself stands six feet high and runs parallel with the road under the nearer trees.

At Limestone Corner the line reaches its apex. Higher here even than at Heaven Field, the Wall at this point commands all the western approaches to the North Tyne valley. From it its sentinels could see clear to the Cheviots; they could watch the river valley where Chipchase Castle was built a thousand years after they went south; to the north-west over Simonburn and Haughton Common they were immaculately positioned to observe the approach of an enemy across the barren moors of Wark. Beyond these military virtues it has a wider and an historic importance. Despite its prosaic name, Limestone Corner for more than two and a half turbulent centuries was the northern limit of the Roman Empire.

Archaeologically it is noteworthy for yet another reason. In Chapter 5 the abrupt abandonment of work on the Fighting Ditch was briefly discussed. The evidence is here. Along the north-west crest of Teppermoor Hill the ditch ceases in a scree of broken stone. In the centre of the deep gully that marks the last stages of the work there is an enormous block of stone, perhaps ten tons in weight. On its upper surface, carefully and patiently, the quarrying legionaries have driven wedge holes in the thin quartz veins that seam the dolerite. The rock is prepared to the very last moment before demolition—but the wedges were never inserted. Up on the lips of the ditch on either side are other boulders ready to be splintered to form the glacis or broken to fill the berm between ditch and Wall face. They lie as the working party left them—halfway through a shift perhaps—untouched for the two hundred and sixty years of the Wall.

Across the road, perhaps two years later, the Vallum ditch was cut through the same stone triumphantly and conclusively. The matter was never one of the hardness of the rock. Clearly the Second Plan abandoned the requirement for a Fighting Ditch.

There is a third item of importance on Teppermoor Hill. For the first time the Military Way asserts itself. It follows at the summit the unusual bastion-shaped projection that is established here by the course of the Wall and it plunges with the Vallum, using its north mound for a foundation and thereby proving its later date, to Carrawburgh Fort—the fort that the Romans knew as Brocolitia—almost a mile down the slope.

Carrawburgh is still largely undiscovered ground. Excavation has been tentative and hesitant. Enough has been done, however, to prove that it is the afterthought of the central sector, the fort that was built when the engineers of the Vallum had long since passed that way, an infantry fort established to strengthen the eight-mile gap between Chesters and Housesteads on the Great Whin Sill. It was known before Horsley, but it was Horsley who first ascertained that its side walls made right-angled junctions with the main Wall, that it had no northerly projection, that its *vicus* lay mainly to its western side, and that close to it there was a well. In his account he wrote:

> It is a good spring, and the receptacle for the water is about seven foot square within, and built on all sides with hewn stone; the depth could not be known when I saw it, because it was almost filled up with rubbish....

Horsley was not interested in "rubbish", whereby he missed perhaps the most fascinating single find in the history of the Wall.

After Horsley the well was for a time lost. A century and a half later it was rediscovered and Clayton excavated it. Below the rubbish of stones that choked the top he found at once thirteen thousand, four hundred and eighty-seven coins. Many more were carried away in a raid on the treasure by the locals, but in Clayton's haul were four coins of gold, a hundred and eighty-four of silver, and bronze coins covering three hundred years of Roman history. The most numerous were of the reign of Antoninus Pius and they included the famous disconsolate Britannia struck to commemorate the pacification of Northern Britain in 155.

With them in the well were altars, incense burners, brooches, carved stones, and a variety of votive offerings. Horsley's well had been a sacred spring, the spring of the Celtic goddess Coventina. It stood within a shrine of which the foundations remain, about forty feet square, and it must have been demolished in one of the great disasters of the Wall after its guardians, in despair, had thrown the sacred treasure into its concealing waters.

Down the slope from the spring and close to the south-west corner of the fort, shrinking peat in the hot summer of 1949 indicated another building. A trial excavation uncovered three important altars still in position. In 1950 Professor Richmond and J. Gillam, one of the original discoverers, carried out a careful investigation for the two excavation committees. The shrine proved to be a Mithraeum, more complete than any other so far located in Britain. This is the Mithraeum of the remarkable reconstruction at the Museum of Antiquities at Newcastle. Its altars and its inscribed stones are preserved in the Museum from the future ravages of time. Out here on the bare moor the Ministry of Works has admirably consolidated the foundations, the low walls, and the benches that fringed the nave. The altars, reproduced in cast stone, stand in their traditional positions. The timber that screened the ante-chapel has been in part restored, and the ancient floor has been made permanent. In the immensity of the moorland it is a place of dignity.

The fort itself is all but virgin. Horsley described it without excavation; Haverfield sank trenches in an unsuccessful attempt to decide its relationship to the Vallum; and finally Birley, in a neat and professional operation, discovered that the rock-cut Vallum ditch across the site had been filled carefully with rammed clay before building of the fort began. The southern part of the angle tower at the north-west corner was uncovered below the verge of the Military Road and some other small fragments were cleared and recognised. The fort itself awaits a careful excavation. It is obvious from the state of its surface that much of its buildings remains. The area to the west and south of its walls has clear indications of at least one major structure and a number of minor ones, and the site cries for full investigation.

From Carrawburgh the road runs straight again for almost two miles to Shield on the Wall. Once more it is the prisoner of ditch and Vallum, hemmed between the two and kept to a most un-English straightness. Just past the position of turret 32b, however, the rampart trends a little to the north and the road follows the Vallum line to the Coesike, and at the narrow water in the pine plantation swings finally and positively to the south as the Great Whin Sill lifts clear of the valley slope like a breaking sea.

At this point car and the Wall part company and for almost sixteen miles this is walking country, perhaps the most splendid walking country left in Britain. As the line of the Wall lifts up the shoulder of Sewingshields Crag, it sheds the centuries. This is the high country, the peaceful country, silent, save where the plover cry or the larks sing or the grouse break out beneath one's feet in a whirr of angry wings, silent as it was for years of the *pax* of Rome, silent almost as it was before the Romans came. The ditch marks its course up the first half mile of the steep as far as the site of milecastle 34. It is bare of stone-work here. The builders of the Military Road, not content with twenty-seven miles of devastation, robbed the Wall naked far up the slope to feed the soft stretches of the valley bottom past the Coesike. Beyond the milecastle it was robbed again to build the farmhouse at Sewingshields, and at a much later date it is recorded that stone was taken from it "for the building of certain offices" at the farm.

It matters less here perhaps than at any other point on the eastern slopes, for, as has been said, this is the start of the splendid country. Here the Marches open out. Sewingshields Farm stands on the nine-hundred foot contour sheltered by the ridge of the crest itself. Beyond it the Crag rises in a great upsurge and the Wall climbs boldly for the first time to the thousand-foot level. Below the farm is the site of Sewingshields Castle, the dour keep that figures in Walter Scott's interminable and off-putting *Harold the Dauntless*. Earlier than either Scott or Harold this was the focal point of one of the oldest and quite the most disreputable of the sagas of Arthur and Guinevere. The legend runs that Guinevere, combing her hair on a rock like a North Country Lorelei, said something that displeased her king, and Arthur hurled a rock at her. They point out the stone today; it weighs a minimum of twenty tons. Demonstrably this was never the smug but chivalrous Arthur of the *Idylls of the King*.

The Fighting Ditch ends here, a little below the clumps of trees that mark MC 34. The line of the Wall thereafter is faced by cliffs and on Sewingshields Crag brief lengths have been consolidated and stand, time-defying again, on the skyline of the northern world. For the rest, field walls built almost wholly of Roman ashlar follow the Roman line.

Past turret 35a, excavated ten years ago, the line turns sharply south and drops down the steep slope to the King's Wicket. This was Camden's Busy Gap, the place "infamous for thieving and robbing" where he dared not go, and the King's Wicket was the passage through the Wall of a drove road to the north that was established long after Rome had passed away. Again the line lifts steeply over King's Hill and Clew Hill and Kennel Crags, lifting and falling to the wind gaps in the ridge, utterly indifferent to the steepness of the slopes, until, level with Broomlee Lough, it reaches the shallow valley of the Knag Burn.

Housesteads stands triumphantly above the Knag Burn Gap.

The Romans called it Borcovicium—according at least to the *Notitia Dignitatum*. But the *Notitia* has certain doubts attached to it. It is a Civil List and Army List combined, naming the principal Imperial officials and the senior officers of military units throughout the Empire—"... *tam civilium quam mili-*

tarium, in partibus Orientis et Occidentis." In the form in which it has reached us it is unquestionably of the fifth century—early in the century perhaps, but substantially after Maximus had abandoned the Wall and certainly after the last semblance of ordered garrison of the area had ceased.

Its list both of officers and of units of the Wall therefore derives from an earlier period. To follow it uncritically is a little like using a British Army List of the Boer War period for enlightenment on the dispositions of World War II. None the less, it is the best list of the establishments that is available and the section that begins: "*Item per lineam Valli . . .*" which can be translated "In addition, along the line of the Wall . . ." is inestimably valuable. It notes at the eighth place in the list the Tribune of the First Cohort of Tungrians at Borcovicium.

The *Notitia* is one of the five recognised sources for names in the frontier area. There were in addition to it two road books, early predecessors of the A.A. books, which described the infinitely complicated road network of the Empire. The first and the best of these, the Antonine Itinerary, is invaluable for Britain as a whole but of relatively little purpose for the Wall. It lists the two roads which cross it: Dere Street going south from the fort at High Rochester (which was called Bremenium) through the Port Gate to Corbridge (which is listed as Corstopitum) and the road from Birrens (Blatobulgium) running south through Carlisle (which was listed as Luguvalium). The second list, the Ravenna Cosmography, exists only in a sixth-century copy of a second-century map, but it enumerates thirteen forts on the Wall itself—if one includes Chesterholm and Castlesteads—and its names agree, with the usual differences in spelling, to an important degree with the list of the *Notitia*.

In addition there are two drinking vessels—the delightful Rudge cup, which was found in Wiltshire and now occupies a place of honour at Alnwick Castle, with an excellent reproduction in the Museum of Antiquities, and the Amiens skillet, which was found at Amiens twenty years ago. The Rudge cup lists five forts, beginning with Banna (which has been identified as Carvoran) and ending with Maia (which is identified as Bowness). The Amiens cup begins at "Esica" (which is identified as Greatchesters) and lists the others. Precise identification of the entire series is, in view of the variations, perhaps impossible. The cups, for instance, agree on Banna, but the *Notitia* calls it Magnis, and as far as Housesteads is concerned the *Notitia* names it Borcovicium and the Ravenna list calls it Velurtion, and one of the two undisputed names in the inscriptions from the Wall itself refers to it as "Ver——", the rest is lost. Professor Birley in the excellent Ministry of Works guide to the fort says, in a mildly disgruntled tone: "It will be best to keep the name of the modern farm on which it stands, Housesteads."

Borcovicium—Velurtion, it scarcely matters. Triumphantly surviving, splendidly excavated, Housesteads is the classic fort of the Wall. It is more perhaps even than that—it is the type example of the Roman camp in Britain. Most admirably in care of the Ministry of Works on behalf of the National Trust to which it belongs by the rich gift of Dr. G. M. Trevelyan, it stands plain and defined against the surge of the Great Whin Sill, open for every man to judge the military excellence that was the frontier of Rome.

Its very excellence indeed postulates a series of unanswered questions.

Was it in fact planned as a fort of the Wall—an integral part, that is, of a single construction from Tyne to Solway—or was it built to stand in independence? When was it built? When was it joined to the Wall? What was its real relation to the general pattern? What was its area of responsibility? How did it function over it?

Some of these questions must be left to a later chapter which will deal with the military capability of the system as a whole, some of them should be asked now.

The academic chronology of the Wall is scarcely sacrosanct. For a century and a half at least it has been bitterly argued by historians and archaeologists. Feuds have developed over it. Scholars have savaged scholars. Controversy has been extruded to an ultimate art form. As late as 1967 C. E. Stevens, redrafting a Horsley lecture originally delivered in 1945, published a devastating attack on almost every view that had ever been put forward in connection with its construction in an intricate fervour of Byzantine disputation.

Yet Housesteads presents certain plain and fundamental facts in relation to that chronology which to the layman appear to require answer before almost anything else in connection with the Wall.

The First Plan, it will be remembered, provided for a stone rampart ten feet wide from Pons Aelius to the Irthing crossing. It may less certainly have provided also for a wall of turf from the Irthing to Carlisle. The main line of the Wall was determined absolutely in accordance with that plan. On the high ground of the Great Whin Sill the surveyors used the immediate crest of the Crags—the vital defensive summit. Along the crest the legions laid the Broad Foundation except where the bedrock made it unnecessary. At every mile, in accordance with the plan, they started the construction of milecastles, between each pair of milecastles they began the turrets. Then, abruptly, as has already been outlined, work ceased.

In the first chapter it was suggested that the suspension was ordered shortly after Hadrian arrived in Britain and that the Second Plan was drafted immediately.

Though the Housesteads site has been included in the study of the Wall since Bainbrigg sent Camden an account of it in 1601, no single piece of evidence has so far been discovered which provides an approximate date for the start of construction. Its place in the academic chronology is determined therefore by a single negative fact. In the course of Simpson and Richmond's excavation of 1945, the foundations of turret 36b in their appropriate position according to the spacing of the First Plan were exposed under the structure of the fort itself. Enough existed—and is preserved—to demonstrate clearly that it had been partially built in accordance with the First Plan, that work had ceased with the suspension of that plan, and that it had been demolished to make way for the great infantry fort demanded by the Second Plan.

In the light of this it is certain, however, only that Housesteads is later than the First Plan.

How much later?

The majority of the earlier forts of the Second Plan show a parallel ruthlessness with regard to work already accomplished. With the cavalry forts it was a necessary ruthlessness. The part-built Wall was torn down to enable the *praetentura,* the front third of each fort, to be erected north of its line so as to provide three gateways for rapid cavalry sorties.

At Housesteads there was no such requirement. At five points in its surviving fabric, on the other hand, there is evidence that it was designed and laid down in blunt and absolute disregard of any plan for the Wall at all.

One: Not merely was a turret demolished but the Broad Foundation—the designated line of the main Wall—was obliterated. A wall five feet wide, in accordance with the normal specifications for an infantry camp, was built to the north of the original surveyed line—on the descending edge of the Housesteads Crags. This involved not only substantial cost in terms of extra man-hours but an equally substantial delay in time. The academic explanation is that the fort's planners found it necessary to create level ground to enable the stock pattern for an infantry camp to be followed.

Two: The outline of the conventional infantry camp has been described as that of a playing card. The rounded corners of the playing card at Housesteads overrode the existing line of the Broad Foundation at the western end and projected beyond a change in direction laid down in the survey for the Wall itself at the eastern end. No academic explanation of this is offered.

Three: Two short sections of defensive ditch were dug east and west of the fort. At the east the ditch ended inconclusively. At the north-west angle it undercut the Broad Foundation so that when at some undetermined date the Narrow Wall was finally built it was necessary to fill and consolidate the ditch. The parallel with Chesters is here self-evident. Stevens argued oddly that this indicates that the fort ditches were dug "earlier than the laying of 'Broad Foundation', there is nothing else for it." It appears an astonishing claim.

Four: The normal plan for infantry forts provided for a turret in the centre of the quadrant at each of the corners. At Housesteads the turrets were built in accordance with normal practice. At the north-west corner it proved possible at the undetermined date when the Narrow Wall was eventually brought to the fort to adapt the north-west turret to give access to the patrol path of the Wall. None the less, the major part of the turret remained behind the fighting face of the Wall and towered pointlessly over an irregularly shaped cul-de-sac between the curve of the fort wall and the back of the Wall proper. In the most charitable terms it is a military untidiness. At the north-eastern corner, because of the fifty-degree change in the direction of the Wall for the Knag Burn crossing, any question of a tidy junction with the fort at the corner tower was altogether ruled out. The quadrant was substantially beyond the planned line. As a consequence the north-east tower was razed, the hole was filled in—the foundations still exist and the wall is patched—and a new tower was erected at the point where the main Wall reached the north face of the fort. Once again academic opinion appears to accept rather than to explain. In Birley's words: "The historical priority of the fort *seemed* to be established."

Five: The result of these contrivances is that the rampart in the Housesteads area in its final shape consisted of Narrow Wall eight feet wide on Broad Foundation to the east; Narrow Wall eight feet wide moving back into Broad Foundation to the west; and a five-foot-wide infantry camp wall of hardly more than half this strength between the two points of junction, bulging to the north of the general line. Academic opinion appears to disregard this altogether. It is, however, scarcely too much to call it military nonsense.

It seems possible to extract from these anomalies a single logical conclusion—that the engineers of the fort were ordered to build a traditional infantry camp in isolation. The destruction of the Broad Wall foundation suggests belief that the Wall had been cancelled over this area. The decision to extend the fort wall north of it on the face of the cliff indicates that the builders searched for a stronger line for a fort in isolation than the surveyors of the First Plan had required for the Wall itself. The rounded corners, the quadrant turrets and the cutting of the north-west ditch together demonstrate that no allowance was made for a future junction with any other work. More simply then, Housesteads was designed and built to stand alone.

For how long did it so stand?

Again no positive date is available and it seems improbable now that one will be discovered. Two pieces of acceptable evidence, however, exist. Close to the eastern gate at Greatchesters, the next fort along the Wall, a portion of the tablet customarily erected over the principal entrance on completion of a military establishment has been recovered. The tablet records the name of Hadrian with the letters *pp*. The abbreviation stands for *pater patriae*, the title which Hadrian first refused and finally accepted only in the year 128. A coin with the same ascription comes from below the backing mound of the north wall of the fort.

The structure of the argument is simple. If the evidence of the tablet is accepted, Greatchesters was not completed until after 128. But the relationship of its ditches to the Broad Foundation of the Wall and the pattern of its junctions, as at Housesteads—and equally as at Chesters—proves that the Narrow Wall reached it only after the completion of the fort building. No clue exists as to how long after, but considered in conjunction with the date of A.D. 128 the scheme—fort, wall and all—cannot have been completed for considerably more than six years after the departure of Hadrian. This fact appears to make hay of the intricate time-tables evolved by the time-and-motion enthusiasts on the basis of the amount of work possible per legion per season. The one fact that emerges clearly from this is that the central forts were built in isolation and that for the indeterminate period Housesteads and Greatchesters stood alone.

If then Housesteads was not built initially to stand in the line of the Wall, why was it built upon this site? The question must have been asked with an acidulous repetition by the Tungrians from the low Belgian hills around Tongres, who formed its earliest garrison, as they faced another winter on the windiest corner of the Empire.

The official view—the academic view at least—is succinctly expressed by Professor Birley in the Ministry of Works guide to Housesteads:

> The site is one of considerable tactical strength... but here, as in most cases, it was for its strategic value, at a meeting point of roads and guarding one of the few practical lines for advance into the northern wastes, that the Romans seem to have selected it....

It appears desirable to question these assertions. Was the site really of "considerable tactical strength"? Housesteads, it is true, has its northern face safeguarded by the beginnings of the Housesteads Crags. To generations of enquirers the sight of this not very horrendous drop has proved sufficient. But the site, militarily, is in fact weak on its western side where it is approached over virtually level ground, weak on its southern side where it runs down a diminishing slope, and weak to the east where it runs into the easy meadow of the Knag Burn.

The underlying strength of the Roman infantry camp seldom depended, however, upon topographical advantage. Essentially it was a base camp; it was not in reality tactical at all except in the most limited sense of position. Its tactical quality lay fundamentally in the mobility of its garrison, the excellence of its weapons, the superiority of its training and discipline. No more than a hundred other camps in Britain was Housesteads selected for the strength of its position.

Was it then selected for "its strategic value" in relation to a meeting point of roads? Was there, in fact, a meeting place of roads at all? The nearest highway to the north was Dere Street, twelve miles away across the North Tyne valley. There may have been a track north from Chesters fort but that was the province of the Chesters garrison. There was a drove road north through Busy Gap but it was not established until late medieval times. The Ordnance Survey map shows the Military Way doubling up in a hairpin bend to the Knag Burn gateway, but the Knag Burn gateway was not cut through the Wall until the fourth century, two hundred years or so after Housesteads was built. A service road indeed crossed the Vallum below Housesteads' south gate but it stopped at the gate. The ramp from the north gate led down to the valley bottom but one half of the northern gate, the most imposing of the four gates of Housesteads, was blocked before Housesteads was finished, before even, as Richmond says, "the arrangements for hanging the doors were complete".

One of the difficulties of the academic approach to Roman fortification is an observable tendency to evaluate it in terms of the medieval castle. The type castles of the Middle Ages—Ludlow or Stirling or Edinburgh—were built because the ground fell from the base of their walls so steeply at most points that an enemy was desperately placed for the attack. Castles like Caernarvon and Pembroke and Leeds in Kent were built to exploit the utmost advantages of a water barrier. The most valued site for a medieval castle was one which had only a single relatively easy approach. Traditionally this approach was covered by the strongest element of the fortifications.

Housesteads had three easy routes of approach and no "strongest element". It was not built for siege but for sortie, and it could in effect have been built anywhere. There was no reason, for example, why the comparatively level ground to the west towards MC 37 should not have been used. The water problem might possibly have been more acute there but in any event it proved necessary to collect water from roofs and turret tops where it *was* built. It might, on the other hand, have been built on the not impossible slopes of the Knag Burn Gap itself with the burn in a culvert against its eastern wall—which would at least have solved the water problem permanently. It might, in fact, have been built at a different point of the Wall altogether. A mile or two would have made little difference to the interlocking system of time and distance in support that is the basic military feature of the Wall.

That it "dominates" the Knag Burn Gap is wholly immaterial. There were six major gaps on the line of the Great Whin Sill and a dozen lesser ones, and all of them provided "lines for advance into the northern wastes" and—equally—lines for invasion to the south.

But name, site, strategies are here parts only of a greater whole. By any title Housesteads as it was built is magnificent. From the low ground of the northern approach route past Broomlee Lough it must have imposed itself monstrously across the southern skyline. Four great towers lifted above the line of the Wall, ten more rose to the south of it. The crenellations of three of these at least were visible because of the lie of the ground. The wide double gateway—with its single gate—opened to the north down the sloping ramp that ran athwart the beginning of the Crags. To the tribesmen—the Selgovae, the Maeatae, the Caledones and, in due course, the Picts—it must have stood like a bar against the roadway to the south.

Housesteads is six hundred and ten feet long, three hundred and twenty-seven feet wide, and its walls enclose five acres. This is the bald statistical approach; there is much more to it than that. Its north gate is still enormous and threatening. The heavy foundation blocks that its builders had to use because of the line they chose are grey and weathered as the Crags themselves.

From the hollow of the Knag Burn it is approached by way of the newly-restored sector of the Wall across the Gap. The fourth century gateway, discovered originally by Clayton in 1856, has been carefully reconstructed. The culvert by which the burn underran the Wall has been rebuilt following Clayton's slightly suspect repair. The Wall itself, largely re-piled by Clayton's men, has been consolidated up the slope to the Housesteads rampart. It looks aggressively new now but it will weather.

The fort is reached at the botched-up junction of the north-east corner. One of the rewarding things about this site is that the layman can here see for himself the anomalies of its origins, can trace the indecisions, the alterations of the plans.

Just past the western guardroom of the gate, for example, there is one of the capacious stone cisterns that they were forced to use to supplement the water supply. Just beyond the cistern is the substructure of the demolished turret 36b of the original plan, carefully extricated now from the tangle of masonry around it and consolidated. Down the *via principalis* towards the south gate the granaries are on the right-hand side. Below them are the wide ruins of the *principia*—not Hadrian's *principia* but the rebuilt headquarters of Severus' time—still rising out of the first of the three great disasters of the Wall, its boldly planned interior courts clear, its offices, its *sacellum* (the chapel of the standards) easily identifiable. Below the *principia* is the house of the commandant, little enough of it above ground now but still in process of excavation, and behind it is the hospital. The barracks lie east and west of the great central group, long ranges of buildings to hold a thousand men.

Silver in the green of the upland turf, Housesteads is the exemplar of the forts of Britain. All forts were built to a standard pattern, "Roman Fort, Infantry for the Use of, Mark I". All derived ultimately from the marching camp. It is an article of academic faith that all Roman detachments on the march dug themselves in at nightfall. Obedient to this standardised scheme, they enclosed the formal lay-out of their tents in formal earthen walls so that every man, however newly joined, wherever in the Empire he came from, knew where to go in the emergency of a night attack, knew where his duty lay. There is a strong element of truth in the belief but like others it goes too far. Three hundred years of marching and counter-marching would have made the soil of the small Province of Britain a palimpsest of military dispositions. Beyond question in hostile country detachments entrenched—the line of Agricola's camps stretching north from the Strath Mor is the classic example of the use in Britain—but not even the relentless eye of the aerial camera has discovered earthworks enough for the countless nights of the legions.

Here at Housesteads the marching camp is translated into stone, and in the museum, small but rich, there is a model to show how it stood in the eye of the British weather, a model complete down to the splendid latrine in the south-east corner with its waterborne sanitation—even if this was not often more than a scouring out in times of heavy rain.

Below the walls and to the eastward was the *vicus*.

It has been claimed that the Housesteads *vicus* was the largest on the Wall. The matter has still to be put to the proof of excavation but much has already been examined, much has been planned, and much is visible in a dry summer from the air. There was to start with a large building, perhaps a *mansio*, by the south gate. There were taverns and most certainly brothels. There were the homes of the common law wives of the soldiery before the adjustment of the marriage laws. There were narrow shops and work buildings, and homes for the farmers who farmed, probably from the very beginning, the southward-facing slopes of the hill. Across the Knag Burn there was a bath house, possibly as large as Chesters but desperately robbed. It was fed by a spring carefully cased in Roman masonry with an apsidal end that must have been primarily a sacred fountain. Over the valley there were temples: a Mithraeum half underground from which was recovered the famous relief of the arising god illuminated by light from behind, which has its lit place in the museum at Newcastle; a temple to Mars Thincsus, with its attendant Germanic godlings; a shrine to the Mother goddesses; and another shrine to a more esoteric cult, the worship of the three strange, cloaked Celtic deities whose sculpture is one of the treasures of the museum.

By the third century Housesteads *vicus* was a small but prosperous town, having apparently a measure of self-government—a parasite town perhaps, dependent basically upon the pay of the thousand men of the garrison, but still a major centre of civilisation in the bleak simplicities of the frontier.

The departure point from Housesteads is by way of the less-botched-up job of the north-west corner. The Wall leads swiftly to the much photographed pine tree spinney. It achieves at once another place in the inevitabilities of academic disputation. The National Trust turfs the surface of its share of the Wall—skilfully cleared here from the tumble of the centuries. The Ministry of Works consolidates its share with mortar. Opinion is splendidly and rancorously divided—but under the trees after rain the Wall has sometimes a notable surface of mud. Perhaps it does not matter. It leads at least to milecastle 37—Housesteads milecastle.

Like both the fort and the Wall, Housesteads milecastle itself inspires controversy. It was built by II Augusta. When John Clayton cleared it in 1853 he found a fragment of the customary gateway tablet which acknowledged Aulus Platorius Nepos as governor. Normally it is held that gateway tablets record the completion of work—but the north wall of milecastle 37 was certainly built after the decision to build the Narrow Wall was taken. From the gateway proper, palpably constructed to Broad Wall standards, it tapers east and west until it reaches the junction with the curtain wall at approximately the narrow gauge. The tapering is unique, 37 otherwise is a normal "Wall, milecastle, Mark Ia". It follows the regimental plan of the Second Legion. It measured internally forty-nine feet six inches by fifty-seven feet six inches; it lay lengthwise along the Wall. Its own walls were nine feet thick, its southern corners were rounded, its northern corners were built into the Wall at right angles, and it had the customary gates—monumental, arched over, ten feet wide and fifteen feet high, capable of handling not merely infantrymen but cavalry and any type of military vehicle known to the Romans.

The first problem that arises is the simple one of where the traffic went.

The Crags may have altered a little since Roman times, they

MAP OF
HADRIAN'S WALL

Beginning at Wallsend on the Tyne, Hadrian's Wall runs from the North Sea to the Solway Firth. Milecastle 80, later superseded by the great fort at Bowness, was its western end. The Wall proper, with Ditch and Vallum, was, however, a part only of the Roman frontier system. This section of the map indicates the strength of the northern holding pattern, with forts at Dalswinton, Carzield, Fairholm and Burnswark. Other forts of the Agricolan pacification held down the hill country. In the last days of Trajan or early in Hadrian's reign the so-called outpost forts, Birrens among them, were added (Chapter 10). South of the Wall a line of fortlets formed a refused left flank for 40 miles down the coast to St. Abbs Head, reinforced by four forts of which the first—Beckfoot—is here shown. The sites of all these forts, together with the three main components of the Wall, have been identified. The general lines of the interconnecting roads are shown schematically.

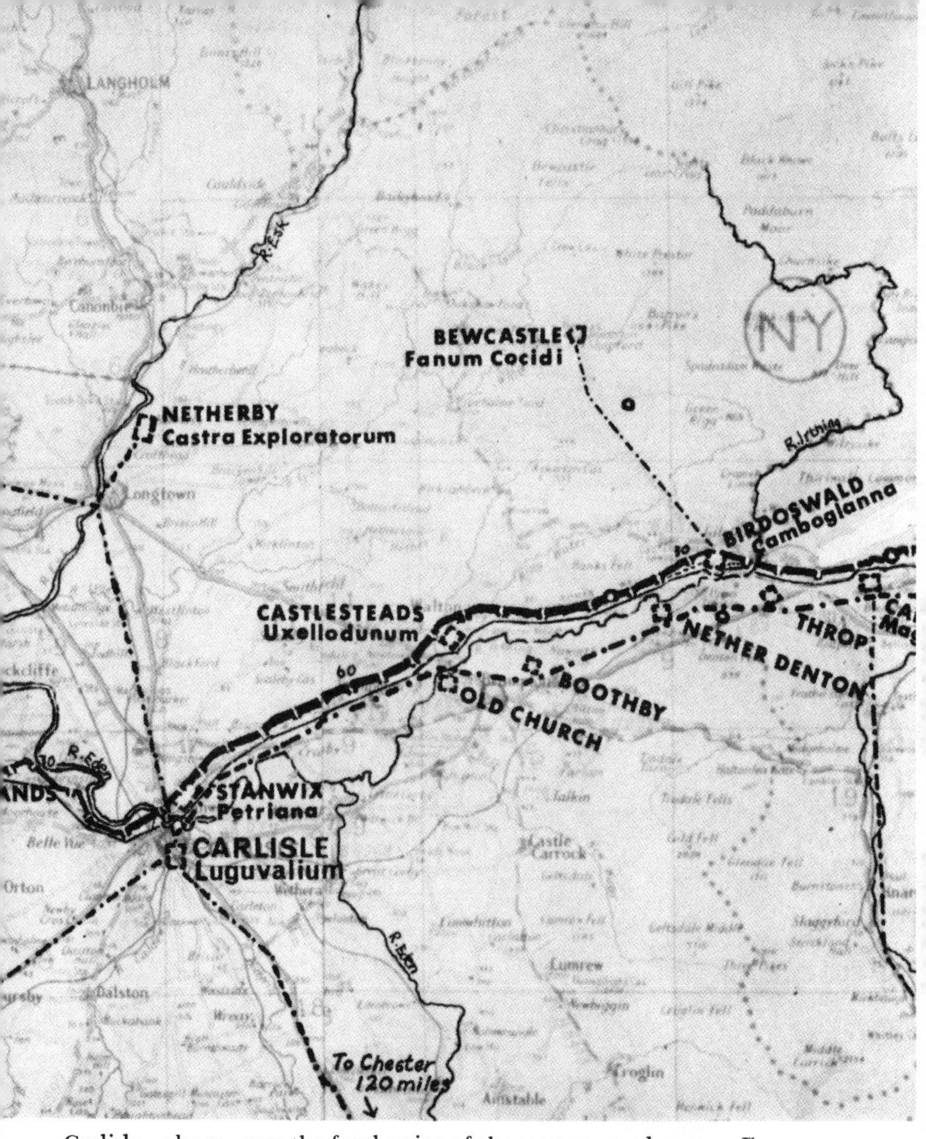

Carlisle—above—was the focal point of the western road system. From its Agricolan fort roads ran north to Scotland, east to Corbridge, south-east to York and south to Chester. The strength of the holding system based on the northern road determined here the character of the Wall. From Birdoswald above the superb gorge of the Irthing its line is militarily weak and, past the Eden, militarily irrational. It was planned as Turf Wall and subsequently rebuilt in stone. Little remains above the surface but it can be traced by Ditch and Vallum. The dauntless little fortress church of Burgh-by-Sands, Lanercost Priory on the Irthing, and a host of lesser structures are built of its splendid ashlar. Birdoswald, with magnificent stretches of Wall on either side and the tremendous Irthing bridgehead, is immensely important. Here alone the Turf Wall survives, shown as a dotted line on the map. Across the Irthing behind Gilsland village Milecastle 48 is the finest of the surviving gateway fortlets of the First Plan.

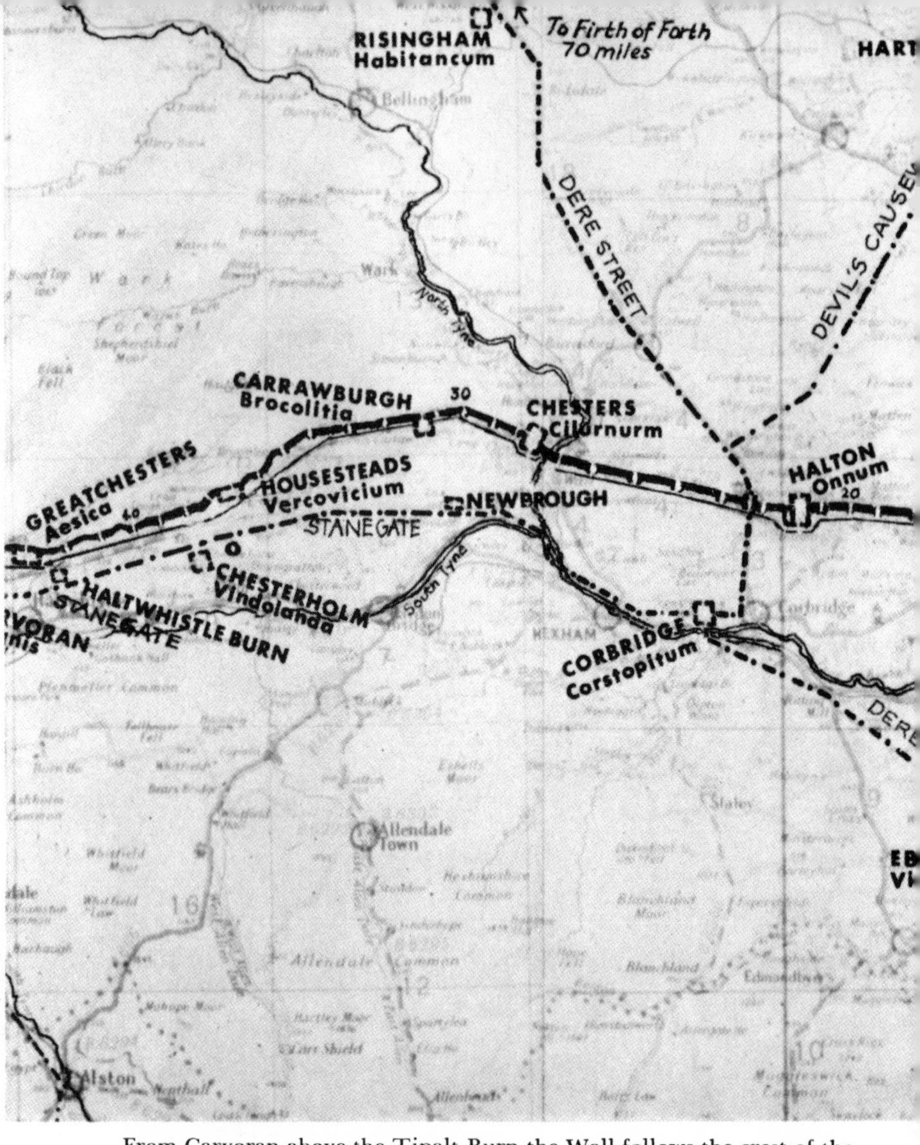

From Carvoran above the Tipalt Burn the Wall follows the crest of the Great Whin Sill. Past the ruin of the Greenhead quarries it soars over the 1,200-foot peak of Winshields Crag. This is the walker's Wall, rough, sometimes difficult, always splendid. Four minor roads cross it. At Greatchesters the first of the two great infantry forts of the central sector awaits recovery. Housesteads, the second, is magnificent. Headquarters buildings, granaries, barracks, walls and gates are intelligently preserved. From the Knag Burn crossing the Wall lifts over Sewingshields Crag and, past Carrawbrough with its Mithraeum, turns south-east at Limestone Corner. For four centuries Milecastle 30 was the north-west bastion of Rome. Chesters, with its superb bridge structure, is the first of the five great cavalry forts of the west. Built athwart the Wall at the change to the Second Plan, its splendid bath house and its museum are essential to any comprehension of the frontier. Chesterholm typifies the support forts.

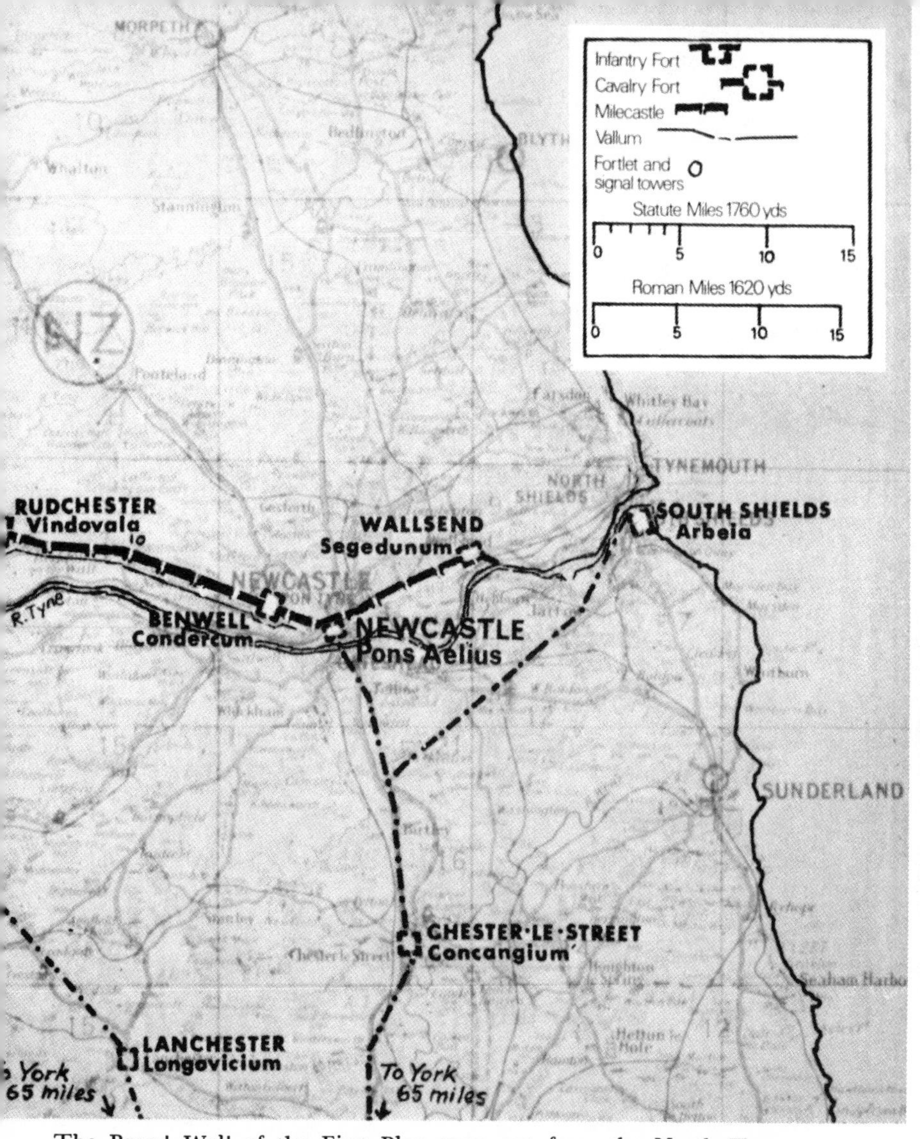

The Broad Wall of the First Plan runs east from the North Tyne bridge. It was largely demolished to make the Military Road but enough remains beyond Chesters and again at Heddon-on-the-Wall to show its strength. Miles of Ditch and Vallum survive, magnificent on either side of the Road. Haltonchesters, where Agricola's eastern road —Dere Street—crosses the Wall, Rudchester and Condercum, with its temple and Vallum crossing, were cavalry forts of the Second Plan. On the Tyne to the south Corstopitum—at Corbridge—successively bridgehead fort, cavalry base and munitions factory—has been elaborately excavated. Hexham Abbey "unequalled for size and magnificence north of the Alps" and Corbridge Church were built of its robbing. Little remains in Newcastle's central sector, but the bridge of Pons Aelius survived in part for close on 2,000 years. Little also remains at Wallsend, but South Shields, entrepot and harbour defence at the river mouth, was linked to the Wall by road.

cannot have altered much. Infantry in broken formation might have passed down that battered slope. Nothing else could have done so.

The second problem, as always along the central sector, is: when was it built? Certainly the gates were built in Nepos' day. Equally certainly the north wall was not. It appears reasonable to assume that MC 37 stood incomplete for at least as long as Housesteads stood independent.

The Wall moves on to Cuddy's Gap. Disregarding the speculative attribution of the name to St. Cuthbert (who was popular over these parts), Cuddy's Gap raises automatically the question of the rigidity of the Roman Military Mind. Why was milecastle 37 not built here? The Gap is wide enough, the slope in front of it is possible even to wheeled traffic. Infantry and cavalry could negotiate it with ease.

One major military objection is of course obvious. The milecastle could have been commanded from the high ground on either side in the event of any break across the Wall. But two Roman miles farther along the line, MC 39—Castle Nick—was built in the face of precisely those objections. Snugly ensconced in one of the narrowest of all the gaps, the garrison of MC 39 would have been at the mercy of a boy of twelve with an accurate stone-throwing arm.

The positioning of the milecastles of the central sector is patently not determined at any point by tactical consideration but at all points by the rigidity of a set plan. One milecastle, one mile.

From Cuddy's Gap the Wall rises steeply over the Crag past the favourite camera position for the well-known Great-Wall-of-China effect. The miles here are beginning to be "on end". Almost immediately it reaches the formidable slope into Rapishaw Gap. Through the bottom here an old limestone road leads easily across the Sill and down to the ancient kiln in the valley. The platform of the kiln is perhaps the best of all the vantage points from which to see the Wall as the Picts saw it, black and ominous, lifting from crest to crest, arrogant still—and lonely.

Out of Rapishaw it climbs steeply again to the Hotbank Crags. The turret at the summit stood here at a height of a thousand and fifty feet. Then and now it commands one of the greatest of all the views of the Wall, the superb stretch of the Sill as far as Winshields with the Crag Lough under the rock face of Highshield flashing on a windy afternoon like summer lightning.

Milecastle 38 stands squarely in the low ground of Milking Gap almost opposite Hotbank Farm. You can see the bones of it in the sloping meadow. "Tactically" it blocked the Gap—but not by design. Its site, like the others, was determined by the distance rule. Milking Gap was covered by a section of Fighting Ditch dug across the low ground before the cancellation from a point beyond the Hotbank Farm to the water of the Lough. Above the water the Wall exists only as tumbled ashlar but from the edge one looks down vertically on the backs of the swans who possess that remote and solitary lake, and the widgeon, the mallard and the teal who share its lonely beauty.

Normally even over the Crags the Wall flows with the contour of the ground. The size of the ashlar with minor adjustments of mortar makes possible a smooth and easy construction in deep accord with the nature of the country. At the west end of Highshield Crag beyond the lough, however, and at an increasing succession of points along the heights the angle of the gradients made it necessary to step the construction. Building began at the bottom of these steeper notches in the crest. From the bottom layers, anchored wherever possible to the solid rock, the builders worked up horizontally—core, facing stone and flags alike rising in a giant stair, while the crenellations necessary to protect the patrols must have presented curious problems.

From the stepped area the Wall line lifts sharply over a ridge that is almost a knife edge and drops on Castle Nick. Milecastle 39 was another of Clayton's excavations. It is a Type 2 construction, almost certainly erected by the Second Legion and, as was said earlier, it is so tucked between the slopes of the narrow notch that its defences south of the Wall are illusory.

Above the Peel Crags the Wall is solid again until at the end of the height it bends sharply south in a deep re-entrant—a U-shaped bend, the side walls of which in military terms covered the Gap from east and west. It is traditionally believed that the re-entrant was planned for the purpose; in fact it appears to have been dictated primarily by the uncompromising character of the steep Peel slope. It would have been difficult to build it in any other way, and the western side appears to do no more than seek the quickest possible way back to the general line of the Wall.

Peel Gap has a special importance for the motorist. For the first time for six miles a road crosses the Wall. Turning north from the Military Road at "The Twice Brewed" crossroads, it bends after a quarter of a mile sharply to the left on to the Military Way, holds the Way for a couple of hundred yards and turns right again to cross the line of the Wall at right angles.

Across the Wall the Northumberland National Park authorities have established a car park—perhaps the most discreet car park in the north of England. Screened by fir trees, well equipped, entirely unobtrusive, it is a model for its kind. It is also a perfect starting point east and west for the finest stretches of the high Wall.

For almost half a mile in this area the work was destroyed and rebuilt in Roman times. The turrets, which stood equidistant either side of the Gap, were torn down and the recesses in the Wall filled in, but the Fighting Ditch ran firmly here from the end of the Peel re-entrant up the bold shoulder of Winshields. It ends at MC 40, a third of a mile from the summit, and Winshields is halfway across the Wall, halfway across England, and one thousand two hundred and fifty feet up in the windy sky.

From Winshields on a fine transparent day you can see the Cheviots and the Scottish border in the north-east, you can see clear into Scotland to the north-west, to the west you can see Criffell fifty miles away and the blue water of the Solway Firth between, to the south-west Skiddaw, and to the south the vast prospect of the Tyne valley and the fells beyond.

The Wall runs downhill now, its height diminishing past each of the little gaps—Lodhams Slack and Bogle Hole, Caw Gap (where the road from Peel, curving west to join the road from Edges Green, crosses the Wall again to rejoin the Military Road at the standing stones of "The Mare and Foal"), Bloody Gap and Thorny Doors—until at Cawfields milecastle it comes to tragedy.

A few score feet from Cawfields Gap it ends, cleanly and brutally, as if cut by an axe at the lip of Cawfields quarry.

There is no point here in attempting to retell the lamentable saga of the Wall quarries. The line is safe now. The damage done cannot be repaired; but at least from Cawfields quarry back to Thorny Doors the Wall is now in course of permanent consolidation and the slow patient process of grouting and restoration at the careful hand of the Ministry of Works is a partial recompense for grievous disaster.

Past Cawfields quarry the Wall crosses the Haltwhistle Burn. There was a mill here almost at the point where the road from Haltwhistle cut through the Wall. It is lost now under quarry refuse, but this was the second of the known mills of the Wall. Half a mile beyond it lies Greatchesters.

The Amiens skillet calls it "Esica". So does the Ravenna list. The *Notitia* calls it "Aesica". Latter-day England christened it Greatchesters, and the name holds—not because it is "greater" than the other Chesters but because its walls in that remoteness stood longer perhaps and taller than those more conveniently robbed. As late as 1724 Alexander Gordon described the structure as standing "thirteen feet high". Farm buildings, field walls have robbed it since, but its outline is still clear even to the lay eye—a wide oblong, running east and west, four hundred and nineteen feet by three hundred and fifty-five. It enclosed almost exactly three acres. Until 1925 it was accepted as a part of the main scheme of the Wall.

In that year Simpson chose the site for the first excavation by the Durham University Excavation Committee. The results were remarkable. Earlier excavations had wholly failed to discover the essential significance of the site. Greatchesters was in fact built *behind* the Broad Foundation—behind, that is, the planned line of the Wall. As at Housesteads, an element of the fortification of the Wall was destroyed in the process—milecastle 43, already partly erected in accordance with the First Plan. Once more the plan itself was ignored, the possibility of an eventual conjunction with the Wall entirely disregarded.

At Housesteads it will be remembered that the fort wall was built north of the line; on the solid rock of the crags this was expensive but practicable. Here at Greatchesters to have built north of the Broad Foundation would have meant building on the berm between the foundation and the Fighting Ditch, and therefore on unstable ground. The substitute line selected by the fort's engineers was immediately behind the Broad Foundation and ran directly through the east and west walls of the milecastle which was levelled to take it.

Notable conflicts of opinion derive from this. Richmond, in the eleventh edition of the *Handbook,* says positively:

> The most curious part of the defences is the north-west angle, excavated partly in 1894 and partly in 1925. The angle of the fort is rounded, which suggests at first sight that the fort was built independently of the Wall; but the angle-tower has been planned with a projection so as to bond with the Wall, which is here the Narrow Wall and clearly contemporary with the fort as it stands.

Professor Richmond's dismissal of the possibility of "independence" is categorical. Yet, to defend it, it is necessary to accept a Wall junction even more unsatisfactory than the two at Housesteads. The *Handbook*'s diagram of Greatchesters shows a relatively smooth and "tidy" solution of a difficult problem employing, apparently, the original standard turret.

The diagram in Birley's *Research on Hadrian's Wall*—derived from M. R. Hull's original drawings in the report of the 1925 excavations published in *Archaeologia Aeliana*—shows a wholly different solution. The oblong tower drawn in this is clearly not the normal tower of a standard fort. It is wholly out of alignment with the curve of the fort wall and overlaps it. It is equally out of alignment with the face of the running wall. It is clumsy in its actual jointure in the angle between the curve and the back of the main Wall and, unless its own north wall was remarkably extended, out of touch with the front face of the Wall as built. It bears, in fact, every possible indication of botched-up adjustment at a substantially later date than the building of the fort.

Both solutions cannot be correct.

The ditch system of the fort reinforces this doubt. To the west there are four ditches. The first of these—the one nearest the fort wall—was dug in a curve through the Broad Foundation into the original Fighting Ditch of the First Plan. A subsidiary ditch to the north was cut partly along the berm and partly where the Broad Foundation had stood and ran on in a matching curve at the north-west corner. The outer three of the four western ditches had to have their ends partly filled in to take the foundations of the Narrow Wall when it came, and the first ditch had to be altogether bridged across. Richmond's contention that the ditches of the fort were dug after the change from Broad Wall to Narrow but before the walls of the fort were constructed appears to be strangely outside logic. Everything about the north-west corner of Greatchesters suggests that, as at Housesteads, it was built in the certainty that the Broad Wall was abandoned, in the belief that the fort would have to stand alone, and before the necessity for a junction with the Narrow Wall was considered.

The plurality of ditches, unique to Greatchesters, is a complication not yet adequately explained, though Dr. Swinbank in the course of the Swinbank-Paul investigation of the siting of forts suggests that the original intention may have been to build a larger fort upon the site.

Little of all this is apparent above the surface. Greatchesters for the most part has sunk back into the green of its pastures, and the black-faced sheep are its custodians.

The gap here is the widest on the central Wall. Measured by the Fighting Ditch, always the basic indication of easy approach from the north, it is a mile and a quarter in width. Strangely it is here, as at Limestone Corner, that the evidence of the decision to abandon the Fighting Ditch is most clearly discernible. On Cockmount Hill, half a mile to the west of the fort, the ditch is dug to barely half its depth and the glacis was never raked. A third of a mile farther along at Allolee, though even in Roman times the approach patently demanded a ditch, it was not dug at all!

At MC 44 begins the last stretch of the Great Whin Sill, the saw-toothed escarpment that has been called since time out of mind The Nine Nicks of Thirlwall. Sharp, steep notches in the crest, the Nicks make hard going for the walker. Yet they are astonishingly exhilarating. The Wall here seems to leap, almost to fly, from height to height and the view to widen. To the north the valley of the Irthing runs up into the Wark Forest. To the north-west the towers of Spadeadam stand against the skyline. To the south the Tyne drops strongly from the fells. Even this high remoteness has not, however, been protection enough.

Just beyond MC 45 is the second of the disasters of the quarries. Above Walltown Farm a quarter of a mile of the Wall has disappeared for all time.

Beyond the shambles a fine sector leads to turret 45a, which offers a puzzle of its own. It was built before the Wall. It has no bonding wings and it must clearly have existed first as an independent signal station between the Stanegate forts and the North in a harsh and hazardous isolation.

Turret 45b has disappeared. With the Wall, with the last of the Nine Nicks themselves, it has vanished altogether in the final disaster of the Greenhead quarries. Once more it is perhaps unnecessary to revive the backgrounds of that bitter and long-continued feud. Encroachment at least is checked today—barely checked—but above the quarry the Wall ends, as it ended at Haltwhistle, in a high precarious solution of continuity.

Beyond the quarry floor it runs again as a grassy bank, straight and level for a quarter of a mile—the road to Old Shield crosses the start of it and Carvoran lies detached below it. At the end of the level it plunges magnificently down the straight slope to the Tipalt Burn. There must have been a bridge across the burn when the Wall was garrisoned, but it has gone now, gone perhaps with the stones of the Wall into the keep of Thirlwall Castle which still hangs dangerously above the cottages of the Tipalt crossing, wholly and economically built of Roman ashlar.

Downstream from it the Wall climbs across the Gilsland road and cuts, its ditch deeper here than almost anywhere along the line, cleanly across the watershed of England. To the west of this the rivers flow into the Irish Sea.

The first of these, the steep and brawling Poltross Burn, the boundary between Cumberland and Westmorland, is flanked by what is probably the best preserved of the milecastles of the entire work. Its twin barrack buildings, built up a singular slope, have been consolidated and explain themselves. Part of a flight of steps to the patrol walk remains. Extrapolation of their angle indicates that the Wall was here almost fifteen feet high.

Across the railway line the Wall appears once more and runs high to the Denton road and beyond it again, in an admirably consolidated stretch, to the Willowford bridge. All this sector is

Type B construction, and Type B presents another of the academic connundrums of the Wall.

Birley describes it as "Standard B construction associable with the Sixth Legion". Briefly, it consists of three, and in some cases four, courses of ashlar on the normal Broad Foundation with Narrow Wall superimposed upon it and the north face flush with the original stone-work. The orthodox suggestion is that this was an idiosyncrasy of the work of the Sixth Legion.

It seems an unnecessary elaboration. The simplest reading is that here the Sixth began working eastward from the Willowford bridgehead to build Broad Wall in accordance with the instructions of the First Plan, that they had reached a height of four courses when the plan was countermanded, and that the Twentieth Legion, coming after it, levelled the core where it was essential and built Narrow Wall above the existing work.

The ditch supplies the deep road to Willowford Farm, and at the edge of the farmyard, ditch, Wall and Vallum together plunge arrow-straight down the steep slope to the Irthing meadows. There were here, as at Chesters, two bridges. The earliest work carried the Wall itself on low round arches across the stony gully which formed the river bed eighteen hundred years ago. Little of it survives: the debated evidence of a tower at the end of the Broad Foundation, a mass of masonry identified as the first abutment and, again as at Chesters, portions of an original pier in the first pier of the later bridge.

This second bridge seems to have followed basically the pattern of Chesters. It was wide, designed to carry the Military Way, and consisted of a timber decking on broad piers. It too was guarded by a tower abutting against the Narrow Wall, and it too had a mill.

What remains of the piers and of the western abutment is lost now under the river meadow. The Irthing has retreated from it, cutting back the face of Harrow's Scar. No indication of the manner in which it climbed the Scar exists, but looking down from milecastle 49 on the summit, the western end of the central sector is as clear-drawn today as it was in the time of Severus—the strong and purposeful end of one of the major achievements of Roman military engineering.

8

Western Anomalies

West of the Willowford the Wall is anomalous. In the proper sense of that abused word it deviates from the rules, and for its deviations there are still no persuasive explanations.

Logic ends at the Irthing bridgehead.

For the fifty miles of the Wall from the Tyne crossing the architects of the First Plan sought every military advantage in a sometimes unhelpful terrain. For the fifteen miles from the Coesike they won, boldly and resolutely, every particular degree of military strength from the precipitous escarpment of the Great Whin Sill. For the five miles west of the bridgehead they planned the Wall along the crest of another escarpment—but the escarpment faced the wrong way, south!

For the first fifty miles they planned a strong stone wall, ten feet wide, twenty-one feet high, covered by a wide, deep fighting ditch. For the last thirty miles they planned a twelve-foot wall of turf with a wooden parapet.

For the first fifty miles they surveyed the line to ensure that the men on the patrol walk had the best possible view to the north. Except at isolated points they achieved their purpose. But one Roman mile from the bridgehead at Willowford, Nanwick Hill blocks out the north, a scant mile later Allieshaw Rigg masks the valley of the King Water. Between Craggle Hill and the Eden flats an enemy could have approached the Turf Wall unseen at four critical points.

Were the surveyors forced by the intransigencies of the terrain to accept reluctantly the defective Birdoswald-Walton line? It seems, to put it mildly, improbable; they had at least two clear options.

A powerful defensive wall could have been schemed along the high ground to the south of the Irthing Gorge. Changing course at the fort at Throp—laid down either just before the Wall or simultaenously with it and possibly with such an option in view—the alternative line would have linked the Stanegate forts, both those of the original Agricolan line and those contemporary with Throp, would have reached the plain approximately at Warwick bridge and would have crossed it thereafter largely screened by the marshes of the Irthing.

A strong defensive line could alternatively have been secured less than a mile north of the position actually selected by utilising the high ground of the south bank of the King Water. It would have run from Birdoswald along Nanwick Hill and the north of Allieshaw Rigg, crossed the ridges between the King Water and the Cambeck, and found a better track down the diminishing eastern slope to the north plain of the Eden.

Both options were rejected. The common factor is clearly that along this sector the planners no longer thought in terms of a serious threat from the north. The Wall as built was a military mess, it is inconceivable that it was set up to face the same dangers as the central and the eastern sectors.

Physically it was a lesser wall. Its turrets, it is true, were built of stone, though without wing walls to bond into the running wall when it came. Its milecastles, on the other hand, were built of turf, approximately of the same overall dimensions as those of the Stone Wall but with their interior accommodation so severely reduced that they were presumably planned for smaller garrisons. Their gates were set in timber frameworks and the gateways were surmounted by timber towers. The Wall itself when it linked them was twenty feet thick at the base but sloped—steeply on the north, less so at the south—to a patrol walk barely five feet wide, allowing for a parapet of timber, and only twelve feet high. It had, broadly speaking, the same Fighting Ditch but the berm between ditch and wall was barely six feet wide.

It is demonstrably, then, weaker than the Stone Wall, not only because of its site and because of its blindness to the north, but because of its construction. Why?

There are four traditional explanations. None of them hold water. The first is that the Wall was built of turf because the lime outcrops of the area cease at the Red Rock Fault. The line of the Fault is marked carefully on the Ordnance Survey map just to the west of Lannercost Priory in tacit confirmation of this claim. To accept it is to accept the assumption that the transport system of the Roman army in Britain was not competent to provide for the limited requirement of lime—a few tons a day at most—for bonding a wall of stone. But the first five miles of the sector are inside the lime area and as far as Burtholme Beck lime for bonding was as available as at any point across Britain. From Burtholme Beck to the Eden the distance is barely twelve Roman miles. It is absurd to assume that the absence of lime was responsible for the decision to build in turf.

There was, in any event, the alternative of clay bonding at least for the core of the wall. It was used in places east of the North Tyne and could have served, if necessary, here.

The second explanation is that the Turf Wall was due to the absence of suitable stone. Again this is a nonsense. There are well-known—and inscribed—quarries along the sector, but the simplest answer is that when the decision was taken to build the Narrow Wall—a decision which appears to have been taken simultaneously both across the central sector and here—it was promptly built as far as the Burtholme Beck, and when in due course the later decision was made to build the nine-foot wide Intermediate Wall, that too was duly built—in stone, *and* lime bonded!

The third explanation, put forward perhaps with less assurance, concerns cost. Cost in relation to the Wall is not a factor of finance but a factor of man-hours. Certainly the Turf Wall saved man-hours. No one appears yet to have worked out a precise figure for the difference in constructional time between the quarrying of ashlar and the construction of a mortared stone wall and the digging of turves, their stacking and the assembly and erection of the necessary timber structures. The Turf Wall itself may well have been the product of unskilled labour, of auxiliaries or even of a local corvée rather than the work of the skilled legionaries, but even this is, in the light of Roman military custom, improbable. In the apparent absence of centurial stones from the Turf Wall there seems to be small way of telling. The only point of agreement is that the work was certainly not beyond the compass of lower grade constructors.

The final explanation is that of speed. Unquestionably, as the man-hour comparison suggests, the Turf Wall could have been built at higher speed in emergency than could its counterpart in stone. But was there an emergency? Was speed in fact necessary? Since the evidence argued in the previous chapter suggests quite definitely that the central sector was left without its running wall for more than eight years from the inception of the First Plan, speed, even if Hadrian himself had expressed his views on the subject, appears to be irrelevant.

No explanation, on the other hand, is offered for the suggested difference between the estimates of the probability of attack in this western sector and the remainder of the Wall. Possibly this is because the question has not presented itself in this shape before. It has, on the contrary, frequently been asserted that the danger of attack was graver here and that the "outpost forts" to the north were built in recognition of that fact. The matter will be argued subsequently. It is sufficient here to say that the sector from the Irthing to the Solway had to the north of it a relatively Romanised population—the northernmost of the Brigantes—and a pattern of holding garrisons which had no parallel elsewhere on the Wall. It appears to have been accepted as an effective shock-absorber in the event of attack. The strength of the Wall defences as a consequence was less important.

In any attempt to adjust ideas to reality the chronology of construction is of the utmost importance. It is presented in this sector with a greater clarity perhaps than anywhere along the line of the Wall.

It begins before the Romans. Immediately to the south of what subsequently became the south gate of the fort of Birdoswald was an Iron Age promontory fort, utilising the headland—larger no doubt in that day—that projects into the Irthing Gorge. North of the Harrow's Scar milecastle were two major earthworks.

The Roman occupation began substantially before the Wall. Inside the promontory fort there is a small rectangular Roman post, not itself a signal tower, but since it occupies a central position in the network of signal towers that connect the high ground to the north from Robin Hood's Butt, the relay point at Pike Hill, the Mains Rigg signal tower to the south of the

Irthing and turret 45a (which was built originally as a signal tower) and the forts which they serve, it appears to have exercised a central function in relation to them. Traces of the walls both of the Roman post and of the promontory fort are still visible. Pottery of the early years of the second century has been found in relation to the post but no definite date has yet been established save that it is pre-Wall.

Presumably in the normal order of construction the milecastles and the turrets came next. The existing milecastle at Harrow's Scar belongs of course to the period of the Stone Wall. Excavation has revealed below it, however, the outline of the milecastle of the Turf Wall and fragments of its structure, with the post holes of its gates. There is nothing to indicate the date of the building of the running Turf Wall. It joined its structures, and it is difficult to be more certain than that. Whether there was a gap in time here, as in the centre, it is impossible to say. Whether the gradient was able to take it or whether a palisade substitute was provided up Harrow's Scar is equally unknown. It ran a little south of west along the broad plateau of the ridge to turret 49a, altered course a few degrees to the south to MC 50 and thereafter ran west-south-west in general terms to the Cambeck. It was ditched to the north, and it can be traced today either by the ditch or by the low segments of the Wall that still show above the meadow grass.

With the Second Plan the same abrupt change was forced upon it as in the east. A cavalry fort was flung across the line immediately opposite the rampart of the Iron Age fort. Precisely as with the cavalry forts of the east, a third of it projected beyond the line of the Turf Wall. The ditch was filled in to take it, the Turf Wall was levelled, and the turret that had been built independently in stone was taken out.

Birdoswald was the eastern anchor of the cavalry concept of the Second Plan on this side of Britain. It was the Camboglanna of the Romans. There are four variants of the name, of which that in the Ravenna list goes so far as to call it "Gabaglanda". Birdoswald will do, however; it has a respectable antiquity. Bainbrigg sent an account of it to Camden in 1599:

> Frome Lannercost I folowed the wall all ruinated, till I came to Burdoswald, wiche doth seame to have been some

> great towne by the great ruynes therof, the inhabitants did shew me the plaice wher the churche stode, the inscriptions ther are either worne out by the tract of tyme, or by the clownishe and rude inhabitants defaced.

Despite the clownish and the rude, Birdoswald survives. It stands today among the greatest of the forts of the Wall. Poised above the Irthing Gorge, it commands one of the incomparable views of England, not this time the beauty of the immensity of space that is the special characteristic of the upland Wall but the intimate particular beauty of a river running through English trees, enclosed in them, almost encased in them, so that the trees themselves seem to move down the Gorge like another river of green.

Its earliest garrison is unknown but it must have been one of the cavalry units of the western side, for it has the obligatory three fast exit gates north of the Wall. But its life as a cavalry fort was relatively brief; by the end of the century—possibly even before that—it was garrisoned by infantry, the First Cohort of the Tungrians. The change may indeed have taken place as early as the building of the Narrow Wall, for with the Narrow Wall is established the fifth stage in the occupational sequence. Standard Narrow Wall, eight feet wide, it was brought straight up the steep of Harrow's Scar to the milecastle, the milecastle itself was rebuilt and the Wall was carried to the fort but *not* on the line of the Turf Wall. A short distance from the milecastle it diverges to the north and joins Birdoswald at the north-east corner turret. From the north-west turret it runs on an independent line to a stone wall substitute for Turf Wall MC 50 and rejoins the line finally at MC 51. The section between Harrow's Scar and the fort is one of the best preserved in the whole line of the Wall and stands superbly above the farm track to the Scar.

Birdoswald has been excavated and filled in again, but the main walls are clear, the gateways excavated and visible. The wheel ruts on the thresholds are a poignant reminder of an ancient active life. Cleared and consolidated, the interior buildings—the rear wall of the headquarters establishment is said to stand fifteen courses high and much of the arches of the front remains—would almost certainly provide the best preserved example of garrison construction along the zone. Even in its present state it has a rare and an abiding dignity.

The enclave between the Stone Wall and the Vallum here has proved of vital importance to the study of the Wall. It will be remembered that the first theory of the antiquarians was that Hadrian built a defensive earth wall from sea to sea—the Vallum—and that this was superseded by the Stone Wall in the time of the Emperor Severus. By 1895 this theory had been largely abandoned, though recalcitrant independents still brought it up from time to time. When in that year the Turf Wall was positively identified in the Birdoswald enclave, the recalcitrants seized on it as a new proof of their theory: this was the remaining fragment of the Hadrianic work; where it was overtaken by the Stone Wall it proved only that if Hadrianic material *was* associated with turrets and milecastles of the Stone Wall, it was merely because Severus had used the same turrets and milecastles in his reconstruction. The solution to the problem was once more brilliantly provided by Simpson. In a series of meticulous excavations Turf Wall and corresponding Stone Wall milecastles, separated by the width of a field, were examined. Hadrianic material was found in the structures of Turf Wall and Narrow Stone Wall alike. Except for the original Roman signal post everything in the area was built between Hadrian's accession in 117 and his death twenty-one years later.

From milecastle 51 the single Wall runs east, straight with the road past MC 52 to Pike Hill and the signal tower twenty feet square that already stood at an angle of forty-five degrees to the line. Pike Hill had deep foundations and stood tall: one face watched Robin Hood's Butt, the tower on Gillalees; one face watched Netherby, the central member of the "outpost" forts; one face overlooked Nether Denton fort and Walltown turret; and one looked down on Boothby fort.

Beyond Pike Hill, at the roadside, turret 52a and an excellent stretch of the Wall have been cleared and consolidated by the Ministry of Works. From there on little shows, not even the clay wall section, until the famous nine-foot ten-inch pinnacle on Hare Hill is reached. But Hare Hill is beyond the road, beyond even the crossing of the road to Bewcastle. After this it is walker's Wall once more and, in absolute contrast to the central sector, there is almost nothing above the ground. The patient may explore it by way of field wall and hedgerow and the almost imperceptible rise and fall of ditched ground to the crossing of the Burtholme Beck and the beginning of the Intermediate Wall. This was nine Roman feet in width, a substantial section of the core is preserved, but beyond it there is nothing, not even ditch, and the winding roads of the lower slope cross and recross it. It must be taken on faith and the Ordnance Survey map, except occasionally where the line of the ditch shows up, positive and unmistakable. It passes Castlesteads—Uxellodunum, the one fort detached from the Wall that is included within the line of the Vallum—and descends slowly, and with an insolent disregard of the slowly diminishing high ground on either side, to the levels of the plain. It can be followed best now by the place names—Oldwall and Wallhead, Walby and Wall Knowe—to Stanwix, which was Petriana, the fortress of the *ala Augusta Gallorum Petriana bis torquata milliaria civium Romanorum*—the senior regiment of cavalry in the Province of Britain.

The *ala Petriana* had a strength of a thousand horse, the only *ala* of its size in the Province. The *Notitia,* drawn up substantially after the evacuation of Northern Britain, still calls the fort Petriana after the regiment, a notable distinction—but only the *Notitia* names it so. It stands on the high north bank of the Eden, three-quarters of a mile from Carlisle (which was Luguvalium). The westernmost of the two major Roman roads to the north passed close to its north-west corner. To house the *ala* it measured seven hundred feet from east to west, five hundred and eight feet from north to south, and covered over nine acres. It was by far the largest fort of the Wall complex.

Little is known of its structure. Not until Simpson, Richmond and Hogg carried out an intensely difficult operation in 1939 was it possible to define its shape and its relationship to the Wall. Even now its junction with the Wall line is inadequately understood, though a brief section of ditch close to its north-east angle suggests that it might have joined the Wall at right angles, as at Carrawburgh. The southern corners were rounded, with normal angle towers. In 1940 a granary in the northern section was examined but apart from this little has been positively identified. It did *not* overlap the Wall like the other cavalry forts and consequently it did not have the customary triple exit gates. It is probable that this was due again to the strength of the Roman held area to the north and to the consequent belief that speed was not as urgent as it was elsewhere. In a sense it was a strategic establishment. For that reason it was the headquarters fort for the Wall system. It held the cavalry reserve but in addition it occupied the key strategic position of the western Wall. In an hour it could bring pressure to bear as far east as the Burtholme Beck, establishing in the process a five-mile overlap with a force from Birdoswald. To the west it could reach in the same period almost to Bowness at the end of the Wall. To the north it could cover Netherby and the crossing of the Esk. The huge demilune between these three points represented its immediate strike capability. Given a day's march, it could bring great strength to bear on any situation from Housesteads in the centre to the latitude of Raeburnfoot on the north and Maryport at the south-west. It controlled, in other words, the northern plain deep into the mountains of Dumfriesshire, the whole western slope of the central spine and the entire north Cumberland plain.

Its precise relationship to the strategic northern road is not yet resolved. The line of the road is tolerably known; it is assumed that there was a triumphal arch or at least a major gateway where it passed through the Wall, but it has yet to be identified under the buildings of modern Stanwix. The Wall itself ran west to MC 66 on a high bluff above the river.

It is confidently claimed that at this point it crossed the Eden by a bridge. Camden described "mighty stones, the remaines thereof" as still existing, and in the course of dredging in 1951 Robert Hogg of the Carlisle Museum identified among the considerable quantity of worked stone blocks removed from the river bed a centurial stone carrying the name of Vesnius Viator. In sharp contrast to the four other principal bridges of the Wall system, however, no remains either of piers or, more importantly, of abutments have been located. The North Tyne, a swifter flowing river than the Eden, has permitted its abutments and its piers to survive. The main Tyne at Corbridge has left both abutments and most of its piers. As far down the river as Pons Aelius fragments of the piers survived even into the nineteenth century, and the remains at Willowford are substantial. It is legitimate to ask whether there was in fact a bridge at MC 66 at all. The stones recovered from the river—the position, incidentally, is "upstream from the conjectured crossing point"—may be the stones of the terminal sector of the Wall undermined by flooding and submerged in the channel. The centurial stone may be a record of that terminal.

Alternatively, it is of course possible that the main bridge structure is under the alluvial meadows of Willowholme. The position of MC 66, however, makes a singularly unattractive site for a heavy bridge. The Caldew river debouches into the Eden precisely at this point. Its course through the alluvial mud until it was banked was clearly shifting and uncertain. Moreover, the necessity for a bridge with its considerable demands on available engineering resources is at least in doubt. The Eden crossing had already been established long before with the construction of Agricola's road to the north. It passed by way of an islet or middle ground in the centre of the river at a point directly between Stanwix and the north gate of Carlisle. The crossing avoided the alluvial river meadows, utilised adequately high ground on either side, and provided for all reasonable communication between Stanwix and the Solway Plain. A second bridge a bare quarter of a mile downstream from this point seems to be at least supererogatory.

From the Irthing to the Eden crossing, the Wall is, as has been said, anomalous. From the Eden crossing to Bowness it is irrational. It offends not only against all the rules which regulated the First Plan from Pons Aelius to the Irthing but even the less logical precepts which regulated it from the Irthing to the Eden. It disregards elementary military principles and it seeks alternate and disparate solutions to problems that are in themselves negligible.

Its almost invisible remains wriggle like the track of a demented mole across the low rolling country of the Burgh isthmus. In so doing it makes thirty-four alterations of course in fourteen Roman miles. Comparisons are interesting. In the twenty-three miles of the Broad Wall from Pons Aelius to the North Tyne crossing there are only fourteen positive changes of direction. In the seventeen miles immediately to the east from the Irthing to the Eden crossing there are only nineteen. The sector of the Great Whin Sill is a special case; the course of the Wall there is not chosen but dictated by the absolute necessities of the cliffs and the gaps between them. It is not so dictated across the Solway Plain. This is easy country; there is nothing here to compare with the eight-hundred-foot rise and fall between Newcastle and the North Tyne, nothing to compare with the inconsequent foothills of the eastern slope from Craggle Hill to Oldwall. It is impossible to believe that the same planners who planned the line from Pons Aelius to Stanwix with such authority planned the line from Carlisle to the sea. It is even more impossible to believe that the same surveyors surveyed it.

It is, to begin with, militarily careless. Though for the first three miles from the Eden to Grinsdale it clings as closely as possible to the Irthing bank to secure every defensive virtue of the deep river—taking thus precisely the opposite decision to that which ruled out the use of the south bank of the Irthing—it then clings to the fifty-foot contour and leaves half a mile of flood plain between it and the water the rest of the way to Beaumont.

At Beaumont it runs on the river bank again for a few hundred yards and then sheers away altogether to cross the isthmus of the Burgh peninsula. The choice of line appears to be capricious and illogical. It leaves higher ground in front of it at North End and beyond, and it ignores the fact that the end of the Burgh peninsula is masked by the fifty-six-foot ridge of the Cassondyke—behind which an enemy crossing the river could have concentrated in absolute secrecy.

From milecastle 73 on Watch Hill beyond Burgh-by-Sands—where subsequently the second planners built the fort of Aballava—it plunges temerariously into the Burgh Marsh, where ultimately and inevitably it sank out of sight. Beyond Drumburgh at the far end of the Salt Marsh, where it eventually emerges, it zigzags wildly and out of phase with the outline of the coast as if it were reaching towards strong points which were never there. Just beyond milecastle 80 on the fifty-foot eminence of Bowness it runs down into the tideway and ends—for no better reason apparently than that at this point it is below the last fordable point of the Solway estuary. Whether those who forded the estuary by the Sand Wath could not have swept past the Wall end on the hard low-tide sand and outflanked the defences, does not appear to have been debated.

Once more, as with the Turf Wall sector from Willowford to the Eden, it is necessary to ask if there was an alternative to the Wall as built. Once more, there were two alternatives.

If a strictly defensive wall was considered necessary, as apparently was deemed to be the case from Carlisle to Beaumont, it could have been carried close to the river clear round the Burgh peninsula. The fifty-foot contour runs as far as the limit of the tide. From this point on the ground is at least firmer than the line chosen by the builders across Burgh Marsh. The north face of the peninsula across the Cassondyke is high again as far as Old Sandsfield, and from Old Sandsfield to Watch Hill it is covered securely by the Burgh Marsh. This line would have required two and a half extra Roman miles of Wall but it would have secured the peninsula effectively against any crossing. And crossing *was* possible given the necessary conditions. The fords of the Sand Wath and the Peat Wath were known and used. It was on the Burgh peninsula that Edward I lay waiting for those conditions as he tried for the third time to emulate Agricola—and waiting, died. From Watch Hill solid ground exists less than half a mile south of the chosen line—solid ground immune to the dangers of the marsh—and from there moderate high ground runs easily to Bowness.

From a purely military point of view this is the best line. The second alternative, however, is shorter and more direct. Briefly, it is the line of the Vallum. Between Carlisle and Bowness the Vallum virtually dissociates itself from the Wall. If, as has been claimed in the east, it was built to secure a military zone, argument about its purpose in relation to such a zone is here shot to pieces. In the previous sixty-six miles the Vallum, except behind the Great Whin Sill, is only on two occasions as much as a quarter of a mile from the Wall. Here at Grinsdale and again at Beaumont and along the marsh sector, at Glasson and at Port Carlisle it is anything up to half a mile away. It ignores the antic diversions of the Wall. Conforming to its general strategic outline, it still requires less than a dozen changes of course where the Wall takes twenty-three, and almost always it runs on what is militarily the sounder line. Even where it does change course it does not, as happens to the eastward, change course simultaneously with the Wall's moves. It seems prepared only to admit the remotest of associations.

The fundamental problem in attempting to understand the reasons for these variations on the normal theme of the Wall is the fact that less is known of the sector from Carlisle to the sea than of any other vital stretch of the work. Scarcely anything solid remains above the surface. Even the three forts of the Second Plan—Burgh-by-Sands (the cavalry fort which was called Aballava), Drumburgh (which, according to the *Notitia*, was presumably Congavata) and Bowness (which by the evidence of the cups was Maia)—have desperately little to offer. Not one of them has been adequately excavated and the entire corpus of knowledge is insufficient for judgment. The general impression that the choice of the line and the points selected for its changes presents, however, is that of a defensive work conceived late to join previously selected points.

South of Bowness the Wall continues, as is well known, for forty Roman miles down the coast in a line of detached watch towers and fortlets built with the spacing and the regularity of the milecastles of the main Wall. It would be a satisfactory solution if it could be shown that this plan was originally intended from the Solway crossing west. The available evidence, however, indicates that detached watch towers and fortlets were protected by ditch systems wherever possible, and the structures along this sector of the Wall are not independently ditched.

Yet there were works which had at least a quasi-independence. At Drumburgh the stone fort that was pulled down when "Lord Dakers Father builded upon old Ruines a prety Pyle for Defens of the Contery" was quite certainly preceded by a fort of clay.

The forts of the Second Plan were always stone forts. They were built independently of the Wall in the central sector and, as has been argued, joined up with it later. Even in the Turf Wall sector Birdoswald was thus built—of stone. Drumburgh stone fort, however, was built inside the clay ramparts.

This clay fort was small—barely two acres—and its ramparts were demolished when the Stone Wall was built. The plan produced after the Cumberland Excavation committee's operation in 1947 shows it joining the Turf Wall at right angles—after the style of Carrawburgh. But did it? With every possible respect to a careful survey, nothing shows in the diagram which ought to be accepted as proof of a phenomenon which occurs nowhere else along the line of the Wall, except in stone at Carrawburgh, doubtfully in stone at Stanwix, and demonstrably in stone at a much later date here.

It appears to be generally accepted that the Intermediate Stone Wall replaced the Turf as late, probably, as the year 162 in this area. No stratification data exists for the clay fort. The analogy of the linking of Housesteads and Greatchesters is alone available to suggest that this was a fort built in independence before the Turf Wall and incorporated in it when it arrived—later.

Is there other evidence to support a theory of independent forts linked, afterwards, by a hastily planned Turf Wall? Birley in *Research on Hadrian's Wall* says firmly in the section on Bowness:

> An earlier fort, with ramparts of turf or clay, must be postulated here as elsewhere in the western sector, but as yet there has been no opportunity of trenching for it.

Burgh-by-Sands shows no evidence for such a fort, but Burgh-by-Sands shows remarkably little evidence for anything except its eastern wall and enough material to hazard a guess at its dimensions—a little less than five acres. Moreover, it seems an unlikely place for a fort in isolation, for the commanding ground lies at North End, just *beyond* the estimated north-west corner of the cavalry fort. Beaumont, the most probable site on the eastern side of the peninsula for an isolated fort, is so confused with the earthworks of the motte castle of the de la Fertés that it is unlikely to produce anything positive, and Kirkandrews, the last of the appropriate positions, has only a quantity of unexplained stones, which might have belonged to anything from a signal tower to the now vanished church.

There remains one unlinked fort—Kirkbride—three miles south-west of Drumburgh and connected with it by a Roman road. Recent excavation suggests that it was a Trajanic fort contemporary with the Throp type and accepted, therefore, as a fort of the reserve.

The evidence is inadequate for the logical development of the theory that this area was first held by small forts in isolation which subsequently, in the face of new threats from across the Solway, were linked by a turf wall. Inadequate or no, however, it is at least a theory. The archaeologists appear to have disregarded even the need for one to explain the frenetic zigzags between Carlisle and Bowness.

9

The Building of the Wall

Whatever the explanation of the last eccentric sector, the Wall ends at Bowness, probably at what the maps list as the now vanished turret 80a somewhere about the high-tide mark.

How was it built?

The broad general picture has already been sketched in. There remains the question of the actual fabric. It has produced as many theories as any other element in the unsolved problems of the frontier. Today the theorists appear to divide into two factions: those who support what C. E. Stevens calls, sardonically, "the hypothesis of simplicity" and those who back Mr. Stevens' own theory which might justly be counter-called "the postulation of complexity". Richmond in his 1957 edition of Bruce's *Handbook* puts the first theory clearly.

> The original building of the Wall itself was organised by centuries, each unit building a length of about 45 yards, and seems to have been almost entirely confined to the legions. The lengths thus constructed were normally marked at each end by a small inscription mentioning the name of the century (and sometimes its cohort) which had done the work.

Stevens elaborates this in an ingenious intricacy of argument derived from the systematic analysis of the centurial stones. From it he interprets the movements of the sub-divisions of the legions involved from sector to sector of the Wall, argues their progress and explains away the irregularities that arise. One whole block of what he calls "dislocation" (but might reasonably be described as a failure to meet his time-table) he claims was caused by Nepos' taking out gangs that were working on the Wall in order to build a trial sector of the Vallum for Hadrian to see. A further "dislocation" he attributes to the fact that Hadrian was dissatisfied with the result "and directed that forts should be built on the line of the Wall itself". The dislocations, he suggests, reduced the efficiency of the legions and as a result, he claims, "the natives" rose in 124. Nepos, he declares, misjudged the effect of the campaign of 124 and announced a victory, but the natives rose again in 125 and the "dislocation" on the Wall continued. In this second campaign, Stevens maintains, the Ninth Legion was defeated, Nepos was recalled, and a new Governor

> ... determined to re-establish Roman prestige by showing not only that building of Wall could be resumed, but that more Stone Wall could be built. The fact, however, that his building force had been reduced incited him to reduce the thickness of Wall to be built.

This seems to include everything except perhaps the Roman equivalent of the kitchen sink. The theory is worked out with the tortuous ingenuities of Bavarian baroque backed by genuine and ingenious scholarship. The hypothesis of simplicity may appear to the average man a little more acceptable. It is based at least on the clear understanding that the military art is not logical but conditioned by circumstance.

Mr. Stevens' explanation of the reduction of the thickness of the Wall, however, raises another point. It is the latest in a long succession of such explanations. They vary from cheapness to speed, from the availability of stone to the difficulty of construction on the steep slopes of the crags. It is therefore of interest to see what precisely was involved.

The bottom layers of the well-trimmed ashlar of which the Wall was constructed were larger than the upper stones, but a convenient average appears to be about six and a half inches by ten and a half. This indicates a Wall twenty-seven courses high with about five thousand five hundred blocks to the linear mile, giving a rough total of a hundred and fifty thousand per mile for each face, plus an allowance equivalent to about six running miles for the milecastles and perhaps another mile for the turrets and milecastle gate towers.

Simple arithmetic indicates that the First Plan called for a grand total of twenty-five million carefully squared blocks tapering towards the back and neatly faced, probably with a bravura of feather tooling.

The real work of the building of the Wall was in fact in the quarries!

How much would the switch to Narrow Wall have saved? Narrowness *per se* would have saved nothing except a little rough filling. Birley, however, argues that the Narrow Wall would have been three feet lower than the Broad. Precisely what the assumption is based on is not altogether clear. The only early figure available is Bede's and, early as that is, it was arrived at long after the abandonment of the Wall and, as Bede's own monastery showed, after at least the first of the robbing.

But even if a difference of three feet can be justified, it amounts only to one-fifth of the Wall facing. Parapet, turrets, milecastle towers and flags for the walk would remain about the same. Perhaps all told it would have represented a saving of fifteen per cent in man-hours over the narrow sector—one-third only of the total length of the Wall. Would Rome, of all nations, have bothered about saving five per cent of a legionary's time in the face of a military necessity?

Two constituent parts of the Wall remain—the Vallum and the Military Way.

In *Roman Britain and the English Settlements* Collingwood describes the Vallum as

> . . . a broad and deep, flat-bottomed ditch, whose upcast earth has been neatly arranged in two parallel mounds set back some twenty feet from its north and south sides. This symmetrical section makes it tactically neutral: no force of troops on one side of it has any advantage over one on the other.

With this splendid simplicity Collingwood demolishes four hundred years of battling historians. As has already been suggested, it may all have started as far back as Bede. Certainly Camden in Holland's translation declared that "the said *Vallum* or Rampier was nothing but a wall of turfes".

By the eighteenth century battle was magnificently joined. Greater and lesser authorities argued as to whether it was actually the frontier built by Hadrian and, alternatively, whether the Stone Wall was built long after by Severus. In the early nineteenth century a rival theory developed for a short time: according to this the Vallum was a frontier set up by Trajan when the retreat from Scotland became a bitter reality, long before Hadrian inherited the throne. By the end of the century the preferred faith was that it was constructed to defend the Wall from the hostility of the Brigantes. At the century's turn Haverfield decided that it was a civil and legal demarcation, and achieved a following. But Simpson built up an ingenious theory in the next decade that the Vallum was a frontier line by itself supported by small forts of its own, and drew powerful adherents, including at first Collingwood. The Simpson theory was demolished by the results of his own excavation of milecastle 50—round which the Vallum was diverted, proving that it was later even than the Turf Wall. It was followed, since archaeology like nature abhors a vacuum, by a completely new orthodoxy. The Vallum—insidiously at first and vociferously later—was declared a customs barrier and immigration control line set up to regulate the frontier traffic. C. E. Stevens, in a splendid sub-faction of one, stated authoritatively in the revised version of his Horsley lecture—published in 1966:

> The Vallum would both seal off the garrison from intruders and make it harder for the forced levies who occupied mile-castles and turrets to drift back to their homes.

The Vallum was, however, assuredly, an integral element of the First Plan. The evidence for this exists mainly in its alignment. It follows the course of the Wall—and of the Fighting Ditch—with such meticulous care that it is clearly part of a single concept and a single survey. At ten points between Pons Aelius and the Coesike it alters course exactly as the Wall and the ditch alter—or at most within a few feet of the change point. Its few brief essays in independence are dictated by the terrain.

Precisely what its character would have been had the First

Plan been completed is not anywhere clear. Would it, for example, have had a crossing at each milecastle? There is no archaeological evidence of such intention, but without crossings how would the reserves from the valley forts below have moved into action? And if there had been eighty crossings, one at each milecastle, who would have provided the guards for them? Who would have protected the gates, most particularly in the area behind the Great Whin Sill where for miles the Vallum was distant and invisible from the Wall?

But if it was part of the design of the First Plan, it was equally assuredly part of the construction of the Second. Certainly its line had been surveyed before the sites of forts were selected, possibly the markers were already placed in position, but in no case is there the slightest evidence that digging had started anywhere in the vicinity of the forts. The broad angular deviations round them are in all cases cut in virgin soil, and the earth of the causeways opposite their southern gateways is equally undisturbed. Intermittent attempts have been made to argue this relationship and to claim that the deviations were spaces left in which to build forts if and when a decision was finally taken. They seem irrelevant. If the Vallum had not been planned already, a general line clear of the forts would certainly have been selected. There was nothing in the terrain to make this difficult.

The simplest explanation seems to be that forts and Vallum were built, broadly speaking, simultaneously, using the original planned line to save time and marking the local deviations as the plans of the forts were set out. Of the five forts of the eastern side four were set up at points where Wall and ditch changed course. At all four the line originally planned for the Vallum if extended from either side would have met within the fort enclosures. The fifth fort, Carrawburgh, is not involved; it was built substantially later—*over* the filled in Vallum ditch.

It has been suggested that there was some special relationship in space between Wall and Vallum which demanded the maintenance of the original line. It seems unlikely. The distance between the two is nowhere sacrosanct. On the flat and the easiest slopes between Pons Aelius and the Eden it does, it is true, keep close to the Wall, but the matter is clearly not absolute. At Harlow Hill, for example, the Vallum takes the base line across a long deviation of the Wall and at the apex of the triangle so formed it is as much as a quarter of a mile from the rampart. At the Coesike, more dramatically, it abandons the Wall altogether and permits the great bulk of the Whin Sill to interpose itself between it and the main defence. For the next twelve miles it is widely separated from turrets and milecastles and the garrison of the system.

Finally there are the eccentricities of the trans-Eden, already discussed in Chapter 6.

There is enough evidence here already to eliminate the earlier disputations. It was plainly not Hadrian's original Wall. It was not replaced by Severus. It was not a new frontier set up by Trajan, and—accepting Collingwood's accurate definition of its neutrality—it was not constructed to defend the garrison from the Brigantes, or anyone else. And it was certainly never constructed to keep in Mr. Stevens' "forced levies" for whose enforcement, incidentally, no scintilla of evidence exists. A section drawn through it (see diagram on page 27) clearly proves the point.

Its central feature was a ditch twenty feet wide at the top, eight feet wide at the bottom, and ten feet deep. From the earth of its excavation a mound was constructed on either side. Since the bases of the mounds were twenty feet wide and the section of the ditch was one hundred and forty feet square, the section of each mound could not have exceeded seventy square feet, making each mound at the most five feet high, allowing generously for a revetment of turf. An active boy could have negotiated it in five minutes given a stone sharp enough to hack out toe holds on the turf of the farther slope.

Clearly it was not designed simply to keep out trespassers. A stout timber fence would have served that purpose better—though suitable timber might in that area have been hard to come by. The Vallum was in reality vulnerable everywhere to a determined man. At night or in the frequent mist of the high ground it would have kept out no one.

Was it, then, established in accordance with modern dogma, as a customs barrier and an immigration control line? A customs barrier implies trade. Not to put too fine a point upon it, it would be singularly irrational without it.

What trade?

The economy of the Province of Britain divided itself into the four parts customary to that period: agriculture, livestock, mining and manufactures. It differed drastically in importance between south and north. But even in the south there was no trade in grain until the Belgic invasion, half a century or so before Caesar, brought an effective plough to the southern kingdoms. There was no Belgic invasion of what is now Scotland, and it is in the highest degree improbable that there was ever enough grain produced there to do much more than supply the Highland tribes through the savage northern winter.

What was the position with regard to livestock? At Hadrian's accession the northern tribes were only just recovering from the depressed conditions of life after Mons Graupius. It is doubtful if before 120 there was any real surplus of beef on the hoof—or, conversely, any real requirement for it in the south. There may have been a surplus of hides. It is possible that a small horse trade went on. And there was always the traditional movement of hunting dogs, though the best of these were the wolf hounds from Ireland.

There were no mines in Scotland as early as this and no mineral trade of any significance.

There is left, then, the possibility of manufactured goods. Brooches made in Northern Britain—how far north is unclear—were certainly traded up the Rhine but they are brooches of an early type, produced long before the Wall. There is little other evidence of manufactured articles in trade and little enough evidence of manufactures at all beyond the limited needs of a still primitive if warlike people.

There *was* trade with the north, of course; excavation of the Roman sites in Scotland and the distribution maps of Roman finds—despite the notorious capacity for misguidance of distribution maps—proves this. But it was trade of a late date, for the most part long after the time of Hadrian.

If there was trade before, how did it move? Trade implies trade routes. At one time certainly there was a moderate degree of seaborne traffic, but on the land there are only two lines of movement—Agricola's road through Carlisle and Annandale, and the earlier and perhaps prehistoric track that he used for his eastern axis of advance and which became in due course Dere Street.

Eighteen hundred years later there is still no north-south road between these two, and effectively there is only one new route across the eastern coastal plain.

All movement between north and south—certainly all heavy trading movement—was canalised down these two lines. The Knag Burn gateway, the possible road north-west from Pons Aelius and the drove roads are all of later date. These two main routes of communication between north and south tapped also the only two local areas from which, in the military situation which impelled the establishment of the Tyne-Solway frontier, extended possibilities of trade might still have been expected.

The most important of these was the Annandale-Solway Plain district. Before Agricola it sheltered a relatively dense Iron Age population. It has over thirty major earthworks designated as forts. It has more than fifty lesser defended dwelling places and scores of minor sites. Even after Agricola it was sufficiently populated to require a considerable military holding system. It is probable that it represented an important outlying sub-tribe of the Brigantes. But even if it produced a surplus in any of the four categories listed previously (above the requirement of the resident Roman garrisons), that surplus must inevitably have gone south through the Stanwix gate.

Similarly, the only other heavily populated area immediately north of the Wall—the North Tyne Valley—must, if it produced a surplus, have sent it south through the Portgate. More than fifty defended dwelling sites are recognised over this general area—plus a handful of hill-top forts—and it is at least conceivable that they might have wanted to trade with the rich potential market first, of the Stanegate forts and, later, with the complex of the Wall; but at best the total surplus must have been minute.

It seems necessary to ask again the question: what trade? What evidence of commerce at all exists to justify the establishment of a customs line estimated—by Collingwood himself—to have cost the Romans "a million man-days of labour in mere earthwork"?

And it must be remembered that apart from "mere earthwork" the Vallum was cut for long stretches through solid rock, it was revetted in stone through sandy patches, it was built up on embankments through marsh, and it was furnished with monumental gateways at all the forts.

The gateways provoke more questions.

Collingwood, in a masterful dissection of the relationship between the finance branch of the Roman administration—the procurator's men—and the military branch, suggests that "friction and jealousy were not unknown". Therefore, he claims, customs officers in the forts were a significant problem.

> Hadrian, a stickler of military discipline, may very well have thought it unwise to give the procurator's men an official position at fort gateways, where the authority of the commandant should be undisputed. The simplest solution, though a cumbrous and expensive one, would be to have a second barrier behind the Wall; to make this barrier look as unmilitary as possible, consistent with efficiency; and to provide it with a crossing opposite each fort, where the customs officers could do their work.

And all at the cost of a million man days? Roman economics must have been even more eccentric than our own!

Whether it is possible to accept Collingwood's scholarly thesis or not, the Vallum at any rate was built. Its sole apparent function thereafter was to provide a track between the mile-castles—this was early christened the patrol track. The academic assumption was that the Vallum was patrolled by the garrisons of the milecastles, but nobody appears to have examined the capability of the milecastles in this respect. They constituted units, at the maximum of the First Plan, of fifty men. Out of these they had to man a turret on either side which obviously had to provide for patrols in crisis on a twenty-four-hour basis, supply their own share of the Wall patrol, defend their own gateways and maintain a fighting reserve. There remains the question of what precisely a Vallum patrol was supposed to be able to accomplish. Along most of the Wall the sentries on the ramparts could see far more than a man walking the south berm of the Vallum. Along other sections, notably behind the Great Whin Sill, the man on the Vallum walk could perhaps see more—but could certainly do even less about it.

From MC 40 the Vallum was eight hundred yards away down the steep five hundred feet of Winshield slope. What was the lone patrol supposed to do? The patrol walk, so called, was in reality the lateral communication, possibly unplanned, probably unofficial, between the milecastles, the alternative to the flagged walk way of the Wall itself.

The Vallum, then, was built—it lasted for barely fifteen years. On the move forward to the Antonine line it was abandoned and the ditch was slighted. (The slighting is an excellent example of the extreme rigidity of the Roman military mind; it was filled in regularly at intervals of forty-five yards, though bored troops here and there scamped the work.) Part of it was briefly cleared out after the final return from Scotland, but in the end much of its north mound was used as the foundation for a proper lateral road connecting forts, milecastles and turrets as well.

This Military Way is the fourth and final element in the construction of the frontier. It is a small masterpiece on its own, exquisitely surveyed, boldly engineered. Along the Whin Sill it follows a brilliant line behind the crest but close enough to the points that it was its task to supply, sheltered as much as possible but planned so that its gradients were always reasonable to traffic. It is still there today. For miles you can trace it, sometimes by its cambered mound, sometimes by its flagstones, sometimes by its cuttings—most often by the brighter green of the grass that grows along it. It is notable even among the notable Roman roads of Britain.

So the Vallum ended.

Is there an easier solution for its origins than Collingwood's and the infinite variations of the academics? Surely it lies in one of the simplest games of boyhood, in one of the most primary expositions of challenge and response.

There is a ploy common to the children of all peoples and in all ages whereby the boy on the defensive draws across the ground a strong line with a stick and says, in every variant of every tongue: "There's my mark." And the crossing of the mark thereafter is an act of war.

The Vallum was Hadrian's mark, a strong clear line equally apparent to north and south, neutral by one assumption, equally hostile by another—a line not to be crossed except for the purposes of war.

Whether such a demarcation was laid down in his original charge to Falco cannot perhaps now be discovered. Certainly, as has been argued, it was Falco who drew the first line for it. But equally certainly its integration in the Second Plan must have been confirmed by Hadrian himself, for it was adapted to meet the necessities of that plan, strengthened at least visually by the grandiloquent gates that led to the new forts and dug simultaneously with their building.

It was in itself the symbolic expression of empire, the marked frontier, defended by the potent complex of the Wall, authorised by an emperor who, more than a soldier, was a planner, a constructor, and throughout his reign an architect.

10

Forts of the Frontier Complex

The four structures of the Wall formed a narrow military belt from sea to sea across the Province. By themselves, as has been argued, they were militarily sufficient to prevent raiding, to discourage medium-scale attacks and—with the warning inevitable to any campaign *en masse* from the north—to concentrate within the necessary consideration of time forces strong enough to meet and destroy the strongest possible combination of the northern tribes.

They did not, however, stand alone. They were the principal part—but still a part only—of a wider-spreading military complex that covered a zone approximately thirty miles in depth from the North Sea to the hills of Kirkcudbrightshire, and the coast of Cumberland as far south as Moresby. Within this general area there are thirty-four identified Roman forts—twice the number of the forts of the Wall—that should be included in the larger pattern of the defence of the frontier. In addition there is a substantial number of fortlets; of these the earliest date from the period of Cerealis and Agricola, a large number were established during Agricola's campaigns as Governor. Five were built in Trajan's reign but the majority of the remainder, together with the forts of the Wall, were built in Hadrian's reign. A small handful is attributed to Antoninus. They were not, of course, all occupied simultaneously. The pattern is a shifting one, adjusting and adjusted to the requirements of successive crises. A few clearly had ceased to exist before Hadrian came. Of the rest almost all at one time or another were linked operationally with the Wall complex.

They fall into four categories, divided by function, and it is simplest to deal with each category separately.

The first, the series most directly associated with the Wall, are the support forts of the garrisons of the immediate rear.

Two of them have already been dealt with—South Shields and the possible fort at Jarrow. South Shields, it will be remembered, may have owed its original foundation to Cerealis or Agricola. As a defended entrepot it was clearly developed under Hadrian to supply the eastern end of the new frontier. Jarrow, in the light of the paucity of evidence, cannot yet be assessed. The first important military establishment of the Tyne valley other than South Shields, therefore, is Corbridge—Corstopitum of the Antonine Itinerary—eighteen miles from the bridgehead at Pons Aelius. The empty zone between Corbridge and the North Sea, as has been said, is one of the puzzles of the frontier. No indications either of fort or fortlet have been discovered, no road to the mouth of the River Tyne has been traced. It is possible that an explanation lies with the character of the coastal inhabitants, that they had come voluntarily under the Roman aegis at the conclusion of the Northern campaign, that it had been unnecessary to establish a holding area. Yet the strategic importance of the Tyne with its harbours still makes such absence remarkable.

The first fort at Corbridge was earth-walled like all the forts erected by Cerealis and Agricola. Construction of this period is generically referred to as Flavian, after Vespasian's wife, to cover the twenty-seven-year dynasty of Vespasian and his sons Titus and Domitian, who occupied the throne a quarter of a century before Hadrian's journey. It was large, capable of holding two cohorts, and it was built to guard the bridgehead across the Tyne in the opening phase of Agricola's invasion of Scotland. As the conquest of Scotland proceeded, the necessity for a fort of that size progressively diminished, and it was reduced to a single cohort fort on a different axis and equipped for cavalry. Its new status was that of a fort of the road, accommodating the bridge guard for the only bridge across the Tyne on the vital main-road system to the north and providing a mobile force able to operate at substantial distances from the bridge. Subsequently it was redesigned for infantry, and it was this infantry establishment that was in being at the time of the planning of the Wall. With the decision of the Second Plan to place the forts on the line of the rampart, the garrison appears to have been moved north, probably to Haltonchesters.

Corbridge, however, was not abandoned. It became largely a civilian centre with important supply and armament responsibilities. Two military enclaves were established inside the walls, and the manufacture of weapons and military equipment appears to have reached a considerable level. With the increase of the civil population temples were introduced inside the area of the original walls. Eight of these have been identified, perhaps the most remarkable assembly of religious building in Roman Britain. Finally, one of the largest of the known buildings of the Province was begun—a series of "storehouses", approximately two hundred and twenty-five feet square ranged round an inner quadrangle and built of exceptionally well-tooled stone. Barely half completed, the scheme was abandoned. To the north of it there was to have been a hall of similar proportions, and the plan bears strong resemblances to the forum of a legionary town. The workmanship is of the time of Severus, and in its extent and its quality there are indications that it may have been the Emperor's intention to move the eastern legion from York to the north of the Tyne on a successful outcome of the Scottish expedition. Certainly the death of Severus and the final withdrawal from Scotland put an end to the plan. Admirably tended by the Ministry of Works, it is, even incomplete, one of the most impressive monuments of the Province.

Corbridge's size and its proximity to Saxon settlement in the Tyne valley made it in due time a mine for the stone robbers. Among the earliest and most enthusiastic of these were the Saxon monks. Hexham Priory, "the fifth Church of stone in Britain", was declared by Eddius, who wrote the chronicles of St. Wilfred, to be "unequalled for size and magnificence north of the Alps". Something of its magnificence came from the "men brought from Rome" by St. Wilfred, most of it came from the stone of Corbridge, and the wholly perfect Saxon crypt under the nave is built throughout of well-tooled ashlar with the marks of the Roman masons clear yet upon its facings. The splendid tombstone of Flavinus, Standard Bearer of the *ala Petriana,* was presumably looted by the monks at the same time. Still closer to home in the church of St. Andrew's in the Saxon town of Corbridge, the arch which joins the seventh-century tower to the nave was stolen entire from the pagan buildings of Corstopitum, and its sturdy thirteenth-century fortress vicarage was built of ashlar from its ruins.

The main axis of the frontier until Agricola moved forward to the conquest of Scotland was the Stanegate—the admirably engineered military road that ran west from Corbridge to the Solway Firth and the Irish Sea. It has been traced over most of its length from Corbridge to Carlisle and long stretches are visible today. At the village of Fourstones, just beyond its still undiscovered crossing of the North Tyne, it forms the lonely and beautiful central road of the modern valley system. Service roads ran from it to the frontier defences.

On the Stanegate from Corbridge to Carlisle there are thirteen permanent forts. There are in addition at least thirty identified temporary camps of a wide variety of size and elaboration. For the greater part of the Roman occupation it is apparent that this moorland slope between Wall and river was militarily the nerve centre of the Province of Britain.

Of the thirteen permanent forts, seven belong to Agricola's frontier: Corbridge, Newborough, Chesterholm, Carvoran, Nether Denton, almost certainly Castlesteads, and Carlisle.

Of Newborough, a mile and a half along the road from Fourstones, little remains. St. Peter's church is built within the limits of the fort, the churchyard covers it and the churchyard wall rests on a late Roman wall that was fronted by a fifteen-foot ditch. This probably was the rampart of a small fortlet, built of the materials of an earlier fort somewhere about the time of Theodosius; excavation has been difficult and inadequate.

Chesterholm—Vindolanda of a well-attested inscription—has been and is being, on the other hand, examined with a brilliant professionalism. It stands on a high plateau above the Chineley Burn, a site wholly typical of Agricola's eye for the defensible position. Three and a half acres in extent, it barred the track through the gorge of the Chineley Burn to the Tyne valley and effectively covered the central section of the Stanegate. In 1930 it was excavated by Professor Birley, who demonstrated that the visible fort belongs to the early fourth century—the period of Diocletian. The fine fourth-century headquarters building belongs to this era, four other occupation layers exist, and the earliest fort was unquestionably occupied well into the first years of Hadrian's reign. Chesterholm was presented by Professor Birley to the nation and is safely in the custody of the Ministry of Works.

The third of the Agricolan forts is almost certainly Carvoran. Precisely positioned at the junction of the Maiden Way from Kirkby Thore with the Stanegate, it has been identified as Banna of the Amiens skillet and Magna of the *Notitia*. Whether identification is positive or not, Carvoran is one of the odder eccentricities of the Wall. Though nothing to prove the existence of a Flavian fort has so far been located, all the experts are in remarkable—indeed improbable—agreement that there *must* have been one here. Its existing outer wall offers no help at all, for it dates definitely from the end of Hadrian's reign. But the most notable circumstance is that though Carvoran is less than two hundred and fifty yards from the rear face of the Wall, it was never regarded as an integral part of it. Astonishingly the Vallum makes a careful, well plotted angular deviation to the north of it, though not in precise alignment with it, coming thereby into awkward contact with MC 46.

Officially the theory seems to be that the Vallum deviated to avoid a marsh. There is no marsh today and the contour of the slope suggests that the theory is improbable. Elsewhere, after all, the Vallum took marshland in its stride. Finally, if it had continued along its original alignment, it would, without any deviation at all, have missed the fort by a hundred and twenty-five yards. It is, as the experts refuse to say, all very puzzling.

For reasons best known to themselves, Agricola and his engineers ignored the far side of the wide and vulnerable Gilsland gap. The next fort of his period is four and a half miles from Carvoran along the Stanegate. Nether Denton (its Roman name is entirely unknown) was a cohort fort of about three acres facing towards the east, well placed on the high ground of the Church Hill steeply above the Irthing and covering a ford. Its site is occupied by church and churchyard, but excavations in 1933 located a thirty-foot turf wall, unquestionably belonging to an early fort, and cobble foundations and stone structures of a second.

It is in this churchyard that F. G. Simpson, first and still in many respects greatest of the modern archaeologists of the Wall, is buried. To make his grave it was necessary to dig through a stretch of the cobble foundations. No more appropriate resting place could have been chosen.

Castlesteads was built five miles to the west of Nether Denton. Doubtfully a fort of the Stanegate, it lies a mile to the north of the road across the Irthing valley and it is yet another of the anomalies of this anomalous sector. If the evidence of the cups is accepted, its Roman name was unquestionably Uxellodunum. It was a fort of the Wall, the work that still exists is late Hadrianic, and equally certainly the Vallum was diverted—this time to the south in order to include it in the Wall complex. It was none the less still separated from the Wall by the strong stream of the Cambeck and at no point was it closer to it than a quarter of a mile. It is the only isolated fort to be thus taken into the Wall system. Carvoran—barely two hundred and fifty yards to the south of the Wall—was, it will be remembered, excluded.

The reason may lie in the importance of the first fort on the site. This was an earth-walled structure, discovered and proved by Richmond in 1934. It stood on an entirely different alignment, almost certainly set up to guard the approaches to the road zone from attacks by way of the Cambeck valley. The available evidence is slight and difficult to assess, but from its site and from the type of the turf rampart it must have been, like Nether Denton, Flavian. As an element in the quick reaction policy of the Second Plan, it was at best a clumsy addition. Effectively, however, it was the last of the earliest series of forts of the Stanegate.

Carlisle, its eastern anchor, should more properly be regarded as a fort of Agricola's western road. It stood at the vital strategic point of the Solway Plain. Well sited above the first effective ford of the Eden at the crossing point of the ancient track of the Brigantes, it controlled the junction of the western road, the

---

The North Tyne bridge abutment, probably the most important ▶ engineering work still standing of the Roman period in Northern Britain. The beautifully finished masonry exhibits the traditional feather tooling. The basement of the tower to the right housed an undershot mill and the millrace was covered by heavy slabs of stone, now largely broken. Remains of the western abutment and the piers of the bridge can be traced at low water in summer. *Photograph: Ian Yeomans*

important diagonal road from York and the Stanegate itself. It commanded the level coastal plain beyond. The Roman walls that had so wide a reputation as early as the time of St. Cuthbert were, however, the walls of the civil town that succeeded it; the fort that Agricola—or, according to another school of experts, Cerialis—built was a fort of turf and timber, first discovered when Tullie House—now the Museum and just beyond Carlisle Cathedral—was enlarged at the end of the last century. Its dimensions are unknown, its character was that of the period, its site occupied the present site of the cathedral and stretched towards the castle but did not apparently make use of the bluff of the castle hill. Beyond this it is difficult to build a picture save that it was occupied as a fort at least until the building of the Wall.

There were, however, two distinct generations of Stanegate defences. Beginning at the Haltwhistle Burn, halfway between sea and sea, there is a chain of six fortlets, substantially later in design, wholly different in character, and quite certainly the products of a changed requirement: Haltwhistle Burn itself, Throp, the first fortlet at Birdoswald, Castle Hill, Old Church and High Crosby, and to these should be added the lately determined fort at Kirkbride. In addition, Carvoran may have been reconstructed to take its place in the new line, Nether Denton may equally have been adjusted, and Castlesteads almost certainly was included in the scheme.

The date of Castlesteads, like so many dates along the Wall, is still matter for disputation. What may be called the official view attributes it to the early part of Hadrian's reign—to, that is, the period of the First Plan, as a reinforcement of the forts of the rear. A faintly heretical school claims that it belonged to the time of Trajan. The evidence seems capable of being inter-

◀ The Willowford bridgehead. The recently excavated sector of the Wall from Willowford farm which ends in the abutment of the Irthing bridge. The photograph shows the Broad Foundation built up here to a height of five courses before work was suspended and the Second Plan with its Narrow Wall superseded it. Not as imposing as the North Tyne bridgehead, Willowford was none the less a major engineering work; the bridge, covered by a tower, was equipped with a millrace and undershot wheel. *Photograph: Ian Yeomans*

preted either way. No inscriptions are available for any of the fortlets. Finds in all of them are limited, the surest indication of a short period of occupation. Coarse pottery gives an approximate range that would be compatible with any date in the last five years of Trajan or the first five of Hadrian, and the notoriously uncertain evidence of coins triumphantly reaches a new level, for at Old Church the sole coin found was a *denarius* of c. 88 B.C., struck, that is, when Julius Caesar was fourteen.

The dating of the scheme must, then, rest upon military probabilities.

Were the fortlets built as an essential part of the First Plan for the Wall to strengthen the possibilities of close support? It appears in the highest degree improbable. The original forts of the Stanegate were adequate to provide the mobile reinforcement required for that plan—very substantially more adequate, for example, than was considered necessary east of the Great Whin Sill. Moreover, if the fortlets were planned in conjunction with the selection of the Wall line, the siting of some of them is remarkable.

Haltwhistle Burn, it is true, is close to the Wall at MC 42, well placed to cover the Haltwhistle Gap at its eastern end. Throp, equally close to the Wall, covers the Gilsland Gap at its western end. But Castle Hill, Old Church and the putative second fort at Nether Denton were all on the wrong side of the Irthing and execrably placed to render any assistance at all. High Crosby, the last of the line except for Kirkbride, is actually on the Stanegate, but for no obvious reason almost three-quarters of a mile from the nearest milecastle.

As a reinforcement for the elderly Agricolan forts of the Stanegate, on the other hand, the plan makes sense. Haltwhistle Burn is almost exactly midway between Chesterholm and Carvoran. Throp is midway between Carvoran and Nether Denton. Castle Hill is midway between Nether Denton and Castlesteads. Old Church and High Crosby cover most of the remaining miles to Carlisle. The still smaller fortlet that was ensconced in the Iron Age promontory defence at Birdoswald was, as was suggested earlier, an essential post in the signal system that connected all these forts. The scheme may even offer a partial explanation for the eccentricities of the sector beyond the Eden. The earthen forts at Drumburgh and Kirkbride, and fortlets at Bowness and elsewhere, may have been originally fortlets of the same plan.

It was, in fact, not a part of the Wall but a predecessor of the Wall. Long before Trajan's reign was over, pressure from the North was imminent in this half of the Tyne-Solway isthmus. This was surely a plan conceived by one of Trajan's last governors in anticipation of a collapse of the western holding system above the Solway. It had, to a governor living with Trajan's rising demands for his campaigns in the eastern Empire, the special virtue that it was cheaper than a continuous frontier both in construction and in man-power.

It existed, then, before Hadrian. It was made use of by his governors in the first phase of the Wall building. It may even account in part for the decision to build the Turf Wall since it was of itself strong enough to counter-balance the weakness of that Wall. It may account for some at least of the delays in building by the mere fact of its existence. It was effectively abandoned when the forts of the Second Plan were placed athwart the Wall.

The second category of the forts of the frontier zone comprises the extension of the Wall from Bowness down the Cumberland coast to Moresby. This, as described earlier, is the refused left flank of the Wall, a line of fortlets spaced precisely in the manner of the milecastles of the Wall, with towers matching the turrets of the Wall between them and strengthened, partly presumably in accordance with the Second Plan, by four forts: Beckfoot (the Roman name of which was Bibra), Maryport (which was Alauna), Burrow Walls (which was Gabrosentum) and Moresby (which was Itunocelum). Beckfoot was on the coast of the Solway Plain with high ground behind it. Maryport was firmly placed in the mouth of the valley of the Ellen. Burrow Walls commanded the landing place at the mouth of the Derwent, and Moresby protected the landing area at Whitehead.

Here, as elsewhere in the western zone, however, use was made of earlier works, and the condition of the remnants of two of the forts at least makes positive dating difficult. The extension of the Wall was known certainly to Camden. Because perhaps of the paucity of visible remains, little interest was taken in it thereafter until the early eighteenth century and the day of the eccentric Alexander Gordon, and though occasional sporadic investigations were made, it was not until 1928, with Collingwood's swift and energetic survey of the coast from St. Bees Head to Bowness, that the chain as a whole was clearly described.

Beckfoot is approximately eleven miles from Bowness, and since it occupies and overlies the calculated site of a signal tower, it is of the period of the Second Plan. Virtually nothing is visible today, but Dr. St. Joseph achieved one of his finest surveys with aerial photographs taken of the site under crops. These show in almost incredible detail not merely the walls but the plan of its internal buildings.

Maryport is roughly nine miles from Beckfoot. Unlike Beckfoot, however, it was a fort of the Agricolan establishment, built, according to the traditional view, as a defence against possible raiders from across the Irish Sea but equally as a part of the Agricolan consolidation of Brigantia. It was about four hundred feet square, had a double ditch and, in addition to its other responsibilities, covered the Roman port subsequently built on the River Ellen. The existing remains of the fort—much was obliterated in the eighteenth century—are, according to Dr. M. G. Jarrett, most probably of Trajan's date. It may be assumed, therefore, to have been included in such designs for the seaward extension of the Wall as existed in the First Plan.

Burrow Walls, six miles farther on at the mouth of the Derwent, had all but vanished long before the eighteenth century. Horsley, surmising the probability of a fort at this point, "could discover no appearance of it". Most of the *praetentura* was, in fact, already destroyed by erosion. The rest had been reduced to the vestiges of the foundations by the builders of the medieval castle and even the outline had been lost under the plough. As late as 1928 Collingwood came to the same conclusion as Horsley—that anything Roman on the site could not have been more than a fortlet. Once again, however, an air photograph by Dr. St. Joseph provided sufficient evidence for subsequent digging to show that there had been a fort of two and three-quarter acres with two ditches, and pottery finds proved that it continued in occupation until the end of the fourth century. Material for establishing the absolute date of its building is still lacking.

Moresby was five miles south of Burrow Walls. In 1822 a building inscription of the Twentieth Legion, acknowledging Hadrian as *pater patriae,* makes it plain that the existing remains are later than 128. It had an area of three and a half acres and faced out to sea. Beyond it the milecastles and turrets continued to St. Bees Head, the westernmost extremity of Cumberland, forty Roman miles from Bowness fort.

There is one Roman fort below St. Bees, Ravenglass at the mouth of the Esk, but Ravenglass faces inland, a fort closing the valley of the Esk rather than protecting it from the sea—a fort, that is, of the Agricolan holding system. The signal stations and the fortlets are a part of the Wall system, and that system ends at St. Bees.

The signal systems employed on the Wall varied with the areas. There has been, since interest in the Wall began, an engaging legend that a speaking tube ran along the top of the Wall from Newcastle to Bowness and that human repeaters, remarkably like the repeaters of a transatlantic cable, amplified the message along its length. No tubing has been found. The spacing of the Wall turrets and the milecastle turrets, on the other hand, enabled messages to be shouted, at least in still weather, from point to point all the way across. Even if runners had been used, transmission time would have been barely four minutes between milecastle and milecastle—say, six hours across Britain. Simple visual signals, however, existed throughout the Roman army and special codes enabled essential messages to be passed with great speed. Visual signals were also provided by the outlying signal towers. Long-distance transmission existed long before the Romans and even in Britain the tribes north of the Wall appear to have used a primitive code of smoke puffs.

Neglected as it has been, the complex from Bowness to the headland is unquestionably the strongest defended sea frontier in Britain and possibly in the Empire. Even the heavy defences of the Saxon Shore are not to be compared with it. The nine forts of the Saxon Shore listed in the *Notitia* were, it is true, larger and stronger than the forts of the Wall, but they were stretched over almost three hundred and fifty miles of coast and even if there were eleven, as is sometimes conjectured, there was an average distance of almost thirty-five miles between them. In the coastal sector from Bowness to Moresby there were five major fortresses, forty fortlets, and the signal towers were within hailing distance of each other.

What was its purpose? As was said earlier, the established view is that it was built to safeguard the left flank of the Wall against attack from across the Irish Sea. But was attack possible across the Irish Sea in the first half of the second century? The Irish raids began, according to accepted evidence, about the middle of the third century, at least a hundred years later. With the gradual surrender of the Roman grip on the North, they were followed by small settlements, but not until the fifth century was there sufficient strength to set up the kingdom of Dalriada in Argyll. Even as late as this period there were no decked ships. The possibility of raids across the prevailing south-west wind in summer, therefore, was remote at the time of the building of the Wall. Had it been possible, however, the extension as built would have been wholly inadequate, for to ships operating from the north-east Irish coast the area south of St. Bees Head was from a seaman's point of view as easy to make as the area to the north.

What, then, *was* the threat to the Cumberland coast? There was of course the chance of seaborne attack from the Clyde and the West Coast. Because of the type of craft available, however, this is scarcely worth considering. What Nepos and Hadrian were concerned with was clearly the probability of short-range attack in small craft from the deeply indented coasts of the Novantae: Luce Bay in Wigtownshire, Wigtown Bay itself, Fleet Bay, Kirkcudbright Bay, and the complicated indentations of Auchencairn Bay and Rough Firth. Given cohesion and organisation by a strong command, it is apparent that it could have been possible for the Novantae, in co-operation with a general attack from the north, to have landed a substantial outflanking force anywhere between St. Bees and the Bowness terminal.

North of the Wall the military system can be divided into two distinct sectors, one on each side of the spine of Britain. On the east above the Broad Wall there are five forts which were in varying degree associated with it: Risingham, Blakehope, High Rochester, Learchild, and the fortlet at Hartburn.

The first three of these are beyond question forts of the main road to the north. Hartburn is a fortlet of the Devil's Causeway, the fork road to Springhill on the coast of Northumberland. Learchild was built to cover the junction of the branch road from High Rochester to the Devil's Causeway.

The two last can be altogether eliminated from consideration in connection with the Wall. Hartburn was a small affair, probably late, and has not yet yielded information enough to fix its date. Learchild was Flavian and was certainly occupied up to the building of the Wall; it seems to have been abandoned thereafter.

Risingham was Habitancum. It lies in Redesdale on the south bank of the river on a sound if not a strong position, and it owes its first effective recognition to a delightful account by John Hodgson. In 1840 a long investigation of the site was initiated by Richard Shanks; it yielded a remarkable series of inscriptions, many of them from the baths, and other material —enough to plan its history in considerable detail. There may possibly have been a small Flavian fort on the site but it has not been identified. Nor, though it is the nearest of the northern Dere Street forts to the Wall, has it yielded evidence of Hadrian's reign, either in pottery or in structures. The first positive Roman dating is of the time of Lollius Urbicus, and therefore of the period of the return to Scotland. The existing work is mainly of the time of Severus and it was one of the strategic props of Caracalla's plan for control of the North after the death of Severus. Under Diocletian it was rebuilt, damaged again in the middle of the fourth century, reoccupied until the time of Theodosius and thereafter left ruined.

Blakehope has yielded little. A series of investigations indicate only that it was built before Hadrian's accession and abandoned after destruction by fire. Opinions vary as to whether it was one of Agricola's forts of the road or one of Trajan's hasty attempts to hold the pressure from the North. It seems to have been a cohort fort of just under four acres and to have faced south rather than north.

High Rochester was the Roman Bremenium, there is ample evidence for the name, from Ptolemy to inscriptions. Painstakingly excavated in the middle of the last century, it was until the dissection of Housesteads the most detailed surviving cohort fort in the Province. Camden knew of it, Horsley examined it, and

> A poor man of the name of Partis, some time since, in making a garden, adjoining to the north wall, is said to have found so many valuable articles, that he was never after in want.

The first work was a turf walled fort of the time of Agricola. Under Lollius Urbicus it was rebuilt in stone as a part of the project for the reconquest of Scotland. His fort was reconstructed by Severus, Diocletian largely rebuilt the Severan forts, and its vicissitudes are for practical purposes a time-table of the ebb and flow of the frontier. It seems remarkably difficult to claim that it was in any serious sense a part of the Hadrianic frontier scheme except inasmuch as it was a fort of the main road to the north and therefore a bar against its employment by a south-bound enemy. Evidence of actual Hadrianic use is quite unclear, even the first garrison inscription is of the time of Urbicus. That it would have been held as long as possible during the withdrawal from Scotland is obvious enough, but to suggest that it was in any real sense an "outpost" of the Wall needs solid proof.

The general problem of the "outposts" requires more precise analysis than has so far been accorded it. Birley, in his list of outposts, includes these last four forts and the three fortlets of the area—Hartburn, Tweedmouth and Mitford. That at intervals in the long and turgid history of the frontier these in various combinations were occupied, and served at least incidentally the purpose of a forward screen along Dere Street is, of course, not to be questioned. That they were outposts, in the strict sense of outlying works permanently integrated by strategic or tactical design with the main positions, is altogether improbable. The evidence of position suggests little more than that they were forts of the road, the inevitable defended works that ensured the safety and the efficiency of the network of communications by which Rome held down a newly conquered area and maintained her authority in settled country. There are as many forts on Dere Street in the twenty-five miles due south of Corstopitum as there are in the twenty-five miles to the north!

The matter is of the greatest importance to the consideration of the last of the four categories of forts in the frontier zone, the elaborate pattern of the area north-west of Carlisle.

Here in a belt little more than twenty miles deep, north from the Solway to Tassiesholm, there are eleven major forts, five fortlets and an extraordinary number of camps. Of these, three, arbitrarily and for no better apparent reason than some at least of the others, are designated as "outpost" forts—Birrens, Netherby and Bewcastle.

Of the eleven forts in this area the origins of two—Gatehouse of Fleet and the seven and a half acre work at Ward Law—have yet to be determined, five—Glenlochar, Broomholm, Tassiesholm, Dalswinton and Birrens—have been identified as Flavian and probably Agricolan, Netherby may have had Flavian beginnings but the surviving work is Hadrian's after 128, Bewcastle is Hadrian's after 128, Raeburnfoot is claimed by one party as Antonine and one as Agricolan, and Carzield appears to be definitely Antonine.

The pattern of the area, then, is that of a typical Agricolan holding network. The forts are forts of the road or of the glen. They were established to keep a difficult population in check, to stand between the Novantae, the outliers of the Brigantes on the Solway Plain, and the Selgovae to the north-east, and maintain the peace. This is a garrison area as, but no more, densely garrisoned than comparable areas to the south.

At Hadrian's accession seven of these forts were almost certainly occupied, sufficient certainly to form a formidable defence against invasion from the north and more than sufficient to perform the main duty of advanced positions—that of warning.

It is difficult, then, to understand the insistent and specialised designation of Birrens, Netherby and Bewcastle as "outposts".

Birrens (Blatobulgium of the Antonine Itinerary) has yielded definite Hadrianic material, and Birley accepts Pennant's version of a Hadrianic inscription from the site. The position, however, was occupied earlier by an Agricolan fort. The outline of it is faintly visible on the western side of the Hadrianic work and it was spotted from the air before the war. It stands on the Mein Water close to the point where the Roman road from Netherby altered course into Allandale. The site is on the southern slope of a rising hill, it had no outlook to the north, no direct communication with the northern complex of forts and only doubtful visual communication with Netherby twelve miles to the east.

Netherby (Castra Exploratorum of the Itinerary) was positioned on high ground on the east bank of the Esk. The site is largely covered today by Netherby House, and excavation has been limited. No positive indications of a Flavian fort have been discovered. As far back as Leland, however, "... Rynges and Staples yn the Walles, as yt had bene Stayes or Holdes for Shyppes" were known. The topographical evidence for the silting up of the River Esk is considerable, and the inference drawn is that in the days of the first advance to the north this was the lowest point at which the river could be satisfactorily crossed, and that this factor determined the line of the northern road. St. Joseph's survey, however, suggests an alternative crossing close to Longtown at the shallows of the Roost. The possibility of a fort of Agricola's time is considerable, major river crossings were for obvious military reasons almost invariably covered by a nearby garrison. But the position clearly contains the debouchement of Eskdale and Liddesdale and therefore must have been, with the small fort at Oakwood—which is unquestionably Flavian—a major element in the control of the Selgovae. The existing remains, which include a substantial bath house, are Hadrianic and the single inscription omits the *p.p.* addendum and dates therefore from before the year 128.

The third of the three "outpost" forts, Bewcastle, is perhaps the most remarkable of the three. Crowning a low, irregular hill in the centre of a shallow valley between high shoulders of the fells, it breaks most of the acknowledged rules.

It was established, almost certainly, on the sacred place of Cocidius, the war god of the Cumbrians. On the evidence of altars and silver plaques to the god it is certain that his worship continued after the occupation, and from this fact it is assumed that this was the Fanum Cocidi of the Ravenna list.

It utterly disregarded normal practice in the construction of forts. Neither square nor oblong, its walls followed the crown of the hill in six irregular facets, and internally the standard layout of a Roman camp is ignored. The limited excavation that has been carried out has decided the position of the *principia* and the *praetorium*. An elaborate internal bath has been examined, and one gateway of the Severan stone fort, which replaced the turf wall, together with timber buildings of the earlier construction, have been located.

Again there is no positive evidence of earlier work and indeed two inscriptions of Hadrian, both prior to 128, have been found. None the less, there are questions still to be answered. If this *was* an outpost fort, why was it built in a valley so wide as to be almost a bowl but so circumscribed by high fells as to have long-range visibility across barely ten degrees of the arc of its horizon and that to the westward—the most improbable direction for an enemy advance? Why also was it turf walled in Hadrian's day? Militarily Bewcastle is, in fact, another of the unanswered puzzles of the frontier system. Authorities insist on the probabilities of attack towards the Wall from the Bewcastle area. Attacks from the north would, in fact, more probably and more effectively have followed the Irthing valley on the high ground on either side of the river to feel for the weakness of the Gilsland Gap.

That Bewcastle was connected by road with Birdoswald may certainly be significant. That there was a signal station on Gillalees Beacon may also be significant, but it seems at least probable that this was set up before the building of Bewcastle at the time of the establishment of the six fortlets. Any consideration of Bewcastle must inevitably come up against the fact that it was singularly "blind", that its capacity for intercepting forces advancing on the Wall from the north was deplorably limited, and that its communications with the Wall—the Gillalees Beacon in any case was over the skyline—were defective.

The explanation of the three outposts seems to lie basically in the distance between the forts of the glens and the line of the Wall. This was a vast, open and easy country. At some point, possibly even in the last of the Trajanic period, it was decided to extend and simultaneously to repair and modernise the holding system in order to control it. Birrens was rebuilt as the link between the forts of the glens and Carlisle, Netherby was re-established as a fort of the road, and Bewcastle was set up to provide a garrison and patrols for the high ground to the east.

It has today, even at noon, an infinitely lonely and a ghost-ridden air.

11

Military Effectiveness

This then was the frontier defence of the Province of Britain.

What was its military effectiveness?

The single essential of a defensive system is security. Four times in the three centuries which followed Hadrian the security of the frontier was breached; four times the barbarians, breaking like a wave across the Wall, flooded the Province of Britain.

It has been argued that an average interval of seventy-five years between invasions represents a higher immunity than obtained on less elaborately defended frontiers. The argument is unsound. If the modern principle of cost effectiveness is applied to the system of which the Wall is the principal part, it is apparent that it failed to produce results commensurate with its cost—first, in the expenditure of man-hours and material on its building, and second and more importantly, in the cost over three hundred years of its garrison.

It was suggested in Chapter 2 that the historic failures of the Wall were in reality inherent in its concept, that it, in fact, acted as a breeding ground for the discontents which fired successive rebellions. On three of the four occasions on which the Wall was overrun it is accepted that disaster was made inevitable because its garrison had been withdrawn. This is not an excuse for the system but a condemnation of it, for on each occasion the garrison is known to have been withdrawn to support a pretender in rebellion against the Roman throne. The degree to which the seed of rebellion was inherent in too large garrisons too long idle is perhaps debatable, but it is not possible to argue the plain fact that the Province spawned a succession of pretenders, and that these pretenders were either senior officers like the Governor Clodius Albinus or the Admiral Carausius, inciting rebellion on their own behalf, or like

Maximus and Constantine III pushed from behind as the nominees of the men.

The size and density of the garrison is therefore a significant factor in any attempt to evaluate the effectiveness of the system.

Authorities differ. The Roman army in Britain certainly was based on a foundation of three legions—a total of approximately sixteen thousand eight hundred crack troops. Sixty-eight auxiliary units have been traced through inscriptions, discharge plaques and the *Notitia*. Sixteen of these were cavalry formations—one of them, the *ala Petriana,* a unit of a thousand horsemen. The fifty-two infantry cohorts included seven of a thousand men each and forty-five of five hundred—a total of thirty-eight thousand men altogether, making, with the legionaries, an effective strength of fifty-five thousand for the army of Britain.

What proportion of this force was committed to the defence of the northern frontier?

According to Collingwood in *Roman Britain* (1923), published when he was the chief protagonist of the Vallum Frontier Theory, the whole garrison "was probably about 8,000".

According to Collingwood in *Roman Britain and the English Settlements* (1936), published when the Vallum Theory was defunct, the total strength of the forts on the Wall was 8,000 infantry and 2,000 cavalry. The forts of the Cumberland coast, South Shields and the northern outposts brought the figure to about 14,000 and—with a patrolling garrison of 5,000 for the mile-castles and turrets of the Wall—made altogether 19,000 men.

According to Professor Birley in *Research on Hadrian's Wall* (1961) the garrison, with that of "the outpost forts and the nearest units on the lines of communication, totalled 5,500 cavalry and 13,000 infantry."

According to Dr. A. R. Birley in the Ministry of Public Building and Works' illustrated guide to *Hadrian's Wall* (1963) "the total garrison of the Wall was about 15,000 men."

The discrepancies are in part accounted for by variations in the definition of the frontier area. It appears as well, therefore, to attempt to set up a comprehensive list of the defences and the forts properly included in the "frontier", together with the estimated strength of their garrisons. In the absence of positive archaeological evidence in relation to a number of the forts, the matter of strengths can only be speculative but, in general, major forts are assessed at cohort strength—five hundred men —except for the four in the area known to have housed a milliary cohort—which numbered a thousand men. Minor forts, such as the Throp series, are more difficult to estimate and may not have held more than a hundred and fifty to two hundred men.

It is desirable also to attempt to assess which forts were, in fact, intended to be used in relation to the First Plan and which, with the advent of the Second Plan, were abandoned. This task is made difficult by temporary reoccupations and subsequent rebuilding, but the total committed to the frontier is directly affected by their use or disuse as also is the military density of the Wall area.

Finally, a last complication exists in relation to the patrol garrison of the Wall. The milecastles were, as has been described, designed in accordance with the First Plan as units of fifty men, thirty-two in the milecastle itself and the remainder in the turrets on either side. With the Second Plan this total was reduced. Evidence as to a precise figure is lacking, though a total of twenty-five is sometimes suggested, but a proportion—possibly determined by topographical requirements—unquestionably housed the full number. Poltross Burn, at Gilsland, was completed with two barracks buildings each holding sixteen men as in the original design, so certainly were others. Still more may have combined a single permanent block with temporary buildings at critical periods. Last of all, the precise number of milecastles proposed in the First Plan is not known. Possibly for a brief while it might have been intended to end the Wall at the Irthing. More probably, as was discussed in Chapter 8, it was intended to end it at the Eden crossing. Its continuation beyond that point and down the Cumberland coast appears to be almost certainly an addition of the Second Plan. Man-power totals must therefore be judged in respect of these possibilities.

If the First Plan, as has been suggested, covered the line between Pons Aelius and the Eden crossing, it incorporated, on the available archaeological evidence, seven forts of the original

Agricolan chain—Corbridge, Chesterholm, Carvoran (1), Nether Denton, Castlesteads (1), Old Church and Carlisle. With the new bridge guard fort at Pons Aelius, and Maryport on the Cumberland coast, the total was nine. In addition, it utilised eight fortlets of the Throp series, built hastily in the last years of Trajan's reign as a line of reinforcement against threatened attack from the north-west—Newborough, Haltwhistle Burn, Throp, Birdoswald (1), High Crosby, Drumburgh (1), Bowness (1) and Kirkbride. The garrison total for these seventeen forts—of which Chesterholm, the largest, held a thousand men—was approximately 6,000.

The Second Plan used probably not more than ten of these forts on a permanent basis, though others may have been occupied for indeterminate periods. With the new model cavalry and infantry forts on the Wall proper—South Shields, Wallsend, Benwell, Rudchester, Haltonchesters, Chesters, Carrawburgh (probably a late addition), Housesteads, Carvoran (2), Greatchesters, Birdoswald (2), Castlesteads (2), Stanwix, Burgh-by-Sands, Drumburgh (2), Bowness (2), Beckfoot, Burrow Walls and Moresby—the Second Plan involved altogether twenty-five forts between the terminals of South Shields and Moresby and required a fort garrison total of 14,250.

To the fort garrisons must be added the total for the patrol garrison along the line of the Wall. On the assumption that the First Plan ended at the Eden and that the unit figure was fifty men for a milecastle and two turrets, the total for the sixty-two milecastles involved would have been 3,100. If, however, the western extension of fortlets and signal towers in isolation from the Eden onwards was indeed conceived as early as the First Plan, the total would rise to 5,800.

The Second Plan added four more milecastles for the Wallsend extension—but MC 43 was demolished at Greatchesters and MC 80 at Bowness. In addition, as has been suggested, the manning scale was sharply decreased along the line of the Wall proper, probably to twenty-five men, requiring a total of 1,950. It is improbable, however, that it was decreased along the coastal extension to St. Bees Head, and the overall total under the Second Plan must have been 3,950.

To the figures for the immediate area of the Wall must be added the totals for the holding systems to the north-east and the north-west. These have already been examined and the indeterminate nature of the datal evidence in a number of cases makes precise assessment impossible. On the basis of known Hadrianic material, however, it is possible to assume that at maximum strength the north-eastern component—the four forts of Risingham, Blakehope, High Rochester and Learchild, all of which appear to have been manned prior to and in the earliest part of Hadrian's reign—needed for an effective garrison 2,000 men. In the later period Blakehope and Learchild seem to have been abandoned, but Hartburn was added to the list for a probable total of 1,150.

The north-western system in the opening years of the Hadrianic period consisted of Gatehouse of Fleet, Glenlochar, Ward Law, Birrens, possibly Netherby (1), Dalswinton, Broonholm and Tassiesholm. At full strength the garrison for these seven would total 3,500 men, but the occupational periods are still vague and it is possible to proceed on an estimate of probability only.

To these forts under the Second Plan were added Bewcastle (probably late in the day) and Netherby (2) for a total of 4,500. Once again the estimates can, in view of the very substantial work that remains to be done in this north-western area, be only speculative.

Finally, there is the constant figure of the legionary anchors to the line, York and Chester—the traditional strength being 5,600 men for each legion, a total of 11,200.

The overall figures for the frontier complex, then, read:

	First Plan	*Second Plan*
Forts of the Wall	6,000	14,250
Patrol Garrison	3,100	1,950
Western Extension	2,700	2,000
North-East	2,000	1,150
North-West	3,500	4,500
Legions	11,200	11,200
	28,500	35,050

The Haltwhistle angle. Milecastle 42 shows clearly in this picture ▶ of the restored sector of the Wall just before it ends on the lip of the Cawfields quarry.
Photograph: Ian Yeomans

Though the eligibility of certain forts for inclusion in these lists may be questioned, it is probable that doubtful instances cancel each other out. The figures in the second column show a rise of rather more than six thousand men on the total provided for by the First Plan. Considered in conjunction with the figures for the legions at York and Chester, which acted as the eastern and western anchors of the scheme and whose strategic role, after the closure of the frontier, lay essentially with the Wall system, the effective garrison of the frontier, it is apparent, totalled not less than thirty-five thousand men—approximately sixty-three per cent of the entire garrison of the Province.

These men were trained soldiers. In the early history of the Wall it is certain that the vast majority were drawn from distant areas. With the frontier legions it was accepted practice that they were raised in one province and transferred promptly to another. The Ninth—the Hispana—came to Britain from Pannonia, the Second, Augusta,from Strasbourg. Embroilment in local patriotisms was thus avoided. As the new legions became established a measure of local recruitment was permitted but the percentage was generally low. Auxiliaries were raised under similar rules. On the Wall the earliest known garrison at Chesters was the second *ala* of Asturians, at Housesteads it was the First Cohort of Tungrians. Raetae, Syrians, Germans, Dacians—all the provinces contributed to the Wall garrison. Inscriptions even record work by the Durotriges of Dorset and the Damnonii of Devon, but it is probable that these were construction units. It has been suggested that the patrol garrison occupying the milecastles consisted of second grade troops or even forced levies from the immediate locality, but the evidence is highly doubtful and not until very late in the occupation, if at all, were British troops acceptable in Britain. There is, on the other hand, ample evidence of their employment in Gaul and Germany and elsewhere.

The man-power total and the percentage of trained men are, however, alike inordinate. The initial construction of the

---

◀ Thirlwall Castle. Built, like almost every ancient structure for two miles on either side of the Wall, of ashlar looted from the ruins, Thirlwall is a typical Border keep erected to cover the eastern side of the Gilsland gap. The dead moles are a late addition. *Photograph: Ian Yeomans*

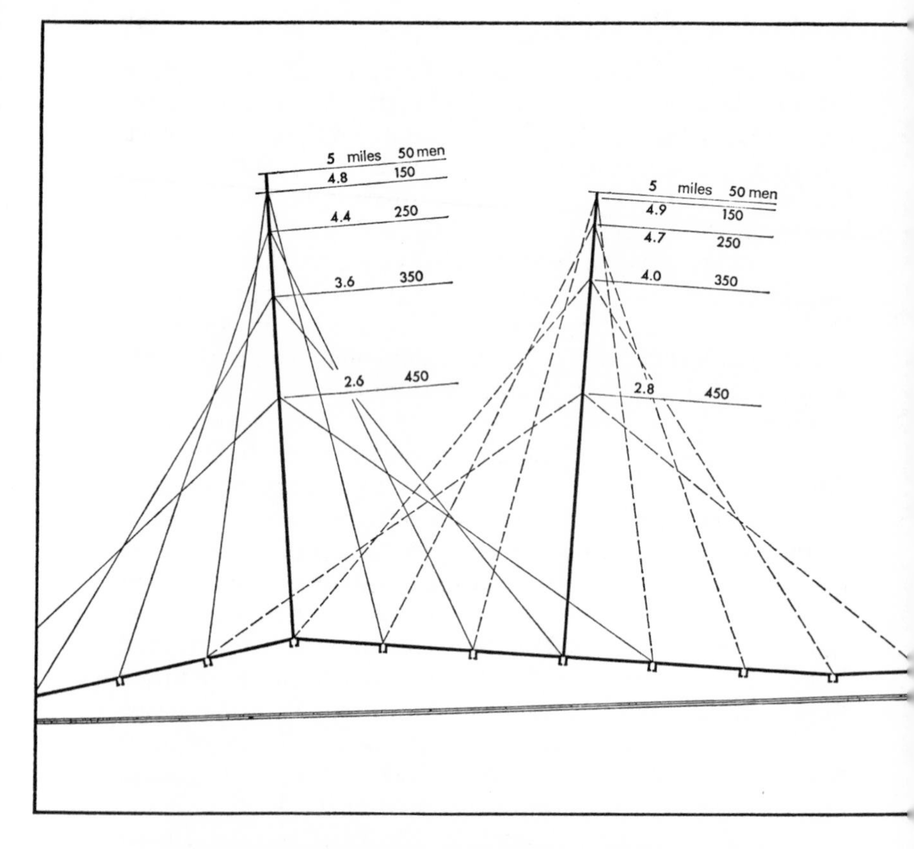

CONCENTRATION DIAGRAM : FIRST PLAN

The concentration diagram for the First Plan for the Wall—the original Milecastle plan with its 50 man garrisons. Calculated on the basis of a reaction time of one hour, it indicates that a continuous zone existed, beginning 3 miles north of the Wall and 2 miles in depth. Concentrations—diminishing with distance from 450 to 150 men—could be brought to bear on an advancing enemy within 60 minutes. Terrain difficulties naturally affected the time schedule but effective interception in strength was at all times assured. Reinforcements from the support forts could reach an average line 2 miles north of the Wall within the period.

Wall unquestionably made large demands on the finances of the Province, but long after its capital cost was amortised the annual cost of soldiers' pay must have been crippling. Militarily the system was undoubtedly effective, economically it was a disaster.

Is it possible to dissect from the surviving evidence the tactical theory which demanded this extraordinary concentration of man-power on a strictly limited front?

In any attempt to do so the two plans must be considered separately. The original plan made provision for a substantially lower expectation of attack than its successor. Reasons for this have already been argued but, at the risk of repetition, it is desirable to recapitulate. In its completed form, then, it called for a defensible wall, for a milecastle system of fortified gateways regularly spaced and realistically garrisoned, and for a strong support system of garrisons in the forts of the rear.

Despite the present fashion of denying the defensive capability of the scheme, a twenty-one foot six inch wall and parapet, fronted by a thirteen foot six inch ditch, was at least as defensible as a high proportion of the medieval English castles. It is none the less doubtful, however—contrary to the placidly accepted general view—that it could ever have prevented determined infiltration. Given a hide rope and a primitive grapnel, or even a stout length of tree branch to lodge between the crenellations, it would have been possible for any active youth to scale it in cloud on the high Wall, in fog on the Lowland stretches, or in night and rain almost anywhere.

Against deliberate attack the case is different. The time-scale of reinforcement for the patrol garrison along the parapet walk has already been examined. The parapet walk—at least in the Broad Wall—was *not* too narrow for defensive purposes; once again, it was wider than vital sectors of many medieval castle walks. The Broad Wall was beyond all question capable of repelling small raids and of holding surprise attacks in greater strength.

Static defensive capability, however, was one part only of an infinitely more sophisticated design. The milecastle system provided, as was outlined in Chapter 5, an offensive-defensive plan for the forward area, and the time and space considerations involved in this part of the scheme are of the utmost importance to the validity of both plans and indeed to frontier history.

The evidence suggests very clearly that the Wall was calculated on a time/space system based on the capability of a milecastle garrison over a period of one hour and to a distance of five miles.

The geometry of the theory is remarkably simple as the diagram on page 178 suggests. A milecastle garrison could advance in one hour at fast marching speed to a point five Roman miles to the north of the Wall. With the neighbouring garrisons on either side it could concentrate at a point slightly more than four and three-quarter miles in front of the Wall in the same period. Five garrisons in the same time could concentrate at a point four and a half miles from the Wall, seven at four miles, and nine at three. Eleven garrisons in all could concentrate on the central gateway inside the required period.

Allowing for the necessity to leave a gate guard at each milecastle and allocating a figure of ten men for each guard, the theory provides for concentrations of four hundred and fifty men at any threatened gate of the Wall. It provides, even more importantly, for an effective zone of interception over a belt roughly two miles deep beginning three miles to the north of the Wall. Within this area, and within the period of one hour, concentrations varying from one hundred and twenty to three hundred and sixty men were possible.

No precise figure exists for the comparable value of trained Roman soldiers and "barbarians". But in the circumstances of the Wall the garrisons would have been able to choose the line of attack, to secure the advantages of the flank of their choice, and to utilise a known terrain to secure every possible assistance. A ratio of three to one, with due allowance for Roman arms and Roman training, does not seem inordinate, but even at two and a half to one, a concentration of three hundred and sixty men, given the advantages of choice and time, would probably have been considered adequate to deal with a tribal foray of a thousand men. The prospect must have been daunting to any enemy unless he was prepared to scale up the weight of attack substantially beyond this level.

At this point the third factor in the tactical theory of the Wall comes into play. Though nothing is known of the inten-

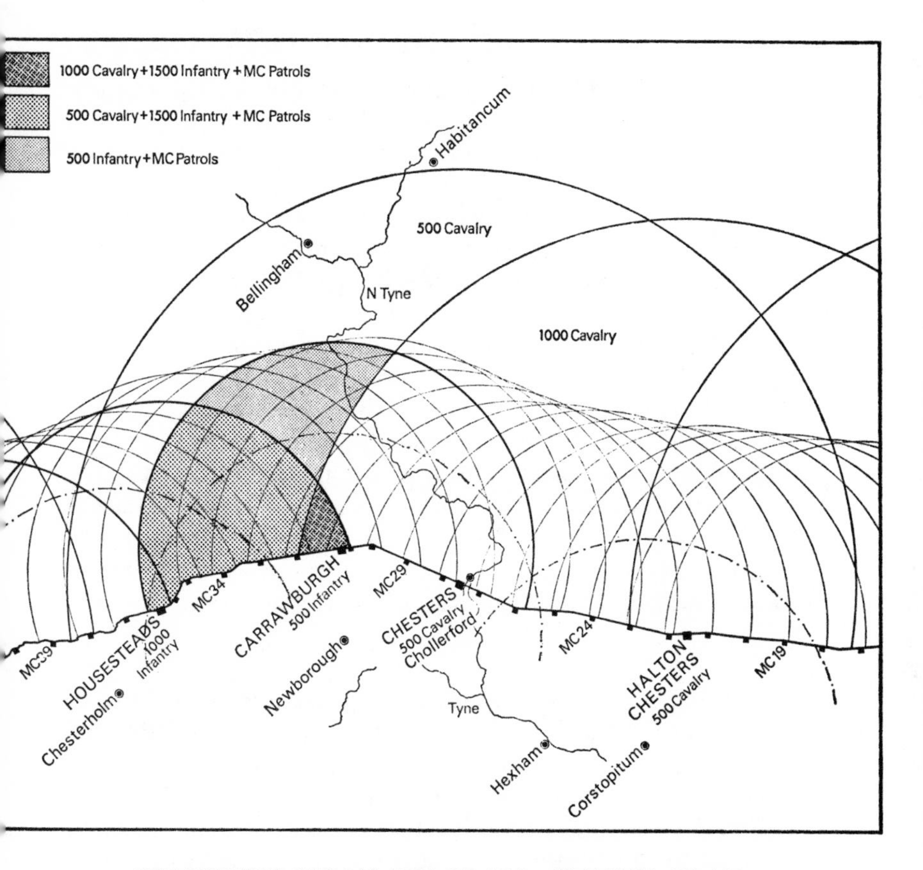

CONCENTRATION DIAGRAM : SECOND PLAN

The advent of the cavalry forts enormously enlarged the possible reaction of the Wall system in time and distance. The small interlocking circles of the diagram contrast the possible infantry concentrations of the First Plan with the increased potential of the cavalry forts of the Second Plan (indicated by the large circles). Mutually self-supporting, the cavalry forts provided for a concentration of 1,000 horse at an approximate distance of 9 miles north of the Wall with overlaps of 1,500 horse at regular intervals. In the central area the new infantry forts on the Wall—Housesteads held 1,000 men—were strategically placed to defend the difficult terrain of the Great Whin Sill. Cavalry support could be brought to bear on an expanded time scale within this area also.

tions of the First Plan for the eastern sector of the Tyne valley, from Corbridge onwards there is a well-spaced succession of support forts. Corbridge actually is the farthest of the chain from the Wall. With due allowance for a relatively slow speed up Stagshaw Bank, the Corbridge reserve could have been at milecastle 22 within thirty-five minutes of an alarm. It could have been well over two miles north of the Wall within the hour. Corbridge is the worst case. All other forts could have reached the zone of maximum concentration within the time limit. With the ease of the lateral communications along the Stanegate and the Vallum, concentration was possible to astonishing degrees.

The Wall of the First Plan, then, provided not merely for a sound defence but covered itself with a fighting zone adaptable to almost any scale of enemy attack and almost any combination of forces, and always behind it there remained the ultimate sanction of the legions. York on the east was two and a half days in an emergency from Corbridge, Chester was four fast days from Carlisle.

The Second Plan enormously enhanced the possibilities of the forward zone. The diagram on page 181 illustrates the degrees and variety of concentration obtained in the altered circumstances of the cavalry plan.

The milecastle garrisons, it is true, were probably reduced to less than twenty-five men except at critical points by this plan, and the weight of the concentration was therefore approximately halved at the infantry level. But this loss was powerfully counterbalanced by the advent of cavalry. With an alternation of trot and canter a cavalry formation could make good ten miles in the hour. The immediate defended zone, therefore, was doubled in width. The position of the cavalry forts—there were five from Wallsend to the North Tyne crossing—permitted immense overlaps within the time-scale.

The arc of a ten-mile semicircle centred on Chesters—the last cavalry fort of the eastern sector—covers Carrawburgh, Housesteads, and overlaps by a mile and a half the arc of a ten-mile semicircle from Birdoswald—first cavalry fort of the western sector. The arc of Haltonchesters covers Chesters and Carrawburgh to the west and reaches far beyond Rudchester to the east.

Within the intersections of the arcs, concentrations of a thousand cavalry were always possible within the hour. Within the overlaps of three arcs, where they occur, the total is raised to one thousand five hundred.

The Second Plan, however, in addition, placed two major infantry forts, as has already been described, on the line of the Great Whin Sill, and Carrawburgh was added to these a few years later. In the eastern approaches to the Great Whin Sill opposite Housesteads it was possible to effect concentrations of five hundred cavalry, one thousand five hundred infantry, and the garrison of the milecastles at an hour's notice, a notable and formidable expansion of power.

The theoretic possibilities were diminished at points by the character of the terrain. It was not always possible, inevitably, to proceed in a straight line; bogs, deep rivers, crags and forest affected the time of concentration and the speed of advance. Yet these same factors affected an enemy to a greater degree. The foreground of the defensible zone was the home ground of the garrison of the Wall. In the constant patrolling of periods of strained relations every detail of every sector, every advantage of every feature must have been known to all subordinate commanders.

The conversion to cavalry added other vital advantages to the defence. The possibility of extended patrols in great strength offered stringent guarantees against surprise. Carter Bar on the watershed between Northumberland and the Tweed valley was only slightly over thirty miles north of the Wall. The seaward plain opposite Berwick was hardly more than twice that mileage from the bridge at Pons Aelius. The Solway Plain and the dales of Dumfriesshire were well within the operational range of detachments of the thousand-strong regiment of the *ala Petriana* at Stanwix. Aggressive patrolling in time of imminent attack was, over this terrain, entirely possible, and infinitely the best form of defence. So important was the conversion from a defence based on infantry to one based on cavalry in real terms that it raises inevitably the question as to whether the change was not, in fact, forced upon Hadrian by major advances in the enemy cavalry potential.

The Caledones in Agricola's time clearly possessed both chariots and horsemen. It is at least possible that applying the lessons of the defeat at Mons Graupius over the intervening period, they had achieved a higher proportion and a more effective tactic for the cavalry arm. If the Ninth Legion was in fact slowly worn down over the latter end of this period, it is entirely conceivable that this was due to the traditional problems of infantry in the field against well-used cavalry. The advantages postulated for the cavalry of the Wall applied unquestionably in a substantial degree to the cavalry of the barbarians in open country.

The control and the employment of the enormous forces which these varied considerations established between the Tyne and the Solway by the end of the building of the Wall, required a high degree of expertise. The chain of command is therefore of importance. Under the remote control of the Emperor, the forces of the northern frontier were administered by the *legatus legionis* at York—the senatorial commander of the VI Victrix. Tactically the senior officer of the Wall must have been the commander of the principal unit—the milliary unit of the *ala Petriana* at Stanwix.

No positive evidence has been discovered to suggest a more central command post, though it is possible that the unconventional lay-out of the buildings of the fort at the Haltwhistle Burn indicates a control headquarters during the period of the Wall construction. Objections to Stanwix have, however, been put forward on the grounds of its distance from the eastern coast. They are scarcely acceptable. Stanwix, if the coastal extension of the Wall as far as Moresby is taken into consideration, is sixty-six Roman miles from Wallsend and fifty-four Roman miles from Moresby. More importantly, it is the nodal point of the whole western system with its essential holding pattern of forts and fortlets to the north-west. At Carlisle the road network of the west centred.

It is therefore properly of the commander at Stanwix that Professor Birley says:

> He could quickly concentrate, if need be, a force larger than Agricola had used to fight and win the battle of Mons Graupius in A.D. 84.

12

The Antonine Adventure

The significance of Professor Birley's estimate of the potential of the frontier force has escaped the attention of most commentators on his work. Its implications are extensive and salutary. It seems highly probable that similar conclusions rapidly arrived at by Hadrian's immediate successors account for the brevity of the first phase of the existence of the Wall.

Built, as has been described, at a staggering cost in man-hours, designed with great military brilliance, elevated by Imperial escalation into the strongest defended frontier of the Empire, Hadrian's Wall in its first phase lasted barely ten years.

Remarkably little is known of those ten years; the interval is one of the infuriating lacunae in the history of the Province. Nothing is known of attacks by the barbarians on the frontier zone, nothing is recorded of pre-emptive attacks by the Romans to the north. Hadrian in these years lived out his life, diminishing in tragic convolutions of suspicion and disillusion, and died—and that, so far as the Province of Britain is concerned, is all.

Antoninus Pius succeeded him. Frontier policy changed. The dating of this, like all the chronology of this confused period, is difficult. In or about the year 138 Lollius Urbicus, a not particularly distinguished soldier, was appointed Governor of Lower Germany. Two years later, so far as the evidence serves, he was moved to Britain to reorganise the northern zone. By the opening of the campaign season of 141 it is apparent that he had completed plans for an advance through Lowland Scotland. No immediate *casus belli* is recorded. No explanation of the urgency of the decisions involved is available.

What little can be gleaned from archaeology suggests that one column moved north along Dere Street and another, and possibly a larger force, from Carlisle by Agricola's western road through Annandale. His primary objective appears to have been the line Newstead-Lyne-Castledykes-Loudoun Hill. No evidence of hard fighting exists, but the operation, together with the rebuilding of the Agricolan forts on the Newstead line, seems to have absorbed the first campaign season. In rear of the new line Urbicus restored the major forts of the Flavian period and built a chain of fortlets along the road between Birrens and Crawford to cover his communications in the west. The rebuilt Agricolan forts along Dere Street covered his eastern route.

Over the whole area between the Newstead line and Hadrian's Wall the Flavian security system was re-established.

It would be intensely illuminating to know if military headquarters in Rome at this date maintained a filing system of campaign dispatches. From the opening of the operation Lollius Urbicus appears to have followed meticulously the operational precedents set up by Agricola. In degree he was, of course, constrained to this by the topography of the area, but the parallels are direct and compelling. Like Agricola he moved on two main axes, like Agricola he brought all three legions up at the outset of the campaign, like Agricola he concentrated them on the start line of the Tyne-Solway isthmus, and like Agricola he used his first season in Scotland to consolidate his rear position in the southern Lowlands.

For the second year of the campaign the evidence is, until its conclusion, as indefinite as for the first. Wherever he effected his final concentration, Urbicus moved down from the high ground of the Lothians with his main force basically intact. Where he fought and defeated the northern tribes is unknown. Whether they were broken in a single battle or whether he drove them to the Forth-Clyde isthmus in a series of debilitating skirmishes is nowhere made clear. History rests upon a simple sentence written by Julius Capitolinus in the fourth chapter of his life of Antoninus:

> *nam et Britannos per Lollium Urbicum vicit legatum alio muro caespiticio summotis barbaris ducto....*

An epoch is concentrated in fourteen words. "Lolius Urbicus overcame the Britons. After driving back the barbarians, he built another wall, of turf."

The simple descriptive sentence has been translated in every conceivable manner to prove every possible variant of probability. It is not necessary to drown here in this particular morass. The sense is clear enough: Urbicus drove back the barbarians and built another wall, of turf.

Logically, then, the "barbarians" must have come south out of the Highlands. He drove them *back*! Logically he built another wall. Logically he built it across the Forth-Clyde isthmus. The whole thing is plain and it is confirmed. In the fall of 142 a centurion with the coveted privilege of a bearer of great tidings reached Rome. For the second time Antonius was declared *imperator*—a great victory had been won. New coins declaring the subjugation of Britain were issued.

Thus far the parallel with Agricola is absolute; as has been described earlier, he had established a *limes* on the Forth-Clyde line. How far, however, did Urbicus propose to follow him? Agricola's *limes*, after the pattern of his day, consisted of a lateral road studded with forts built in accordance with his particular talent for the selection of commanding sites. It was, in origin, a winter line, designed, in effect, to form the start line of his final offensive to the north—perhaps also to serve as a switch line in the event of trouble in the first phase of a northern campaign. It was demonstrably temporary!

Was that of Urbicus?

The question opens a wide range of speculation. Was Urbicus' strategy in essence to repeat that of Agricola to its ultimate victory? Did he propose to thrust forward through Strath Mor to challenge the main Highland strength, to envelop the Highland massif, to crush the tribes with the Caledones at their head, and to pacify and consolidate the whole of Northern Scotland?

There is at least *prima facie* evidence of intention.

Sir George Macdonald is categorical. "We know," he says in *The Roman Wall in Scotland*, "that during the period of occupation a line of forts stretched northwards from Camelon into the heart of Perthshire." Collingwood, discussing the strategy, describes Urbicus as "following Agricola once more in throwing out advanced posts beyond the isthmus as far as Inchtuthil". Richmond, criticising the qualities of the Wall, says: "All Fife had to be encircled in order to prevent its use as a spring-board for an attack on the east."

Evidence for these claims is singularly slender. It seems indeed fair to say that no proof of serious occupation at any time of more than the road through Camelon to Ardoch, the key fort in Strath Allan, exists.

The implications of this are significant. The real problem was never to establish the parallels between the operational plans of Agricola and those of Urbicus, but to define the precise point at which the plans diverge. In time and place this point was Ardoch.

It need not be assumed that Urbicus here suffered a defeat. It is more probable that here he took time to assess the profit and loss account of his advance. After two seasons of hard campaigning his casualties must have been at least substantial. To reach Strath Mor he had still to force his way through the gap into Strath Earn. Certainly his troops must have been tired. Probably he had outstripped his logistics. But heaviest of all was the drain on his forces caused by the necessity to establish the garrisons of the rear. As Birley properly estimated, the man-power total of Hadrian's frontier system was greater than the force which had defeated the Caledones under Agricola, but the army which finally reached Ardoch under Urbicus was no longer adequate to the conquest of the North.

To Agricola the forts of the winter line were an integral part of the drive to the north. His road led past Ardoch and past Strath Mor to the succession of the great marching camps that mark the way beyond Ythan Wells to the Moray Firth and the envelopment of the Highland massif. It was a means and not an end—a means to secure his winter line and to enable him to rest and refit for the resumption of his advance. Urbicus' "wall of turf", on the other hand, was an end and not a means. It was the northern limit of advance; with its construction he abandoned any intention of the final conquest of Scotland. The Antonine Wall was a harsh confession of failure.

It was too solid and not solid enough, it was too strong and too weak. It was too hurried and it wasted a whole indispensable, irreplaceable season of campaigning time.

How does it compare with Hadrian's Wall?

It is not within the scope of this book to attempt a detailed examination of Urbicus' design. In general terms, however, the Antonine Wall was forty-one and a half Roman miles in length, just over half the length of the walled sector of Hadrian's complex. Starting with Carriden and ending with Old Kilpatrick, it had altogether nineteen forts, spaced just over two miles apart, as against the five-mile spacing of the southern plan. In size its forts ranged from the six and a half acres of Mumrills to Rough Castle's single acre. It was long accepted that it had no milecastles, but Dr. St. Joseph has established the position of three fortlets between the main enclosures, and evidence of at least two others exists.

The Wall itself was built by large gangs from each of the three legions. The magnificent series of sculptured distance slabs, one of the glories of the scheme, name the detachments which took part and record the work done. It was built of turf on a laid foundation, the kerb stones of which were approximately fourteen feet apart; at the point where the road to Camelon cut through the Wall just beyond Rough Castle it changed, however, to clay. Its height was not more than ten feet with a parapet walk six feet in breadth. Probably there was a wooden "crenellation" but no evidence of it remains.

The Wall was fronted by a fighting ditch over most of its length almost forty feet in width. Its profile varied, but for substantial distances it had the typical square-sectioned bottom ditch. At Bar Hill and at other points it cut through solid rock. Unlike Hadrian's ditch, it was completed.

The forts themselves were built, in part at least, by the units that manned them. All except two, Balmuildy and Castlecary, were of turf or clay; these two were of stone. A lateral road, the Military Way, passed through the forts with by-passes where desirable.

There was no Vallum. Despite this, the diehards of the "customs barrier" still cling valiantly to their theory. Collingwood held that its absence merely meant that "a *modus vivendi* had been reached by which the customs officers could be accommodated in the forts". The point seems scarcely worth arguing. For most of the life of the Northern Wall Rome was bitterly at war with the Northern tribes.

The plan bears evidence of urgent uncertainties. It has nowhere the craftsmanship of the Southern Wall and it was not at any time designed to employ its techniques of the offensive-defensive. It bears, in fact, every evidence of a decision hastily arrived at to extract the best out of failure. Its line is not at any point planned, as was the line of the First Plan of Hadrian's Wall, to provide effectively for the defence of an area forward of the Wall itself. Urbicus, faced with the abandonment of his attempt to emulate Agricola, sought simply for a quick solution to his difficulties; and his line follows the high ground from the Firth of Forth at Carriden, uses the cover of the marshes of the Carron through Falkirk, and thereafter links the sites of the forts of the Agricolan winter line. Sir George Macdonald in his monumental survey of the Antonine Wall suggests that nine of the nineteen forts that comprised the plan were originally Agricolan. Subsequent excavation and newer methods have reduced their number. Probably not more than five, at the most six, of the nineteen are indisputably Agricolan, but the choice of the line clearly reflects the state of Urbicus' mind. It determined inevitably both the strategy and the tactics of the system. The sites of the Agricolan forts were selected, as has been said, for their defensive qualities in isolation. It was originally a loose chain, built without any regard for Roman engineering predilections in favour of straight lines, and the men who surveyed the position for Urbicus developed it by placing their markers on the forward slope below the crest of the high ground but, as far as possible, with a steep fall in front of them. There was clearly no thought of elaborate time-space considerations and planned concentrations in a defensive zone ahead of the Wall.

The forts, when not built on Agricolan sites, show no clear evidence of logical development. Nine of them are lost under the damnation of industrial progress. Of those that remain, three at least—Bar Hill, Croy Hill and Westerwood—appear to have been built substantially after the Wall itself, and are without natural bridges across the Fighting Ditch to the north. Bar Hill is built apparently in isolation with a complete ditch system of its own a few yards to the south of the main rampart. Old Kilpatrick, the anchor fort at the western end of the Wall immediately above the Clyde, was also built in isolation, with its corners rounded. The Wall patently reached it late across ditches that had already been dug.

The most remarkable of the anomalies of the Wall, however, are the stone forts at Balmuildy and at Castlecary. Excellently built of ashlar—one probably by the Sixth Legion, the other by the First Cohort of Tungrians from Housesteads—their southern corners were rounded, with watch towers, their northern corners square. Balmuildy was provided with wing walls ready to bond into a running wall when it came, precisely after the pattern of the milecastles of the First Plan for Hadrian's Wall. It is immediately obvious that there was here a serious conflict of planning. None the less, the position is wholly different from that, for example, at Housesteads. This was *not* a fort intended for existence in isolation. It was clearly designed in due consideration of its eventual incorporation in a wall.

But in a *stone* wall.

Castlecary was square cornered to the north but without wing walls. Neither design made for a tidy junction. The turf wall when it reached Balmuildy was brought in with consummate awkwardness behind the stone-work of the wing on the eastern side, and left the area equally awkwardly at an angle of sixty-five degrees on the west. At Castlecary the turf wall foundation was aligned precisely with the footings of the stone wall. As the face sloped, backwards, after the normal fashion of a turf wall, there must have been a highly untidy angle at the point of junction with the vertical wall of stone.

Finally, the ditches in front of both forts were freakish—in front of Balmuildy narrow across the full width of the fort, in front of Castlecary narrow across half of it.

Remarkably little consideration appears to have been given to these oddities.

Whatever their causes, the Wall was completed. Its garrison absorbed about seven thousand men, with perhaps another two thousand on the defences of the road to Ardoch as long as that was maintained.

It lasted in its first phase probably thirteen years.

At some point in time in the first quarter of this century it began to be whispered among the scholars that it was strategically unsound. Professor Haverfield was almost certainly the prophet of the new contention. In *The Roman Occupation of Britain*, published in 1924, he summed it up.

> Tactically the new line was strong.... But we must admit that its strategic weakness was pronounced. At more than one critical point the northern hills rise dangerously near and threatening. On the west its defences could be easily outflanked... on the east its right could readily be turned.

In accordance with normal custom his successors followed him through the same hole in the same fence. In 1936 Collingwood declared himself. In *Roman Britain and the English Settlements* he wrote:

> Granted the insecurity of the Antonine Wall's strategic position, the slightness of its works, the makeshift character of its organisation... it may be thought to resemble a temporary measure.

Richmond, astonishingly, followed them both—with certain reservations—as late as *Roman Britain* in 1963.

> Tactically considered, the Antonine Wall was in fact less an imitation of the great work which it superseded than a skilfully devised improvement upon it. Strategically it is more open to criticism. Its flanks are weak, and the weakness is emphasised by the precautions taken to avoid it.

There are others who take the same view, but these will serve—the view itself is arrant nonsense. The Forth-Clyde isthmus is strategically the strongest internal frontier position in the entire island of Britain. It is the shortest possible military line anywhere between the Straits of Dover and Cape Wrath. It permitted for that reason the most economical and at the same time the most cost-effective frontier garrison conceivable in Britain. Its flanks, far from being weak, were superbly protected by deep tidal water—except at the Dumbuck ford below Kilpatrick, which was carefully covered by the Whitemoss Fort on the south bank of the Clyde. Its potential enemies were weak in respect of shipping, but the *classis Britannica* by 142 was strong enough to deal with any reasonable situation.

Tactically it was neither strong nor a skilfully devised improvement on the Wall of Hadrian. Tactically, in fact, it was a botch, and in due course it paid the penalty of its tactical inadequacy—but not at the time of its first abandonment.

Hastily planned and hastily built, it served for its first thirteen years as a substitute for Hadrian's Wall. Its accomplishment was a tribute to its siting but not to its military politics. Only the conclusion of total victory could have justified this major advance to the north, only the conquest of Scotland. It was not achieved.

13

Regeneration of the North

Essentially the policy of Agricola was dynamic. It relied from the beginning for its success on the impetus of its forward movement. In simple terms, Agricola's plan was to knock the enemy off balance early and to keep him off balance thereafter.

Essentially the failure of the policy of Urbicus lay in his abandonment of the dynamic—his loss of impetus.

With the construction of the Northern Wall, Antonine policy must be paralleled not with Agricola but with Maginot. The inherent defect of the change is that the forces available were as inadequate to secure a permanent defence as they had proved incapable of supporting a dynamic impetus. Orthodox opinion on the Lowland defensive system has in the main failed to attach a proper weight to this fact.

Appreciations of this system are generally muddled and occasionally weird. Perhaps the most remarkable is that of Collingwood in *Roman Britain and the English Settlements.* Drawing an extraordinarily doubtful analogy from Fabricius' suggestion that the shallow advance of the frontier defences in Germany under Antoninus was designed to keep newly established colonies of barbarians "in" rather than to keep the traditional Northern enemies "out", he says:

> If the Antonine Wall, like the "outer *limes*", was designed rather because of what lay behind it than because of what lay in front, its unprotected flanks are no longer a fault. And if we can find reason for thinking that the potential enemies against whom it was built were, through some special cause, unusually weak, the unusual weakness of the Wall itself becomes only reasonable.

The paradox of a northward facing wall, built for the most part below the brow of a northward facing hill, being designed to keep the conquered—and thinned out—Lowland tribes from escaping to their hereditary enemies of the North is militarily farcical. But followers of Collingwood in this matter have in addition claimed that the southern defences of the forts of the Antonine Wall were stronger than the northern. The briefest examination of Macdonald's excellent plans is sufficient to prove the irrationality of this theory. The military logic of the Antonine Wall is straightforward: it was built to keep the Northern tribes at bay.

A second school of thought holds the belief that the two Walls were maintained simultaneously. Once again the proposition is at least doubtful. Purely military demands raise such questions that it requires to be examined in some detail.

Lollius Urbicus entered on his campaign with a considerable handicap compared with Agricola. Where his predecessor had had four legions, he had three—a twenty-five per cent reduction in the indispensable component of his field army. It is possible, though arguable, that he possessed larger auxiliary forces at the start, but the deficiency in legionaries remains unaltered and significant. In Chapter 11, it will be remembered, the effective garrison of the frontier—including the anchor legions at York and Chester, was estimated at thirty-five thousand men, a figure equivalent to approximately sixty-three per cent of the garrison of the Province. Though II Augusta was certainly moved up from Caerleon for the opening of the campaign, and some of the Welsh forts and a large number of the Brigantian forts were shorn of auxiliaries, it is impossible to see how Urbicus could have concentrated a field army large enough for the task in hand without denuding the Wall and its ancillary forts of the greater proportion of their trained troops.

Far too much significance has been attached to the evidence of legionary occupation of the Wall in this period. It is, to begin with, tenuous: an undated inscription at Housesteads set up by soldiers of II Augusta stationed in the fort, building inscriptions at Chesters possibly dated to about 139, dedication slabs indicating constructional work of 139 and 140 by II Augusta at Corbridge, an altar of the same legion at Tarraby and one of VI Victrix at Kirksteads, and a soldier of XX Valeria Victrix buried at Carvoran. Though most of the dating is indefinite, it is reasonably of the period—there is, however, little else. On this slender basis an elaborate theory has been erected which claims that the legions manned the gaps in the Wall when the auxiliaries moved forward and, by extension, the continued manning of the forts as a whole has come to be accepted.

In view of the attenuation of Urbicus' army as it moved north—dropping off garrisons for the forts of the consolidation—it is unbelievable that this could have happened. The manning scale of the forts probably occupied at the time of Hadrian's death was calculated in Chapter 11 at something over thirteen thousand. To suggest that Urbicus could for one moment have considered leaving behind even ten thousand men out of his exiguous forces is absurd.

The presence of legionaries on the Wall may best be explained by the probability that they were positioned—temporarily—at certain forts in reserve. The evidence that there were men of the named formations at Housesteads and Corstopitum suggests a force held in readiness in the vicinity of Dere Street, and the Kirksteads altar with its implications of a return to base from "operations beyond the Wall" might equally be evidence of a reserve of the Sixth Legion stationed in the Carlisle area on the western road. With the frontier now far to the north, Chester and York were out of phase in the support role.

The constructional evidence on the Antonine Wall, on the other hand, indicates that while vexillations only of the Sixth and the Twentieth worked on wall and ditch, the whole of the Second Legion was so employed, which would appear to make nonsense of a formal occupation of Housesteads by the Second in replacement of the First Cohort of Tungrians in the period up to the completion of the northern system.

The most probable position on the Wall as Urbicus moved north is—at the risk of repetition—that garrisons, equivalent roughly to the average density of the Brigantian holding system, were left at selected forts, separated by the customary distances of the holding system and possibly reduced numerically in accordance with a general reduction throughout the area.

The first hard evidence that exists at all in this matter is that, at a date accepted as coinciding with the completion of the Antonine system, the Wall as such was abandoned, the gates of the milecastles were taken off their pivots—the pivot slabs themselves appear to have been destroyed—and the Wall patrol was finally suspended. Simultaneously, and even more significantly, the Vallum was "erased"—the crossings are curiously like the transverse strokes that one would make with a pencil in eliminating a feature from a map—and the frontier was moved forward a hundred miles.

It should not be assumed from this, however, that the Wall system as a whole was written off. Unlike the isolated forts of a holding area in process of pacific abandonment which could be left to rot, the Wall was a gigantic complex still almost brand new, elaborately equipped and capable at any time of serving as a reserve position in the event of northern disaster. It is inconceivable that an army administered as was the Roman army would have jettisoned an asset such as this. It seems probable that some system of care and maintenance was set up at the very beginning of the Northern advance along the whole length from Wallsend to St. Bees Head—parties sufficient to prevent the unoccupied forts being taken over by squatters from the local tribes, to keep the thatch of the barrack blocks in repair and the gates in order.

It is unnecessary to look farther than this. The new frontier was a hundred miles to the north. The area between was garrisoned. The Lowland tribes were subdivided by the roads of the consolidation, and surprise was out of the question.

In a sense this contention is supported by the first campaign that followed the establishment of the new frontier. The evidence indicates that it was a campaign "between the Walls" and its occurrence has been used in justification both of the "southward facing" theory of the Antonine and the continuous occupation theory of the Hadrianic Wall. Neither theory, in fact, applied.

The historic evidence, as always, is perilously slight; moreover, it is disputed. It rests once again on a single sentence—this time from Pausanias, the Greek geographer:

> He took from the Brigantes the larger part of their territory because they had raided under arms into the Genounian area, the people of which were subject to the Romans.

Few more unexceptionable statements of fact have been subjected to more varied interpretation. The passage has been used forcefully to prove that the action of the Brigantes was the reason for Antoninus' abrupt change of frontier policy and the excuse for the conquest of Southern Scotland in 142. It has been used with equal forcefulness to explain the withdrawal from the Antonine Wall about the year 155. There is some slight excuse for the commentators. Not only is the date of the episode obscure but no one knows where Genounia was.

S. N. Miller, editor of the Glasgow Archaeological Society's excellent volume on *The Roman Occupation of South-Western Scotland*, suggests that it was in the country of the Novantae to the west of Nithsdale. The evidence is basically archaeological. It pivots largely on the destruction of Birrens at about this time.

It has been ridiculously complicated, however, by the interpretation of the more or less simultaneous reconstruction of a deserted Agricolan fort at Brough in Derbyshire, twenty miles south-east of Manchester. The coincidence is held by a whole list of earlier experts to prove the existence of a vast Brigantian uprising from the far south of their territory to the extreme north, a rising which, oddly, produced no proven damage except at these two points. If it happened at all, however, it would patently have involved every fort across a hundred and twenty-five miles of the weakened holding system of Brigantia and most of the forts of Hadrian's Wall west at least of Housesteads.

The proposition of a national uprising of the Brigantes at this time is in reality a manifest nonsense. There was, however, an enclave of the Brigantes north of the Wall and stretching across the Solway Plain up the low ground of the northern dales. Precisely where it stood in the campaigns to the north of the Wall is unclear; probably it was always in Roman care and protection, and possibly because of that it waxed fat and kicked. What may be called the Miller theory—though it is shared by others—is that Genounia was raided as the result of a border quarrel between the northernmost of the Brigantes and the Novantae in the area of Nithsdale, and that in 155 the quarrel exploded into general insurrection between the Walls. The timing is appropriate enough. Fourteen years after Urbicus' campaign the Lowland tribes had regenerated, the gaps of the casualties of that campaign had been made good, the tribes were ready for battle once more.

It is, however, the plan of the damage that offers the most tangible evidence. Instead of covering the length of the tribal area of Brigantia, it constitutes an ellipse stretching north-east from Nithsdale through Newstead to the Firth of Forth at Inveresk. Birrens, Milton, Cappuck, Castledykes and Inveresk all appear to have been destroyed or seriously damaged at about this time. The destruction of the Antonine Wall itself follows a different pattern. It suggests if not an orderly withdrawal, at least a predetermined one. The damage is not that of siege or combat but of deliberate wrecking, executed at leisure.

Returning, then, to the Miller theory and extending probabilities, the raid into Genounia disrupted the balance of peace in the area: the Novantae from the west fought back and the holding garrison intervened; Birrens, possibly in the absence of its garrison in the field, was burned, the reserves in the Carlisle area were inadequate to halt the insurrection, and the fighting spread across the width of Lowland Scotland, involving the rest of the tribes and in due course cutting the lines of communication west and east of the watershed. Gathering momentum, it eliminated the bases on which the strategic viability of the Antonine line depended, and with Castledykes and Newstead beleaguered, or possibly even in ruins, the garrison of the Antonine complex was withdrawn, reconstituted as a field army and struck south. Presumably at the same time the reserve forces on the line of the Solway-Tyne moved north to take the enemy in rear.

The campaign and the subsequent pacification of the Border people in the difficult hill country of the area appears to have taken at least two years, and casualties—the implication is explicit in the evidence of the Newcastle slab which records the arrival of fresh drafts—were heavy. All three legions required major reinforcement, and though direct evidence is lacking, balancing reinforcements for the auxiliaries must have been sent about the same time.

With their arrival a methodical repacification of the Border area was obviously possible. The first question in the minds of the Roman command clearly must have been the desirability or otherwise of restoring the Antonine line. Necessarily one approaches the matter in the light of hindsight, yet it must surely have appeared in simple logic that the Antonine line had not in itself failed in any way. Its destruction had not happened because "its flanks were weak", not because its garrison was inadequate, not because it had been overwhelmed by an unanticipated coalition of strength in the North, but because Urbicus and his successors had consistently miscalculated the resilience and the growth rate of the Lowland tribes.

This capacity for regeneration is the crux of the entire situation. It was a capacity which would have been enhanced inevitably by direct communication with the Northern tribes, and the abandonment of the Antonine division could only have served to accelerate and magnify it. The urgent military requirement, therefore, was to re-establish that division and to reorganise the holding system for the Lowlands on a pattern which took a more realistic view of the nuisance value of rebellion south of the Forth-Clyde isthmus.

The orthodox view is that with the arrival of reinforcements a methodical repacification was indeed initiated. The Miller theory claims broadly that a new Nithsdale road or at least a substantial development of known tracks was constructed at this time, and that at Carzield, three and a half miles north of Dumfries, a cavalry fort of four and a half acres was established with stone barracks and wooden stabling to act as a nodal point for an extension of the controlled area into the territory of the Novantae.

The archaeological importance of Carzield in the light of later theories is extreme.

The rebuilding of Birrens, the possible rebuilding of Netherby, of Milton, and subsequently of the other forts of the damaged area by Calpurnius Agricola is by the orthodox view ascribed to this period, and if this ascription is correct, by simple military logic the reoccupation of the Antonine Wall system follows, since the rebuilding of the holding complex, whose sole *raison d'être* was the support of the Antonine system, would have been singularly illogical without it.

Orthodoxy, however, is not enough. In March, 1967, at the Institute of Archaeology, Dr. Michael Jarrett and J. C. Mann put forward a new theory of the time-table of the occupation of Hadrian's Wall and of the Antonine which challenges all existing chronology. Dr. Jarrett accepts that the first period of occupation of Hadrian's Wall ended with the completion of the Antonine rampart, that after this it ceased to exist as a frontier though certain of the forts remained occupied until the trouble of 155. He does not accept a repacification of the Lowland area immediately after the reinforcement of 158, and argues that Hadrian's Wall was re-established as the frontier in that year and maintained as the frontier until 181 when, he claims, *it* was the Wall "crossed over" by "the tribes within the island". According to his theory, Marcellus, sent to Britain urgently by Commodus to restore the situation, accomplished his purpose, and only after he had done so was the frontier moved north again and the Antonine Wall restored. Thereafter, he asserts, it operated as the frontier probably until 207 and finally, after a further abandonment, it was partly reoccupied for two years in the course of the Severan campaign.

The evidence for this theory, as for all theories in this undocumented period, is slight. The reoccupation of Hadrian's Wall, for example, appears to be based on the rebuilding "of substantial lengths of mortared stone wall" by the Sixth Legion in the year 158. Two stones attest this rebuilding. Discovered in the course of the construction of the Carlisle road in 1751, the exact positions at which they were found were not recorded, though the series as a whole was listed as from Heddon-on-the-Wall. The stones themselves have long been missing, and the interpretation of their inscriptions is debatable. One uses the word *refecit*, which clearly implies rebuilding, the other word *perfecit*, which might imply the completion of new work; neither positively relates to the destruction of "substantial lengths of wall" whether by Roman troops or barbarians.

That the Vallum was partially and indifferently cleared again at about the time of the trouble, that some of the milecastle gates were rehung and some of the gateways partially blocked can all be attributed to a brief re-establishment of Hadrian's Wall as a military barrier in this period of extreme threat. None of it is effective evidence of almost a quarter of a century's reoccupation.

On the Antonine Wall the evidence is equally uncertain.

Some of it rests at least on the ingenious interpretation of material assumed to have been cleared from the ditch at Rough Castle and spread across the famous *liliae* in front of the site of the fort. There are two layers of this material and they appear to relate to two long periods of occupation, each succeeded by disaster and then by major reconstruction of the forts. It is extraordinarily difficult to relate this to the Jarrett time-table.

It seems even more difficult to relate the Carzield evidence. Carzield is declared to have had one long occupation only, it was wholly Antonine, and there is no evidence of a break in continuity. If it was built as a part of a general re-establishment of the Roman position in the Lowlands which began in 158, as Miller holds, it had a rational span of existence. If it was not built until the time of Commodus—when Jarrett claims that Marcellus rebuilt the forts of the Antonine Wall for the first time—neither its military rationale nor its archaeological evidence would seem to fit.

The simple fact is that the "evidence" in relation to these years is almost everywhere wholly unreliable, that not enough field work has been done yet to solve satisfactorily even the basic problems, and that it will be necessary to call upon all the resources of scientific archaeology before an acceptable chronology can be determined.

The purely historical evidence is, as always, slender and enigmatic. Once again it is a single passage, an account written by Dio Cassius more or less contemporaneously with the disasters of 181, but surviving only in the eleventh century epitome of his work by John Xiphilinus. The passage says:

> The tribes in the island, having crossed the Wall that separated them from the Roman cantonments, caused great destruction, after killing a certain general and the men who were with him. Commodus was much alarmed and sent Ulpius Marcellus against them.

To the patent fury of generations of scholars, Dio neglected to say which wall.

Jarrett returns to early assumption and chooses Hadrian's. Militarily it is difficult to justify the choice. To have overwhelmed Hadrian's Wall, manned and at full strength, would have required numbers, speed, and astonishingly skilful coordination. Against the forces necessary for such a triumph, the rapidity and ease of the alleged reconquest of Lowland Scotland is altogether unconvincing. If rebuilding between Forth and Clyde was actually completed by 184—as Jarrett implies by his date for the beginning of the second period of the Antonine Wall—the campaign of Marcellus was a masterpiece on a scale previously unattained in North Britain. Whatever the real truths of this most complex period, the Antonine Wall was, beyond question, reconstituted somewhere within this decade and survived at least until the assassination of Commodus.

14

The Engendering of Revolt

The assassination of Commodus and its immediate consequences is one of the tragi-comedies of Roman history. It marks, more importantly from the point of view of the British walls, the first direct intrusion of the Province into the highest level of Roman politics.

Marcellus had been succeeded as Governor of Britain by Helvius Pertinax. Pertinax reached Britain to find the army balancing on the edge of mutiny. It had had five years of relative peace since the last northern campaign, but by this time the irrationalities of the reign of Commodus had spread to and infected all the frontiers of the Empire. The air of Rome itself was full of plot and counter-plot, and at least one attempt—the Priscus affair—had been made in Britain to set up a rival Emperor. Obscurely there had been also a connection in Britain with the conspiracy of Perennis.

Pertinax appears to have dealt promptly and effectively with the one legion which went into open revolt, though he was reported "left among the slain" in the course of the action. According to at least one account, having dealt faithfully with incipient particular mutiny, he was at once offered the option of heading an attempt on the throne himself with the general support of all three legions. The offer was rejected, but in Rome conspiracy developed in complex patterns. Pertinax finally asked to be released as Governor and returned to the capital and to the interplay of intrigue and madness that led inexorably to the assassination of Commodus in a palace revolution. Pertinax was hailed as Emperor—possibly against his sober judgment—by the Praetorian Guard and within three months was dead, assassinated by those who had sponsored him. With the auction of the Empire that followed his death Rome sank to the nadir of political irresponsibility.

Julianus, the man who bought the Empire, accomplished nothing save his own inevitable end. Along the frontiers the generals raised their heads: Pescennius Niger in Syria, Septimius Severus in Pannonia, Clodius Albinus in Britain.

Severus held the central position. Militarily nearest to Rome on the banks of the Danube, he made his bid with ruthless speed. It has been said that no man took off his breastplate between Carnuntum and Rome. By July 193 he had reached the capital, broken the Praetorian Guard and crushed the least shadow of opposition in the city. Julianus was assassinated by a common soldier at the instigation of the Senate. With Rome safe, Severus began the process of eliminating the rival generals. Judging Niger to be the most dangerous, he offered Albinus the title of Caesar—in effect making him his heir and possible coadjutor—and, with immediate opposition from the west checkmated, moved east to deal with Niger. In a brisk campaign the army of Syria was defeated and Niger himself was killed. There remained frontier trouble in the east, and for two years Severus fought a series of campaigns until most of the discontent had been suppressed and he could turn back to Rome to settle the problem of Albinus.

The background of the story from the British side is obscure. Albinus had originally been offered the rank of Caesar by Commodus and had rejected it. It is obvious that he regarded Severus' offer with a deep and proper suspicion. Having secured the complicity of the army in Britain, he now appears to have entered into treasonable correspondence with the Senate. Whether Severus intercepted his letters or whether he was betrayed is immaterial; Albinus was declared an enemy of the State. In 196 he crossed the Channel defiantly to Gaul. With him he took the legions, the cavalry, and almost certainly the greater part of the auxiliaries. The legions of Gaul, led by officials loyal to Severus, failed to hold him and he established his base at Lyons, setting up at that city a rival court and, for effective purposes, seizing control of western Gaul. There late in 196 Severus moved against him. At Tinurtium on the Saone north of Lyons the battle hung for hours in the balance. Leaden ballista missiles, mined—to the perennial satisfaction of British historians—in Derbyshire, all but decided the issue against Severus' army. He himself was believed for a time, according to Spartianus, to have been killed by one of them. But almost was not enough. The tactical brilliance and the ruthless leadership of Severus by the end of the day commanded the field. By nightfall Albinus was dead—by his own hand, or dispatched "half dead" by Severus, it scarcely matters.

Behind him, over the deserted Walls of Britain, between the empty forts, along the Roman roads, the barbarians streamed south. Where the flood began is uncertain. If Ardoch was occupied then, it may have begun there—much depends on the identification of the tribe known as the Maeatae as the original aggressors. Certainly the Antonine Wall was overrun. The trail of ruin spread south from it through the great forts of the base line and down past the holding forts of the Lowland country to Hadrian's Wall. What garrisons there were were overwhelmed, what men Albinus had left behind were slaughtered or made prisoner; there can have been no more than a handful. Even if the estimate of a hundred and fifty thousand men on the two sides at the battle of Lyons is exaggerated, he must still have taken with him almost every front-line soldier of the army of Britain.

The tribes, if the evidence of destruction is interpreted correctly, used the two main Roman roads east and west of the central spine, but at Brougham, south of Carlisle, the western force appears to have split, one element changing direction down the diagonal road to York and overrunning the forts of Stainmore to concentrate with the eastern horde, while its main body swept down the road to Chester. The eastern thrust reached the pinnacle of achievement with the stark, deliberate, formidably engineered destruction of the walls of the fortress of the Sixth Legion at York, the western force less certainly with a possible attack on Chester. North Britain lay in the hands of the barbarians.

Once again the historical evidence is limited. The basic facts of the withdrawal of the army from Britain by Clodius Albinus are accepted, the battle of Lyons is acknowledged history, his death is a climactic point in the record of the reign of Severus—but no one wrote the story of the tribes. The basic evidence, therefore, is once more archaeological, a record of wholesale destruction. Such historical backing as there is lies principally in the evidence of the reconstruction which followed.

Severus—the facts here at least are positive—sent Virius Lupus as Governor to the rebellious Province. He made his way cautiously north, presumably at the head of the humbled and disciplined legions of the revolt—the Sixth certainly was building at Corstopitum in Lupus' governorate. Lupus had a strong record as a soldier, but it is apparent that he arrived at once at the decision that the forces at his disposal were wholly inadequate for a punitive campaign.

Again the information comes from Dio in the abridgement of Xiphilinus, who describes Lupus as "buying peace from the Maeatae for a substantial sum, receiving in exchange a few prisoners".

British history has not yet arrived at a conclusion with regard to the Maeatae. Dio locates them as inhabiting the country "near the wall that bisects the island". The Caledones, he says, lived "beyond them"—for a second time he omits to state which wall.

Dio was a contemporary of Severus; he was, it is recorded, on intimate terms with him; but the *Romaika,* his eighty-book history of Rome, was written long after Severus' death. It ends with the reign of Alexander Severus, which lasted until 235. In the decade in which it was written there was, in fact, only one wall operational—Hadrian's! It is perfectly reasonable, then, to read his description of the Maeatae as relating to a confederation of the Lowland tribes under a new and comprehensive name, and to interpret the Caledones similarly as a coalition of the tribes beyond the Forth-Clyde isthmus. Orthodox opinion has fluctuated between this possibility and the alternative that the Maeatae was an alliance of the Venicones with the subtribes of Eastern Scotland, while the Caledones were limited to the people of their original mountain fastnesses.

There is, in fact, no hard evidence for either supposition.

It is necessary therefore to examine the matter from the military point of view. One other clue in Dio assists in this. Lupus is said to have decided to buy the Maeatae off because of the imminent threat of a general coalition with the Caledones—the Caledones, therefore, had taken no part in the invasion.

The implications of this are far-reaching. If the second body of opinion is correct and the Maeatae were the tribes of the eastern half of Scotland north of the Firths, the invasion of the Province represents an enterprise of astonishing rashness. Not, let it be noted, because of the danger of Rome but because of the danger of the Caledones. It seems inconceivable that the entire man-power of the eastern tribes—essentially a plains people living on terms of traditional if intermittent enmity with the Highlanders—could have been placed at risk in a move south across the isthmus of the Firths. The depth of the drive to the south would have been in reality a gamble of incredible proportions. With every mile towards York the risk of the Caledones flooding down from their hills and taking over the fertile plain of Eastern Scotland increased dramatically.

The risk in relation to a confederation of Lowland tribes below the Firths was in a wholly different category. Militarily it would have been possible for such a confederation to have established a rearguard at the narrows of the Forth-Clyde isthmus sufficient, if not to stave off a full-scale Caledonian attack, at least to hold it for long enough to bring the main force back.

Conversely, it is fair to puzzle over the explanation of the failure of the Caledones to take part in the invasion from the first if the group was in fact contiguous and friendly. The richness of the plunder of the Province should have presented an irresistible bait.

The military situation accords better with the possibility that Maeatae was the generic name for a Lowland confederation. The swiftness of the onslaught, the depth of the penetration, the decision of Lupus (clearly apparent in the record of his reconstruction) not to thrust recklessly even as far as the line of Hadrian's Wall, the absence of any attempt at a punitive expedition into the Lowlands or any effort to re-establish the holding system there, all suggest caution in the face of imminent danger—not of a danger removed by purchase a hundred miles to the north across the Forth-Clyde line.

Turret 26b, a typical turret of the Broad Wall, inset into the fabric of the structure. The patrol way was reached by a ladder. The proportions of the turret above the Wall itself are unknown. *Photograph: Ministry of Public Building and Works* ▶

None the less, the peace that Virius Lupus bought lasted. He completed his term of office with the forts repaired as far as Corbridge and work on the rehabilitation of the Wall begun. He was replaced by Alfenus Senecio, and the work progressed. The archaeological picture is one of intensive activity in the forts, and in the outposts which now at least *were* clearly outposts. It has been suggested that the period of rehabilitation was unduly long. It might as reasonably be said that the circumstances of the rehabilitation were unduly difficult. By the year 206 the precarious peace was ending. Dio says that there were successful wars in that year. They may have been successful; they were not, it is apparent, decisive. Herodian states that Senecio reported to Rome that the situation demanded more troops or that "an Imperial expedition was required".

Severus answered the appeal in person. It is apparent in the story of his campaign that he had lost his fire. The man who had stormed from Carnuntum to Rome without taking off his breastplate, who had broken Niger at Issus and swept from Byzantium to break Albinus at Lyons, failed in the foothills of the Highlands.

He was old, past sixty now, worn with campaigning and the intrigue and resentments of his harsh reign. He brought with him to Britain his sons, Caracalla and Geta—and there is small evidence that they eased his task. Tradition says that he brought them to separate them from the debaucheries of Rome. It seems more probable that he brought them to keep them from each other's throats under his immediate eye.

How he reached the Highland country is one of the minor mysteries of the Roman occupation. Again the authorities are split. There is no direct evidence of the passage of a Severan army between the Wall and the great basin of Strath Mor. Repair work of doubtful identity on the Antonine line has been

---

◀ The granaries at Corbridge. Heavily constructed buildings elaborately buttressed to take the weight of the grain they contained, the granaries had flagged floors built on low piles after the manner of a hypocaust to assure ventilation. They traditionally held enough grain for the garrison for a year.
Photograph: Ministry of Public Building and Works

accepted as indicating a possible short-term occupation there, but the evidence is contradictory and tenuous, and if it is valid at all, the work may be accounted for by local alterations towards the end of the second period of the Antonine. Two sites only offer positive proof of occupation in the three seasons of Severus' campaign: Cramond a little to the eastward of the Forth Bridge, where coin evidence suggests a substantial traffic, and Carpow.

Carpow is in many respects the most remarkable single site in Northern Scotland. Built on the southern bank of the Tay, it has been identified with the Horrea Classis of Agricola. The identification is in process of abandonment—excavation has supplied no signs of the Agricolan naval base, but Carpow by itself remains astonishing. It was built as a major base to hold the Sixth Legion. Designed for three thousand five hundred men, it may suggest either that the legion's losses had not been made good after Lyons or, alternatively, that at least a vexillation was held in reserve either for the completion of the rebuilding of Hadrian's Wall or with the standards at York. It was provided with buildings on a scale of extraordinary elaboration; the accommodation for the legate is described by Richmond as a "palace".

Its position on navigable water and the lack of evidence for a march by land has given rise to a widely accepted theory that Severus reached the Tay by sea. This is at least improbable. From the nearest base port in secure territory—South Shields —it is the best part of a hundred and twenty miles of open sea on a harsh coast subject to strong prevailing north-easterly winds for much of the year. That the *classis Britannica* had substantially improved by the end of the third century is possible. That a force large enough to land an army was available is doubtful in the extreme. That a base port existed large enough to handle such a fleet within the time scale necessary for an invasion is absurd. South Shields, important as it was as a port for the Wall, was wholly inadequate. The legion at Carpow numbered three thousand five hundred men alone, but this can have been no more than a single element in the force necessary to deal with the Highland problem. Agricola had succeeded narrowly with four legions plus a strong force of auxiliaries. Urbicus had failed with three. It is difficult to concede that a soldier of Severus' judgement could have been content with less. To have moved the necessary modicum of thirty to forty thousand men and stores by water to Carpow or even to Cramond and Carpow is surely out of the question. To have lifted the necessary cavalry as well would have been impossible.

Despite lack of archaeological evidence, the major part of Severus' army must have gone up by the old roads and the old marching camps, moving fast, leaving little mark of its passage behind it. The Emperor and his sons, on the other hand, may well have gone by sea.

There has been much bickering between the historians as to Severus' campaigns and it is easy to pick from their books views that are diametrically opposed. But one point appears to have escaped critical analysis. Severus launched his first attack not against the Maeatae—who had carried out the great raid and who had had to be bought off with an inevitable loss of face to Rome—but against the Caledones, who had played no part. If Cramond and Carpow were his major bases, one or other must have been within the territory of the Maeatae whichever theory as to the territorial identification of the confederation is correct. Whatever the explanation of this singular circumstance—and it clearly requires explanation—Severus was by the evidence free to make his first thrust into the Highland country. For the first part of the campaigning season, however, he failed to make contact with an elusive enemy. One school of formal historians presents an almost aimless probing up and down the fringes of the central massif, the other then produces a final triumphant battle and the capitulation, in proper form, of the Caledonian nation. It is possible that both are correct, but the evidence, as always, is of the slightest.

Presumably the victory claim is best supported by the fact that the campaign of the second year was not against the Caledones but against the Maeatae, who were in revolt! Relationships between the tribes are always, in the absence of written record, doubtful at any given moment. Yet it appears astonishing that the Maeatae, if their grievance against Rome was heavy enough for revolt in 210 and their strength adequate, in their judgement, for the action they chose, had not struck the previous year, when Severus was deeply embroiled with the Caledones.

Once more it is possible that there is an indication here of the tribal area of the Maeatae. If, in fact, the confederation lay south of the Firths, it was little involved in the first year of the campaign. Severus' army could have crossed it by agreement—or by a fresh purchase. A base at Cramond implied no more than transit rights along fifteen miles or so of the northern fringe of the territory. The Maeatae in isolation, therefore, may have regarded the attack on the Caledones with a cynical and detached eye, trusting that the Romans would be sufficiently occupied in the Highlands to leave them alone.

On the other hand, if their territory was Eastern Scotland north of the Firths, Carpow lay at the heart and centre of it. The lines of communication for the Caledonian campaign radiated from it, wholly unprotected except possibly at Bertha and more doubtfully at Cardean, and it is all but impossible to understand why they delayed once Severus was inextricably engaged in the mountains. Whichever the motive for the delay, the Maeatae in the event were trounced.

Neither the victory against the Caledones nor the thrashing administered to the Maeatae was, however, decisive. In the winter of 210 Severus, ailing, went down to York to the comfort of the rebuilt fortress to plan a campaign of total victory. In York, early in 211, he died. On his death-bed he said: "I leave the State at peace, even in Britain, old now and with crippled feet...." His gout had troubled him to the end.

Caracalla and Geta succeeded as co-Emperors. One of the most brutal and unpleasant of the later rulers of Rome, Caracalla has been subjected to endless abuse. His part in the decisions in Scotland has been harshly criticised, chiefly perhaps because the third campaign was never launched. An unspecified agreement, however, was entered into with the Northern tribes and the army moved south as mysteriously and with as little trace as two years earlier it had reached the north. Behind him Caracalla left an unfinished conquest—and yet, based perhaps on his "agreement", more certainly perhaps on the strength of Severus' reconstruction of the Wall of Hadrian, he left peace for the rest of the century.

In Rome it was different. In Rome he murdered his brother Geta something less than twelve months later.

Peace on a frontier is always relative. There were minor troubles over the period, small punitive campaigns, police raids, but there is no evidence, historical or archaeological, of a major attack by the Northern tribes. Yet in 197 the Wall was overrun again.

And it was shattered once more because it was undefended.

The revolt of Carausius is one of the more engaging chapters in the history of the pretenders to Roman power. Carausius was a seaman. He was born somewhere on the Lower Rhine, and he achieved by sheer force of personality the command of the Channel fleet, which probably at this date included the *classis Britannica*. The Channel was increasingly subject to extensive raids by the Franks and the Saxons from Northern Germany; the British coast itself was probably under attack; Eutropius records that Carausius was given the task of keeping the peace in the sea area, and his principal base was at Boulogne. He was accused of coming to an "arrangement" with the raiders. Acid Roman gossip said that he intercepted their ships only on their return from raids and that the spoil accrued to him.

In 286 Diocletian in Rome, his forces heavily overstretched by troubles in the east, threats in Germany, and a rising in Gaul, divided the Empire into two parts. Maximian was appointed Emperor of the West.

Maximian, scenting insubordination or loot or both, ordered Carausius to report to him, and Carausius refused. Whether, as some writers have said, he fled at once to Britain or whether he held on defiantly in Gaul, it is certain at least that the essential port of Boulogne remained in his possession. Maximian, without a fleet, had small hope of an immediate solution. By 289, however, he appears to have built ships enough for his immediate purpose—probably on the Seine, possibly in Brittany. Sailing from the Seine up-Channel against the possibility of attack either from Boulogne or from the British coast, the new and inexperienced fleet found refuge in the traditional Roman excuse. The attempt was foiled "*inclementia maris*"—by the harshness of the sea.

Maximian, preoccupied elsewhere, abandoned the attempt. The rule of Carausius—Marcus Aurelius Mauseaeus Carausius, as he had named himself on taking the purple—was acknowledged. Coins carrying his head, with those of Diocletian and

Maximian, were struck. They bore the simple heart-warming words: "*Carausius et fratres sui*". There have been less credible inscriptions—but not many.

For three more years Carausius held Boulogne, a strip of North Western Gaul possibly as far as Rouen (where there was a mint), and Britain. In 292, however, Constantius Chlorus, newly appointed Caesar by Maximian because of the growing problems of the Western Empire, closed on Boulogne. In a swift and energetic siege he built a mole across the harbour mouth, hemmed in at least some of Carausius' ships, and carried the vital base. Carausius himself had already withdrawn to the island. The sea became the moat of the new Empire.

Behind the moat Carausius built the third "Wall" of Britain.

The nine gigantic Forts of the Saxon Shore that remain—originally there were probably eleven—were erected, according to the archaeological evidence, towards the end of the third century. No more precise date exists for any one of them.

It is true that the Saxons and the Franks were threatening the Channel at this time—Carausius' appointment to command hinged on that fact. It is true that two and possibly three of the eleven sites of the British forts were older in origin. It is true that a more or less complementary pattern of forts was built along the Gaulish coast from Boulogne to Blaye. But it is also true that there is a major difference between the two systems. The Gaulish forts were built to defend particular places. The British forts were, in almost every instance, built to command navigable estuaries and harbours, particularly in the sensitive area between the Thames and Dungeness where there were five, and always in such a relationship with the sea as to speak a close co-operation with naval forces. In 1961 an American historian, Donald A. White, put forward the salutary theory that the "third Wall" of Britain was built by Carausius not against the barbarians but against Rome.

The theory has yet to be disproved.

The fall of Boulogne in any event opened the way indirectly to the fall of Carausius. Allectus, his finance minister, conspired; Carausius was murdered, and Allectus usurped the precarious throne of Britain. He lasted three years only. The fleet of Gaul was strengthened again; its commanders acquired experience, two forces of invasion were concentrated—at Rouen and Boulogne. In a Channel fog Asclepiodotus—praetorian prefect—reached the British coast, outflanking the defences of the "Saxon Shore". Allectus is said to have concentrated a fleet off the Isle of Wight, and the assumption is that Asclepiodotus landed somewhere on the western Hampshire coast beyond the great anchor fort at Portchester.

Allectus had concentrated his main army near London to counter the force assembled at Boulogne under Constantius Chlorus. In the urgent crisis of the landing he appears to have lost control. The army of the Province was ordered south—the legions from the great bases, the auxiliaries from the Wall. With the force under his immediate control—probably consisting of the London garrison and detachments from the eastern force of the Shore—he moved to intercept Asclepiodotus. The march was incompetently organised, his forces lost cohesion, in confused fighting Allectus was defeated and killed.

And far to the north the barbarians flooded again across the Wall, looting, wrecking, burning. Once more there is no historical record from the point of view of the tribes. It is stated only that for the first time the "Picts" appear in history. Yet the initial attack must have been engendered in the Lowlands, among the tribes close to the Wall, among the men who watched it, who knew to the hour the withdrawal of the *exploratores*—the Border Scouts—the abandonment of the Wall itself, the beginning of the march of the auxiliaries to the endangered South.

How far the tribes swept is uncertain. York was destroyed for the second time, Chester was devastated. The flood may have raced still farther south, but once again there is no alternative except to rely on the evidence of reconstruction.

Constantius Chlorus, according to Collingwood:

> ...restored the walls and public buildings of Verulam, and doubtless other towns too; it may have been he that added the bastions to London Wall.

Certainly an optimistic medal of the time shows him at the gates of London encircled by the words: "*Redditor Lucis Aeternae*"—restorer of eternal light.

The evidence, however, is capable of other interpretation. In view of the strength of the forces landed in Britain it seems extremely improbable that the barbarians could have reached as far south as Verulamium less than seventy miles, as the crow flies, from the southern coast. Yet beyond question the raid was deep and savage, and certainly the great multangular tower at York is Chlorus' work and all along the length of the Wall there are signs of Diocletianic repair.

In due time the Wall was manned afresh. Britain, which had already been divided into two provinces, was sub-divided again into four. The military system was reorganised. Three new commands were set up, the first under the *Dux Britanniarum,* whose headquarters were at York and who controlled the frontier area in general and the Wall in particular, the second under the *Comes litoris Saxonici*—the Count of the Saxon Shore—who commanded the still powerful forts of the seaward defence, and subsequently the *Comes Britanniarum*—the Count of Britain—who led the mobile field army.

Peace broke out again on the frontier.

This time it lasted, with relatively minor excursions beyond the Wall, for seventy years.

15

The Great Overwhelming

> "A philosopher," says Gibbon, "may deplore the eternal discord of the human race, but he will confess, that the desire of spoil is a more rational provocation than the vanity of conquest."

With that acidulous genius by which he underscores his points, Gibbon, discussing the barbarian invasion of the Province in 367, accepts the rationale of the purpose of the Northern tribes —and simultaneously makes a thrust at the too complacent contemporary acceptance of Roman motives.

The barbarian conspiracy—Ammianus in the *Rerum Gestarum* uses the words *"barbarica conspiratione"*—was inspired basically by "the desire of spoil", but it was fed by close on three hundred years of conquest and control. Hadrian's Wall had stood for two centuries and a half, and despite the great raids that had followed each of the temporary failures of governance and the long periods of accepted peace, there persisted in Northern Britain a tradition of bitterness and oppression. It is explicit in Constans' brief campaign north of the Wall in 343 and again in the raids put down by Lupicinus four years later.

The barbarian conspiracy was in reality the cumulative reaction to an age of wrong. Its victory is the greatest single achievement in the history of the early Britain peoples.

It is also the most neglected!

Again the reason is probably that romantic Latinity which reached its full flowering in Victoria's time and which, as has already been suggested, is responsible for the continuing neglect of Boudicca. Something at least of the explanation lies also, however, in the acceptance of the term "barbarian". It was, as has already been agreed, a word first of Greek and then of Roman arrogance, the insolent attitude of a conqueror to a subject people. The basic concepts of this "conspiracy" were in reality in no way barbarian. Behind them there are the clearest indications of political acumen, of judgement and leadership, of military skill in planning and of military skill in execution that place it by itself in the catalogue of Western opposition to Roman arms.

The Wall of the Province was this time manned, the coasts were fortified, the Roman fleet developed and conditioned to sea war, the command organised and practised, the armed forces, so far as contemporary evidence goes, at normal strength. Yet in a campaign of blinding speed the outposts were overrun, the Wall was carried by assault, the commanders-in-chief were killed or captured, and down the familiar roads of conquest and in from the defended coasts the people of the great alliance raced to the rape of the Province. The forts of the legions were wrecked again, the small towns and the villages were burned, London itself was besieged, and the smoke of countless villas drifted across the sky.

This time judgement is not hampered by the limitation of historical evidence to a single sentence. The account of the campaign in the twenty-seventh book of the *Rerum Gestarum* is detailed and explicit. It gives the time and the place of the receipt of the first news of the break, it names the generals, it lists the preparations for the reconquest, and it outlines its success.

Its author, Ammianus Marcellinus, was a sceptical professional soldier. A Greek of Antioch, he had fought in at least six major campaigns, he was with Julian in the war against the Alamanni, and he had suffered in the long retreat from Parthia after Julian's death. He knew therefore both the Empires, East and West, he understood the military aspects of the disaster, and he was a man of sober and detached judgement. He was about forty years of age when the Wall fell.

The *Rerum Gestarum* is a history of Rome beginning approximately and appropriately where Tacitus left off: it was completed finally about the year 391.

> "Having set out then from Amiens and hastening to Treves," Ammianus says, "Valentinian was alarmed by serious news which showed that Britain was brought into a state of extreme need by a conspiracy of the savages."

The first sentence of the account indicates immediately the quality of the surprise achieved by the tribes. It is equally illuminating as to the condition of affairs in the mainland of the Western Empire. Valentinian, the Emperor, clearly had had no intimation of immediate trouble in Britain at this time, though mutiny had been endemic in the debatable country immediately north of the Wall from the time of Lupicinus onwards. His task at Amiens, close to the Channel—probably the stiffening of the local defence system against the growing incursions of the Franks—was complete; he was "hastening" inland to Treves (Trier), the main headquarters of the West, to deal with a further threat of the Alamanni.

> Nectaridus, the commanding general of the sea coast region, had been killed and another general, Fullofaudes, had been ambushed by the enemy and taken prisoner.

This second passage gives the measure of the disaster, both in relation to time and to the high command. The contingent circumstances of the receipt of the message demonstrate positively that the first thrust of the tribes was carried out with unprecedented swiftness. The reports of the deaths of the two commanders-in-chief contained, as they appear to have been, in the first message, cannot be a matter of simple coincidence. They must be accepted as evidence of skilfully co-ordinated assaults at widely separated points.

Nectaridus was Count of the Saxon Shore. Theoretically his area of responsibility began at Branodunum—Brancaster on the Wash. Branodunum was the most northerly of the Forts of the Shore, but it was still a hundred and sixty miles below the Wall. In the circumstances it is scarcely credible that Nectaridus could have been killed at the outset of the campaign unless an impeccably timed amphibious operation had been launched simultaneously against his area.

The one possible alternative to this is that he was killed in battle following an amphibious landing on the undefended Yorkshire coast below Huntcliff. In a stable-door-locking effort after the debacle a chain of strong signal stations was built from Huntcliff south to Filey Bay. The inference is that an enemy attack in this zone played an important part in the main assault. It is difficult to believe that it could have been Saxon. The boats of the Saxons at this time were not dissimilar to the Irish curragh—light frameworks covered with hide. The North Sea at this point is four hundred miles across to the mouth of the Elbe, a distance possible to small formations but out of the question to an "invasion fleet". It seems, therefore, more probable that this was a short-range operation launched from the Northumbrian coast, and designed to threaten or even to turn the eastern and undefended flank of the Wall. A counter-attack against it would have had to be executed from York or from the Wall itself and not from south of the Wash. Moreover, the time scale would not have permitted intervention from the south early enough to be included in the first dispatches of disaster.

The Imperial Post, the principal Roman communications network, established in Britain from the earliest years of the conquest, was normally an extraordinarily efficient organisation. Given its statutory relay system of post horses, it was capable of sustaining speeds of a hundred miles a day and, in cases of crisis, substantially more. York is two hundred miles from London, Dover seventy-two, Amiens is about the same distance from Boulogne. Allowing a full day for the Channel crossing, it should still have been possible to get a message to the Emperor within four days. It would have taken more than that for Nectaridus to concentrate and march north from Brancaster.

The ambush and capture of Fullofaudes similarly indicates a staggering speed of attack.

Fullofaudes was, in Richmond's judgement, *Dux Britanniarum*—the Duke of Britain—commander-in-chief of the army of the Province. His headquarters were at York. The combat headquarters of the Wall, according to accepted theory, were at Stanwix. Only disaster on the Wall itself could have drawn Fullofaudes from his headquarters in the opening phase of the attack. He was, after all, the essential link with the field army, with the civilian government and with the Emperor; and the channels of command ran through York, the northern capital.

Yet he was "ambushed".

The inference clearly is that the Wall was carried in the first rush, that Fullofaudes, racing desperately to take command in the field and restore the situation, misjudged the impetus of the tribes' attack and was caught with a small escort either on the Stainmore road heading for Carlisle and Stanwix or in the Tyne valley aiming for the Corbridge crossing. According to the *Rerum Gestarum*:

> This report aroused great horror, and the Emperor sent Severus, who at that time was still commander of the household troops, to set right the disasters, if chance should offer the desired opportunity, but he was recalled a little later and Jovinus [Master of the Horse], having set out for the same regions, allowed them to return at the quick step, intending to seek the support of a strong army. Finally, because of alarming rumours about that same island, Theodosius, a man most favourably known, having enrolled legions and cohorts of courageous young men, hastened to depart, preceded by brilliant expectations.

The implications here are of extreme indecision and uncertainty on the part of Valentinian and his staff. Faced with the imminent explosion of the Alamanni, his coastal areas under intermittent attack, Valentinian had no reserves to spare for a major re-invasion of the Province of Britain. His quandary is implicit in the description of Theodosius enrolling "legions of courageous young men". It should be interpreted "hastily gathered together a scratch force and set out".

> The Picts, divided into two tribes, the Dicalydones and Verturiones, as well as the Attacotti (a warlike race of men) and the Scots, were ranging widely and causing great devastation; while the Gallic regions, wherever anyone could break in by land or by sea, were harassed by the Franks and their neighbours the Saxons with cruel robbery, fire, and the murder of all who were taken prisoner.

The passage is important in that it gives at least the main components of the land force: the Picts, who—according to this, were a coalition of two major tribes; the Attacotti, who, Gibbon says, lived in the neighbourhood of Glasgow and who, according to Ammianus, "attacked the shepherd rather than his flock and ... curiously selected the most delicate and brawny parts, both of males and females, which they prepared for their horrid repasts"; the Scots, who still lived in Ireland, though it is possible that they may have had settlements at least in the fastnesses of the south-west Highlands. All three were already "ranging widely and causing great devastation".

Necessarily one must concede here a degree of telescoping in Ammianus' account. This passage clearly describes events after the dispatch of Theodosius. None the less, the description unquestionably was already accurate. The tribes were sweeping south against such opposition as still existed at a speed enormously greater than Theodosius appeared able to achieve in his simple approach march to the British coast. Ammianus is here glozing a failure. In his next passage he says:

> Theodosius hastened to the world's end and reached the coast of Bononia [Boulogne]. From there he quietly crossed the strait and landed at Rutupiae [Richborough]. When the Batavi, the Heruli, the Jovii and Victores, who followed him had arrived, troops confident in their strength, he began his march to the old town of Lundinium.... There he divided his troops into many parts and attacked predatory bands who were ranging about and were laden with heavy packs. Quickly routing those who were driving along prisoners and cattle, he wrested from them the booty which the wretched tribute-paying people had lost. And when all this had been restored to them, except for a small part which was allotted to the wearied soldiers, he entered the city which had previously been plunged into the greatest difficulties, but had been restored more quickly than rescue could have been expected.

The "world's end" was, as has already been said, barely seventy miles from Amiens. Even if Theodosius had started from a point halfway to Trier, the distance would only have been about a hundred and fifty miles. Indecision and slovenly organisation prevented any real attempt at a "rescue" operation. Ammianus' final sentence that London was "restored more quickly" than could have been expected is manifest playing to the Roman gallery.

But it is the internal evidence of this passage as to the nature and the extent of the advance of the tribes that contributes most to a reasoned appreciation of the debacle. Before even entering the city of London—which had clearly been under siege—Theodosius had to split up his force to deal with "predatory bands".

Again the implications go infinitely beyond the bare statement. The first is that the military phase of this barbarian conquest was already complete—and wholly victorious—by the time he reached the scene. The armies of the tribes had broken up and were picking the country clean. They were still moving cattle as well as goods and, most importantly, prisoners. It is possible that these were civilians taken as slaves, but consequent comments suggest that there might have been soldiers among them. The inefficiency of the organisation of the relief force was responsible at least for the overwhelming of the extreme south. London, and possibly some others of the walled cities, alone had survived.

Theodosius wintered in London.

> While he lingered there, encouraged by the successful outcome to dare greater deeds, he carefully considered what plans would be safe, and he was in doubt about his future course, since he learned from the confessions of the captives and the reports of deserters that the widely scattered enemy, a mob of various natives and frightfully savage, could be overcome only by secret craft and unforeseen attacks. Finally he issued proclamations and under promise of pardon summoned the deserters to return to service, as well as many others who were wandering about in various places on furlough.

Disregarding Ammianus' comments on the "frightfully savage" enemy, which, if the tribes had ever produced an historian, would have read like any description of any Roman punitive expedition by a Roman army, the significance of this section of the report lies in its conclusive evidence as to the absolute breakdown of the government and the military system of Britain. The army of the Province had been shattered. All that Theodosius could discover, except at Richborough and London, were "deserters". There was demonstrably no coherent organisation left except that which remained in London, and the legions, the cohorts, the centuries had deliquesced into a scattering of "deserters". Because of this, because of the "widely scattered" pattern of the enemy—because too of circumstances on the Continent, where the Alamanni had attacked both in Gaul and in Rhaetia, the Sarmatae and Quadi had broken into Pannonia, predatory bands of Goths were raiding Thrace, the Persians had erupted into Armenia, and the Austoriani were in revolt in Africa—Theodosius could hope for no further aid from the Emperor.

The issue of a proclamation of amnesty for the "deserters" of an army that had fallen asunder in the circumstances of 367 is probably unparalleled. To Theodosius it was the only solution to an intractable problem. The enemy had, it is true, broken down his organisation from armies into "predatory bands", but his predatory bands covered the whole of Britain and to eliminate them was Theodosius' first problem. He appears to have taken the best part of two years to solve it. The optimistic statement that "he rescued the booty which the wretched tribute-paying people had lost" can cover only an infinitely small proportion of the whole. The tribes swept the Province clean.

Out of context it is perhaps permissible to speculate as to how much of the finds of Roman material in both Lowland and Highland Scotland are in reality attributable to the spoils of this and the two preceding raids on the Province. Largely relied upon by the protagonists of the "customs barrier theory" as evidence of "trade", a percentage at least must be attributed to loot, with a consequent upset to neatly developed statistical analyses.

Vindolanda. The Roman fort at Chesterholm is a classic surviving ▶ example of a fort in isolation. Commanding a steep valley leading down to the Tyne, it shows evidence of five periods of occupation covering the Roman history of the Province from Agricola's conquest of the Brigantes to the end. Its gates and the *praetorium* have been excavated and substantial work is now in progress.
Photograph: Ministry of Public Building and Works

Is it possible to extract from Ammianus the roots of this staggering disaster to Roman arms?

They are, of course, implicit in the part of his account which deals with Theodosius' arrival at London. They are evident in the passages which deal with the deserters and the amnesty. The breakdown of control is underscored by his request to the Emperor for a deputy prefect to resume the civil government and for "Dulcitius, a general distinguished for his knowledge of the art of war, to take over the military command". But it is necessary to go to Ammianus' mentor Libianus for the essential clues as to the origins of this devastating collapse. In the *Orationes* Libianus says bluntly, in Gibbon's translation:

> The sums of gold and silver, which had been painfully collected, or liberally transmitted, for the payment of the troops, were intercepted by the avarice of the commanders; discharges, or, at least, exemptions, from the military service, were publicly sold; the distress of the soldiers, who were injuriously deprived of their legal and scanty subsistence, provoked them to frequent desertion; the nerves of discipline were relaxed, and the highways were infested with robbers.

This was a process which had begun certainly under the eunuchs of Constantius. It was probably rectified for a little under Julian, but the attack of 367 struck against a defence that was weakened from within. Desertion was a built-in factor in the defence of the Province, and Ammianus' curious reference to the numbers of men "on furlough" confirms the allegations as to the purchase of exemption from military service.

One other explanation for the failure is offered—again by Ammianus. It has been more curiously misinterpreted in academic comment than any other.

> In the midst of such important events the Arcani, a class of men established in early times, had gradually become cor-

---

◀ Three cloaked figures on a stone slab found at Housesteads. Traditionally described as "deities", they may equally represent local tribesmen. The workmanship is probably that of the limited school of sculpture which flourished in the Romanisation of the Wall area.
Photograph: Ministry of Public Building and Works

rupted, and consequently he removed them from their posts. For they were clearly convicted of having been led by the receipt, or the promise, of great booty at various times to betray to the savages what was going on among us. For it was their duty to hasten about hither and thither over long spaces, to give information to our general of the clashes of rebellion among neighbouring peoples.

By an exercise of academic ingenuity which passes comprehension, this paragraph has been translated into an accusation of wholesale treachery on the part of the frontier scouts. Richmond says, with complete conviction:

> The Wall and the forts of the north again fell, and it is recorded that the cause of this item in the chapter of disaster was the treachery of the frontier scouts, who were bought over by promises of a share in the loot.

Collingwood goes even farther:

> If the garrison of the frontier had not only betrayed it to the Picts, as we are expressly told they did, but had made common cause with them to the extent of joining them in their plundering expeditions to the south . . .

The word "Arcani" occurs nowhere else, but it is reasonable to assume that its connotations are "secret". The Arcani in the passage which both these authorities claim as their source are accused specifically of having been induced "to betray to the savages what was going on among us". This is the entire gravamen of the charge. It is also the very last information which "frontier scouts" stationed in advance of the Wall—Netherby was called Castra Exploratorum and the frontier scouts were the *exploratores*—would have had at their disposal. They would, in fact, have less contact with "what was going on among us" than any other element of the army of the Province. The Arcani (the name is clearly a fear-word for a secret service) were beyond question a part of the Roman CIA, they were the people who moved about "over long spaces to give information of clashes of rebellion". They would have the necessary knowledge of the discontent in the ordinary soldiery, the avarice of the Roman command, the incompetence of the civil government, and the distractions of the rebellious Continent to provide the alliance of the tribes with the necessary information on which to establish its plan.

They were not disbanded as a military force would have been. They were "removed from their posts". It is at least probable that they were, in fact, the senior personnel of the Imperial Post, always suspected of being the spies of the administration.

Is it possible to sum up cause and effect in this, the most dramatic single episode of the entire Roman occupation?

With the treachery of the Arcani as the real starting point, the time-table begins beyond all question with the political efforts to establish a Northern Alliance. Prior to this there had been *ad hoc* coalitions, temporary conjunctions. Never before had there been an attempt to bring in the Scots from the west, to join together the major tribes of the north, to seek co-operation from the Saxons and the Franks. On the fundamental basis of knowledge of the weakness of the Province, of the corruption of the administration and the discontent of the forces, it was possible to induce each of these diverse and scattered elements to coalesce. It was possible equally—and again perhaps because of the venality of the Arcani—to conceal that coalition from the Roman authorities. With astonishing skill the campaign was planned in advance. A doctrine was developed for it which employed in masterly fashion the potentials of amphibious operations. The difficulties of timing, the problems of logistics, the intricacies of communication were clearly settled beforehand. The control was rigid.

Victory was absolute.

The assertions that Theodosius executed a brilliant campaign of recovery need not be accepted literally. The campaign was over before he reached the Province. It was over because if the Northern Alliance had sought a motto for their banners, it would have been something approaching Gibbon's phrase: "the desire of spoil is a more rational provocation than the vanity of conquest." There was within the alliance no intention of conquest; there was only the determination to defeat—as a necessary preliminary to the loot of Roman Britain. Both aims were achieved. There remains only one unanswered question: who led this staggering venture?

There must have been a leader. It was so new, so gigantic in its spread, so beyond precedent in relation to the four nations involved, that it is inconceivable that the necessary diplomacy could have emanated from traditional tribal councils, that the planning could have been carried out by the normal consultations of tribal chiefs or that the war as a whole could have been controlled by assemblies of elders.

There *must* have been a leader! Nothing in Ammianus, nothing in Roman history, nothing in legend or in tribal myth suggests a name.

16

Decline and Disaster

Theodosius reconstructed the Wall. His work has been identified at a score of points. It can be best described as emergency repair—rough, tough and utilitarian. But in reality the years of the Wall were over. The master project of Hadrian had come to an inevitable end.

The evidence is clearest in the forts. Their reconstruction left them as armed villages; the people of the burned *vici* at their gates were taken into the forts themselves. Storehouses and barracks were, where necessary, converted into dwelling houses. The splendid formal plan of the camp was disregarded and built over, the garrisons patently reduced to small bodies of second grade frontier troops. The vast interlocking interception strategy was finally abandoned, and over the whole frontier the guard was reduced to a screen.

Theodosius returned to Trier, accompanied by the plaudits of the populace—and took back most of the army of the restoration with him. Rome was fighting on every frontier of the Empires of the West and of the East.

The new order lasted scarcely fourteen years. In 383 Magnus Maximus, who had served with Theodosius and who held some undefined office in Britain, was, in Gibbon's words, "proclaimed, by the tumultuary, but unanimous voice, both of the soldiers and of the provincials". Gratian, Valentinian's son, was at this time Emperor of the West. Following disastrous precedent, Maximus withdrew the major part of the garrison of Britain and crossed to Gaul. The armies of Gaul in their turn acclaimed him, Gratian was killed, and Maximus was recognised by Theodosius, son of the General and Emperor of the East, as ruler of Gaul, Spain and Britain. It was the supreme triumph of the British pretenders, but it lasted a scant three years; in 388 Maximus himself was dead and behind him there was, inevitably, chaos in the Province of Britain.

No coins have been found on the Wall later than the year of the departure of Maximus. This is, however, no absolute proof of the date of its abandonment; isolated points certainly survived or were patched up when the tribes once more, glutted with the spoil of this lesser raid, withdrew, but it was never reconstituted as a frontier. The northern *limes* of the Province is thereafter nebulous. The Province itself was foundering in a mire of rebellion and crumbling authority.

Claudian claims that Stilicho liberated it once more from Saxon, Pict and Scot. Whatever Stilicho achieved, it was brief and indecisive, and—probably in 401—he once more withdrew troops to fight in the Gothic War. Five years later what was left of the army of Rome in Britain set up another pretender to the Empire—Marcus. Marcus accomplished nothing and was deservedly murdered. Gratian, his usurper—the coincidence of names is confusing—lasted four months and was murdered. Constantine, a common soldier, thrust through the turmoil, was proclaimed by the legions, and at once putting into operation the strategy that by now had become traditional, withdrew the last remnants of the army to fight in Gaul. Briefly victorious, he went on to establish the court of Arles, and in the inevitable eventual defeat was murdered in his turn.

These are the years of the Groans of the Britons, the twilight years. After them even the shadows fade.

The Romans went—the Wall remains. How long it continued to serve as a series of disconnected strong points for a despairing civil population is altogether uncertain. The curtain, with the milecastles and the turrets, had probably long been abandoned. Some at least of the forts survived for a little or were patched up again after the successive waves of the barbarians. The most recent series of excavations at the key fort at Chesterholm hold promise of greater knowledge. At least five occupation layers have been determined under deep soil, and future digging may well yield something of the secrets of the dark years. Yet nothing will alter the essential history of this period. Rome decayed, and Romanised Britain decayed with and before it, and the tribes came down again.

This is the point at which to attempt to arrive at a just estimate of the Wall's achievement.

Any analysis of the Roman frontier system in Britain divides itself into two elements—political and military.

Politically Hadrian's Wall was a failure. That it was the active principle in the defence of Romanised Britain from the year 120 until the final withdrawal of the usurper Constantine is in a strong sense irrelevant. The Wall failed of its purpose, which was to secure the peace, and thereby the prosperity, of a Romanised Britain.

The magnitude of the strategic misjudgement which followed the battle of Mons Graupius has already been assessed in earlier chapters. The historians for the most part have contented themselves with rejecting Tacitus' claim that Agricola was recalled because of the Emperor's jealousy. The matter is without significance. What is relevant is that the decision made inevitable the establishment of a defended frontier to the south, and the solution that was forced on Hadrian is a direct and logical consequence of it. Theoretically, it was a simple solution. If a wall were built strong enough to withstand external attack, the peaceful and profitable development of the Province in its shelter was a logical and indeed an inevitable conclusion. It is the paradox of the Wall that its very strength was a basic factor in the failure of the Province. This circumstance also has been discussed earlier in the book, but it seems necessary to reiterate it here. The density of the military population in the central sector of Britain between Chester and Limestone Corner, in conjunction with the long periods of idleness which the strength of the Wall system secured, appears to have been itself the greatest single factor in what became the traditional turbulence and instability of the garrison of Britain.

The Wall system, it is apparent, engendered its own political problems.

Was any alternative possible? Agricola's alternative was always possible. Antoninus Pius, in dictating the policy which Lollius Urbicus attempted to execute, acknowledged not only this fact but its urgent desirability. The conquest of the Caledones—and with that the conquest of Scotland as a whole—could have been achieved. Though Urbicus in reality failed,

Severus proved the point seventy years later. In a different degree, the commanders of a long series of successful punitive expeditions proved it also.

It has been claimed that victory in battle would not necessarily have brought about the peace of Scotland. Previous experience in Britain argues against the claim. The fundamental holding system—a military road network studded with forts adjusted in distance and in density to the requirements of a particular situation and made possible by victory in battle—secured first, the pacification of belligerent southern tribes like the Iceni, then, of cohesive and politically advanced tribes of the strength of the Brigantes, and finally, even of tenacious and aggressive mountain peoples like the Silures and the Ordovices of Wales. In all these areas pacification began with battle and ended with the network of forts, and in all of them before the end the network had succeeded to the point of establishing its own obsolescence. There is no logic in any suggestion—with all possible deference to Highland pride—that a similar system would have failed even in the rough country of the North.

The result of the establishment and development of the Wall with its demands on man-power was, however, to burden the Province of Britain throughout its history with a garrison more costly than it could afford and more powerful than it could control. The financial situation resulting from this itself influenced the general attitude of Rome towards the Province. The internal aspects of that financial situation led at intervals in a vicious circle directly to military instability which in turn aggravated the economic viability of the Province. The classic illustration of this is the one expressly military defeat of the Wall system in 367, in which an unpaid army, administered in corruption, broke against a barbarian attack and the Province had presumably to shoulder, directly or indirectly, the cost of an army of reconquest, the rebuilding of cities and towns and villages and villas, and, finally and ironically, the cost of rebuilding the Wall.

The financial inadequacy of the Province of Britain is a large subject. Caesar's pearls were an illusion. Internal taxation probably covered little more than the administration and the garrison. Exports, until the fourth century, can have brought small profit to Rome. Lead, copper, hides, those irritating hunting dogs, slaves and recruits for the auxiliaries can have had relatively little significance in the general budget of the Empire. Yet the conquest of Britain was originally undertaken for profit.

If it failed of profit, it failed in everything, for Rome conquered not in terms of imposing political systems or religious doctrines or even moralities on the conquered peoples, but for two essential reasons—profit, and the necessary defence of the Empire against the barbarians.

In these terms the conquest of Britain failed and its failure was primarily political. It is irrelevant that it incorporated the greater moral failure of neglecting to establish within the Province, which it was eventually forced to abandon, a political entity strong enough to defend itself against future aggression.

Rome went. The Wall remained. But Romanised Britain disappeared as if it had never been.

Against this background it is necessary to attempt to assess the military quality of the Wall.

Its history divides broadly into four periods. From its inception in 119 or 120 to the first rebellious withdrawal of the garrison in 196 there is no convincing evidence of barbarian attack. Despite Jarrett's recent suggestion that it was Hadrian's Wall that was "crossed" by the tribes at the beginning of the reign of Commodus, there is no positive proof that the Wall itself was breached or even assaulted throughout this period. That it was reduced in status during the existence of the Antonine Wall is incidental only to the record. In a sense the Antonine Wall was no more than a projection of Hadrian's barrier, built after a failure of reconquest in an effort to find an economic solution.

In 196 Clodius Albinus made his bid for the throne and withdrew the garrison of Britain to fight in Gaul. That the Wall was then overrun is in no sense a military criticism of its concept. Even had a skeleton garrison been left, criticism would still be invalid, for the effectiveness of the Wall depended fundamentally on its concentration plan, as illustrated earlier, and any serious reduction in the garrison would render that plan inoperable. The Wall was by its nature a single instrument of war. Stripped of its garrison, it was as ineffective as a Polaris submarine would be without her crew.

The rebuilding under Severus was followed by a hundred years in which again there is no evidence either of the breaching of the Wall or of serious attack upon it. That something of this derives from the success of Severus' uncompleted campaign in the north, together with Caracalla's deal with the Caledones, is probable. Yet within this period the tribes had unlimited possibilities of regeneration and combination—the rhythm of previous reaction is clearly established—and the duration of this peace must therefore demonstrably be accepted as evidence of the Wall's deterrent effect.

At the end of the hundred years Allectus withdrew the garrison for the second time to oppose Constantius. Again, and for the same reasons, the second overrunning has no military significance, whatever its military results.

This time the rebuilding was followed by approximately seventy years of peace.

Only in the year 367, two and a half centuries after the surveyors of the First Plan had run their line along the crest of the Great Whin Sill, did the Wall fall by assault. Few frontiers in the history of Rome had so long an immunity—few frontiers anywhere.

The concept of the Second Plan, it is apparent, endured effectively for almost two hundred and fifty years. The comparison in modern terms lies between the beginning of Marlborough's campaign and the invasion of Normandy in World War II. The fundamental brilliance of the concept of the Second Plan spanned all developments between.

Yet the Wall fell.

It has already been suggested that the fall was in measure due to the internal weakness of the defending force. It should not be assumed, however, that this was the entire explanation of the defeat. Unquestionably in the course of the two hundred and fifty years the incidence and balance of sea power in relation to the Province had altered drastically. If, as the evidence suggests, the right flank of the Wall—the North Sea flank—was turned, it was turned by a naval capability unknown and inconceivable in Hadrian's day. If, as the evidence again suggests, the left flank—the Irish Sea flank—was turned simultaneously, possibly on the Lancashire coast, this again was an amphibious potential beyond calculation in Hadrian's time. These landings must have been dealt with either from York and Chester—in which case the support plan for the Wall was disrupted—or by withdrawals from the Wall itself—in which case the interlocking concentration plan must have been compromised. In either case the capacity of the system to deal with the frontal assault on the land was affected.

The academic view is altogether too simple. The Wall was carried "because of treachery in the Wall garrison". Once again the matter has already been discussed. It is in the very highest degree improbable that the Arcani were in any sense a component of the Wall garrison. It is, on the other hand, highly probable that the Arcani, themselves clearly disaffected, were able to inform the enemy of a more comprehensive disaffection due, as has been suggested, to the non-payment of troops, the selling of "exemptions from the military service" and the general "avarice of the commanders". There is here, then, a confusion of political and military circumstance. The defeat of 367 was not a clear and simple military defeat. It was a defeat due basically to a political incompetence. The brilliance of Hadrian's concept after two and a half centuries emerges from it unimpaired.

The fourth period, from the restoration by Theodosius through the revolt of Maximus and the ebullitions of the usurpers, does not permit of military judgement. The forces of Britain by this time were anomalous, the administration was crumbling, the loyalties were divisive, command was irrational. The Wall had at last reached its end as a single instrument of power.

With the withdrawal of Maximus it ceased to exercise a dominant role between the Province and the barbarians. Yet militarily, for more than two hundred and fifty years, it had served the purpose for which it was designed.

Militarily it was more than a success—it was a triumph.

Index